Orange Line 5

Workbook

Herausgeber: Dr. Frank Haß

Ernst Klett Verlag
Stuttgart • Leipzig

Unit 1

Exploring Australia

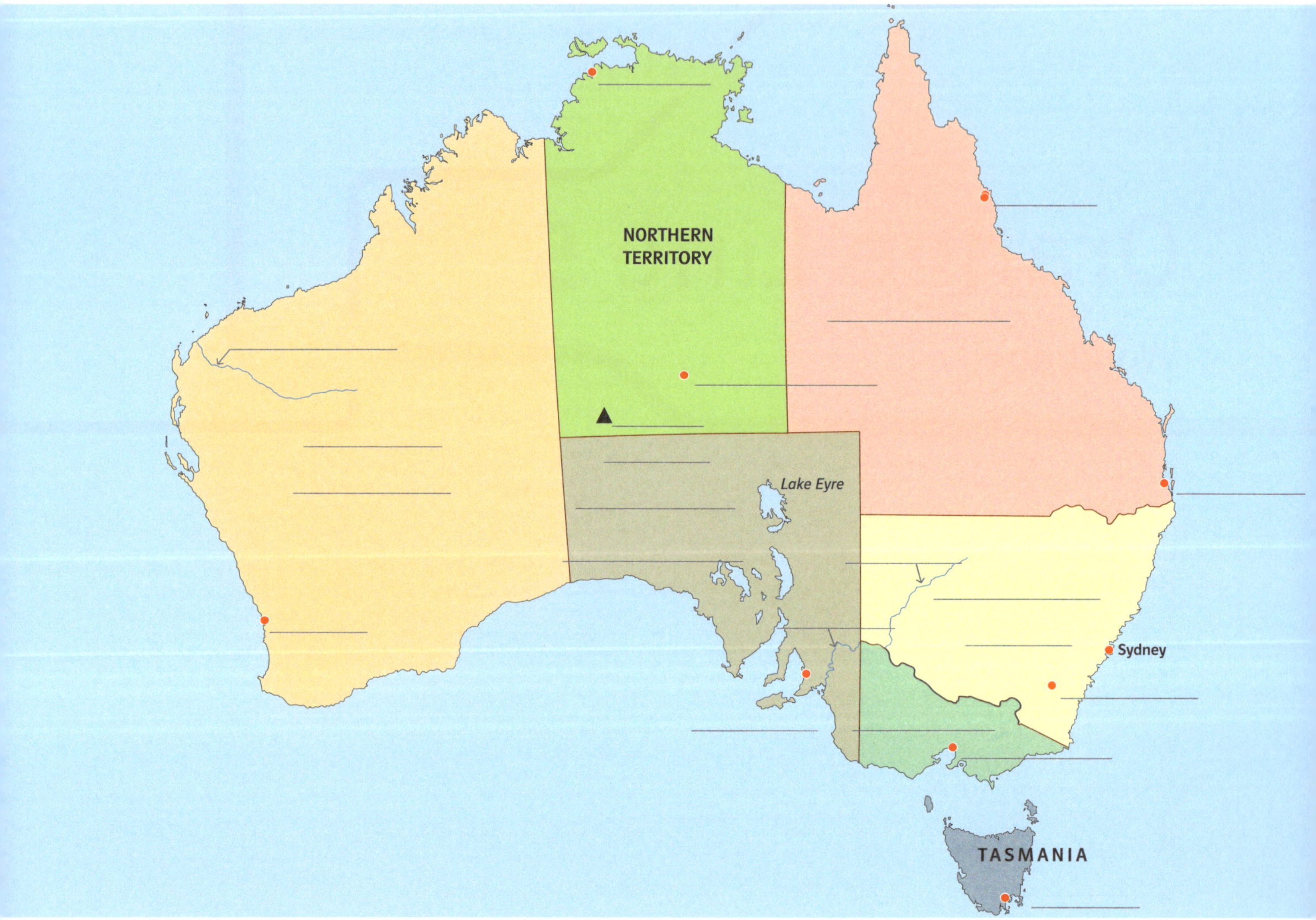

1 A quiz about Australia

10/2

a) Answer the questions.

1. Name two big Australian cities. ______________________
2. Where is the Great Barrier Reef? ______________________
3. When did the Australian continent break away from Antarctica? ______________________
4. Name two species that only exist in Australia. ______________________
5. Who has lived in Australia for over 50,000 years? ______________________
6. What is the name of the huge area in the centre of Australia? ______________________

b) Complete the map with the missing information: the names of the cities and territories, rivers, lakes and the mountain. Use the map in your book or the internet for help.

12/1

1 Write sentences.

a) Think of an example of …

1. someone you respect: I respect ______ because ______
2. something you find offensive: I find it offensive when ______
3. something you try to ignore: ______
4. something you think is disrespectful: ______
5. something sacred: ______

b) Compare your answers with a partner.

/4a)

2 Find the words.

a) Find suitable nouns.

1. to attack → ______
2. to apply → ______
3. to celebrate → ______
4. to begin → ______
5. fantastic → ______
6. free → ______

b) Find suitable adjectives.

1. allergy → ______
2. ambition → ______
3. beauty → ______
4. business → ______
5. to care → ______
6. height → ______

c) Use a dictionary and form more verbs, adjectives and nouns with these words.

1. to write: ______
2. to sleep: ______
3. ground: ______

______

/4b)

3 Noun, verb or adjective? Complete the sentences with the correct form.

1. Tourism at Uluru has been very ______ (success).
2. The tour guides are very ______ (friend).
3. Driving around in the outback in bad weather is very ______ (danger).
4. Snakes are a ______ (real) danger in the outback.
5. It is ______ (ignore) to throw rubbish on the ground.
6. People should ______ (respect) sacred places.

4 (LISTENING) Listen to Merindah talking about respect. Tick the right box.

1 13/5

	right	wrong
1. Respect for the land and the community leaders is important.	☐	☐
2. Nowadays everyone shows respect for Aboriginal culture.	☐	☐
3. Young Aboriginal people just want to have fun.	☐	☐
4. Merindah's dance group mixes modern dance with traditional dance.	☐	☐
5. They only perform in areas where Aboriginal people live.	☐	☐
6. Very few Aboriginal people are unemployed.	☐	☐
7. Merindah wants to fight discrimination against Aboriginal people.	☐	☐
8. More respect for Aboriginal culture is important for Australia as a nation.	☐	☐

5 (WRITING) Describe this picture by an Aboriginal artist.

13/5

This picture shows ______

6 The tourists went to a campsite. Write sentences with modal auxiliaries. Use the simple past.

14/6a)

1. not be allowed to • have fires — *They weren't allowed to have fires.*
2. not be allowed to • bring dogs ______
3. have to • watch out for spiders ______
4. not be allowed to • feed the wildlife ______
5. have to • be quiet after 10 p.m. ______
6. be able to • arrive until 6 p.m. ______
7. allowed to • leave the car near the tent ______
8. not have to • leave until 1 p.m. ______

7 Write sentences about when you were younger. Use was able to, was allowed to or had to.

6b)

1. stay up until midnight: When I was ten, I wasn't allowed to stay up until midnight.
2. eat lots of sweets: When I was ______
3. tidy my room: ______
4. ride a bike: ______
5. say something in English: ______
6. play computer games ______

8 Complete the sentences about Koa's hopes for the future. Use the will-future.

14/7

1. Everyone will have to (have to) respect the local customs.
2. Tourists ______ (not allowed to) go near Uluru.
3. People ______ (be able to) learn about Aboriginal culture.
4. Aboriginal people ______ (not have to) change their way of life.
5. Local people ______ (be allowed to) control tourist activity at Uluru.
6. People and nature ______ (be able to) live well together.

9 Complete the text about Lauren's trip to Australia. Put the modal auxiliaries in the right tense.

15/8

Last summer I was able to (can) visit my aunt in Melbourne. On my last weekend we went on a trip to the countryside. We ______ (must) drive through the hills so my aunt ______ (cannot) drive fast. At the top of a hill she stopped the car so I ______ (can) take some photos.

Suddenly I saw a koala in a tree near the road. I ______ (can) get near it and took a photo. I was careful because you ______ (cannot) touch the animals. Then we drove to the coast and I ______ (can) watch some interesting birds. I really enjoyed my trip and I was sad that I ______ (cannot) stay longer. I've told my mum that next time our whole family ______ (must) go too, and I think we ______ (can) see some koalas again!

16/1

1 Complete the job ad with the vocabulary from the box.

customer service | references | work experience | require | CV | permanent | on-the-job | letter of application

Shop Assistant at Sporty Sports

- We ________________ a part-time shop assistant for our shop in the city centre.
- This is a ____________________ job from 8 a.m. to 1 p.m. five days a week, including Saturdays.
- We are looking for a friendly person with excellent ___________________________ skills.
- __________________________ in a shop is preferred, but we will also give you ___________________ training.
- To apply, please send a ________ and ______________________________ to W.Jones@SportsDX.com. Please also send the details of two ____________________ .

17/3

2 Find the right jobs for the equipment.

1. t ___________________

2. ___________________

3. ___________________

4. ___________________

5. ___________________

6. ___________________

7. ___________________

8. ___________________

17/4

3 Find words for strengths and weaknesses.

a) Sort the words into the table.

efficient | unmotivated | bossy | honest | responsible | ambitious | punctual | hard-working | disorganized | lazy | reliable | rude

strengths	weaknesses

b) Think of more words and add then to the table.

2 17/5

4 (LISTENING) Listen to Sonya and Barry. Take notes.

1. The sheep station: over 12,000 ______
2. Sonya's home: ______
3. Work on the sheep station: ______
4. Accommodation for Sonya: ______

5 Compare these Australian animals.

eastern brown snake about 1.5 m long about 1 kg dangerous 	**koala** about 70 cm tall about 14 kg not dangerous 	**kangaroo** about 2 m tall about 100 kg can attack people 

3/6a)

a) Complete the sentences.

1. The kangaroo is bigger than the koala.
2. The koala is ______ the snake.
3. The snake is ______ the kangaroo.
4. The kangaroo is ______ than the koala.
5. The snake is the ______ animal.
6. The kangaroo is the ______ animal.

big small heavy dangerous

3/6b)

b) Complete the sentences using a comparative or a superlative.

1. I've never seen such a cute animal. → It's the cutest ______
2. This snake is the most dangerous snake on earth.
   → No snake is ______
3. The kangaroo is Australia's most famous animal.
   → ______
4. I've never been to a country which is so interesting.
   → ______

6 Complete the sentences about Sonya's work at the sheep station. Put in the right form of the adverb.

18/7

1. I repaired the fences better than all the others. (well)
2. After I had had a small accident, I drove ______ . (carefully)
3. I was ______ at finding the sheep and got there before anyone else. (fast)
4. Sheep can run ______ than people. (quickly)
5. I was the one who enjoyed working in a team ______ . (well)
6. The team worked ______ than ever before. (efficiently)
7. I've never worked ______ than on that day. (hard)

7 Compare the three people from the sheep station.

19/8a)

Audrey

boss
salary ***
confident ***
friendly **
reliable ***
experienced ***
punctual*

Barry

assistant manager
salary **
confident **
friendly **
reliable ***
experienced **
punctual***

Sonya

student job
salary *
confident *
friendly ***
reliable ***
experienced *
punctual***

1. Barry's salary is higher than Sonya's, but Audrey's ______ .
2. Barry ______ confident than ______, but Audrey ______ .
3. Audrey and Barry ______ friendly but ______ .
4. Audrey, Barry and Sonya ______ .
5. Barry is ______ than Sonya. Audrey is ______ .
6. Sonya and Barry ______ Audrey.

8 Think of six strengths you have, e.g. at school, your hobbies and your personality. Write sentences.

19/8b)

1. I'm very good at ______
2. ______
3. ______
4. ______
5. ______
6. ______

19/9

9 (WRITING) Write an application.

City Guides – Tour Guide Needed

Are you friendly, confident and reliable? Do you have excellent communication skills and enjoy working with people? We are looking for a part-time tour guide in the city. No experience is needed, full on-the-job training is possible. The job will be at the weekends, but it is possible to work more hours during the holiday months. The salary is AU$ 10 an hour.
Please send your CV and letter of application to:
Peter Allen, City Guides, 21 Western Road, Sydney, NSW, 2000

a) You have found this job ad in your local newspaper. Read the job ad.
b) Write a letter of application.

Briefkopf

Wenn du mehr Hilfe brauchst, schau dir die Skill auf Seite 152 in deinem Buch an.

Betreffzeile

Anrede

erster Abschnitt:
Stelle dich kurz vor. Sage, auf welche Stelle du dich bewirbst. Wie hast du von der Stelle erfahren?

zweiter Abschnitt:
Deine Qualifikationen und Erfahrungen, deine Stärken. Warum bist du die richtige Person für diese Stelle?

Schluss:
Sage, dass du dich auf eine Antwort freust.

Grußformel

c) Write your CV.

Persönliche Daten:
Name, Adresse,
Telefonnummer, E-Mail

Informationen zur eigenen Person

Schulbildung

Wenn du mehr Hilfe brauchst, schau dir die Skill auf Seite 153 in deinem Buch an.

Prüfungen

Kenntnisse:
Fähigkeiten und
Fertigkeiten

Berufliche Erfahrungen:
Praktika und Jobs, die du gemacht hast.

Interessen

19/9

1 (SPEAKING) Work with a partner and talk about the photos.

a) What type of disrespectful behaviour is shown in the photos? How should the people behave? Which situation do you think is the worst? Discuss your opinions.

b) Act a dialogue for one of the pictures.

19/9

2 (SPEAKING) Act a job interview.

a) Work with a partner. You have got an interview for a job as a tour guide. Read the job ad below. Act an interview. One of you has applied for the job; the other one is Peter Allen from City Guides. Both of you write down some questions you would like to ask in the interview. You can use the letter of application and CV from pages 9 and 10 in your workbook.

b) Interview your partner.

City Guides – Tour Guide Needed

Are you friendly, confident and reliable? Do you have excellent communication skills and enjoy working with people? We are looking for a part-time tour guide in the city. No experience is needed. Full on-the-job training is possible. The job will be at the weekends, but it is possible to work more hours during the holiday months. The salary is AU$ 10 an hour.
Please send your CV and letter of application to:
Peter Allen, City Guides, 21 Western Road, Sydney, NSW, 2000

Why would you like this job?

I would like this job because ...

How would you describe yourself?

I'm reliable / punctual / ...

Tell me about your strengths / weaknesses / experiences / qualifications / ...

21/5

1 (READING) Read the story.

Fire at the sheep station

I was woken up by the sound of shouting and engines starting outside my caravan. I opened my eyes as my friend Rachel jumped out of bed and opened the door. The first thing I noticed was that the early morning light seemed strange, more orange than normal. And then I noticed the smell – smoke. Rachel and I both shouted, "Fire!" We put on our clothes as fast as we could and ran outside.

We had been afraid of this for weeks. The weather had been hot and windy and the land was dry. There had been several small fires around the area and everyone had been careful when they used machines or put out cigarettes[1]. We knew what to do, but my heart was still beating[2] hard when the moment had come. We could see the smoke. It was a long way in the distance, but the area which it covered already looked huge. Then I noticed the wind. It blew towards the farm, which was bad news. The fire moved towards us. "OK, Sonya and Rachel," shouted Barry, the assistant manager. "Move as many of the sheep as you can into the two fields behind the house. But be careful!" Then he shouted to others, "You! Put all the pets and the chickens into the cages. Luke, drive down to the gates and wait for the firefighters…"

Rachel and I ran over to some of the other farm workers who tried to move the sheep behind the house. All the sheep were already in fields close to the house because of the fire risk[3], but the smoke got thicker[4] and made the sheep nervous. It was difficult to gather them all up and move them, but we got them all on the road and moved them in the right direction. As we got closer to the field, sparks[5] started to fall from the sky around us. Rachel and I looked at each other. "This is getting scary," she said. The wind got warmer around us and the smoke hurt my eyes and throat.

Finally we got all the sheep in. As we closed the gates, we heard the sound of helicopters, which were there to drop[6] water on the fires. In front of the house we saw our boss Audrey. She talked to one of the firefighters. Some farm workers got things ready to leave the farm. "Are we leaving?" I asked Barry. "Maybe. We're preparing everything and waiting for a decision." A fire engine stopped in front of the house and some firefighters jumped out, black with smoke. One of them came over to me. She had a towel with something inside. "Can you take this?" she asked, and held the towel out to me. I took it from her and noticed that something was wrapped in it. As I opened it I saw a black nose and two big furry[7] ears. "I think he's OK," she said. "Just thirsty. He was on the road." "OK…" I stared at the baby kangaroo in my arms.

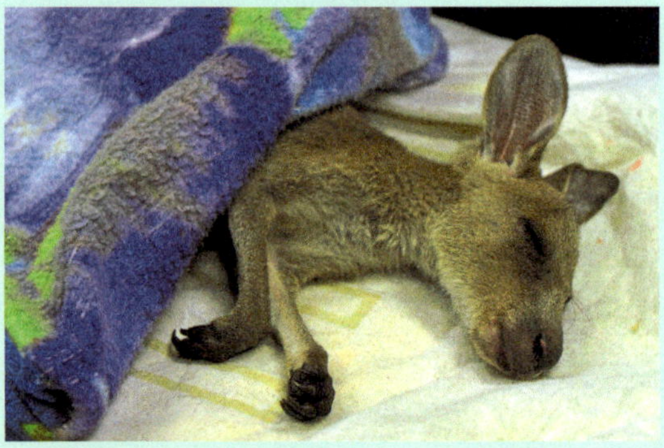

Audrey called to us as I got some water for my new friend. "Right, everyone, good news. The wind has changed direction. The firefighters think they have things under control so we will stay here for now. A group of us must stay here to protect the house and the animals because the situation could change at any time. The rest of us are going out to check the fire doesn't start again." We were all happy but also a little nervous as we looked at the orange and grey sky which was still full of smoke.

1 cigarette [ˌsɪɡrˈet] – *Zigarette;* 2 was beating [wɒz ˈbiːtɪŋ] – *schlug;* 3 risk [rɪsk] – *Risiko;* 4 thick [θɪk] *dick, dicht;* 5 spark [spɑːk] – *Funke;* 6 to drop [drɒp] – *fallen (lassen);* 7 furry [ˈfɜːri] – *pelzig*

21/5

2 Right or wrong? Tick the right box.

	right	wrong
1. Sonya woke up because she heard the sound of people and engines.	☐	☐
2. The farm house was on fire.	☐	☐
3. The weather had been dry, hot and windy.	☐	☐
4. The wind blew away from the farm.	☐	☐
5. They had to put the sheep into cages.	☐	☐
6. Helicopters came and dropped water on the fires.	☐	☐
7. A firefighter gave Sonya an injured koala.	☐	☐
8. She found the animal on the road.	☐	☐

21/5

3 Answer the questions.

1. What did Sonya and Rachel do after they had woken up?

___

2. Why had they been afraid of fires for weeks?

___

3. What did Barry ask Sonya and Rachel to do?

___

___

4. Why was it difficult to move the sheep?

___

5. Why did the farm workers stay on the farm?

___

21/5

4 (WRITING) Make a fire safety leaflet.

a) What can cause fires in the outback? Seach the internet and collect ideas in a mind map.

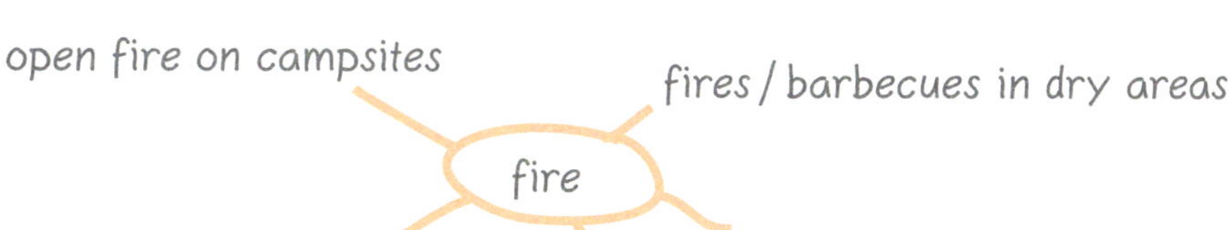

b) Use your mind map to make a fire safety leaflet.

1 (MEDIATION) Wovor warnt dieses Schild? Fasse die Informationen auf Deutsch zusammen.

22/1

2 (MEDIATION) A tour through the outback

22/1

Du machst mit deinem Vater eine Tour durch das Outback. Er macht sich Sorgen wegen gefährlicher Tiere. Vermittle zwischen ihm und dem Führer.

Your dad: Kannst du fragen, ob es hier gefährliche Schlangen gibt?

You: ______

Tour guide: Yes, but they are not dangerous if you leave them alone.

You: ______

Your dad: Was ist mit Spinnen?

You: ______

Tour guide: The spiders here are very big, but they aren't dangerous because they stay in their webs.

You: ______

Tour guide: Tell your dad not to worry. I'll look after everyone! Just make sure you cover your arms and legs so that insects don't bite you.

You: ______

1. Löse alle Aufgaben.
2. Überprüfe deine Lösungen online. Gib dazu den 🌐-Code (nach Ziel 5) auf www.klett.de ein.
3. Gib dir selbst Punkte. Wenn du weniger als die Hälfte der Punkte hast, male das Kästchen rot aus und übe auf den Step by step-Seiten (z. B. bei Unit 1 auf S. 18–19).

Ziel 1: I can understand information about Australia.

→ ⊙ pq88b3

Australia is a country and also a continent with a huge desert at its heart. Most of its cities are near the coast, like the biggest cities, Sydney and Melbourne, although the capital, Canberra, has forests and farms around it. Australia is famous for its unusual wildlife and interesting countryside. From Uluru in the red centre to the Great Barrier Reef in Queensland to the spectacular Sydney Harbour, there is something for everyone to enjoy. There are famous animals too, such as kangaroos and koalas, and also thousands of types of fish, spiders and insects. Many people think of Australia as a country full of immigrants, but Aboriginal people have been on the continent for thousands of years, and have a very old and traditional culture. Tourists from around the world come to Australia for the sun, sea and surf lifestyle.

What does the text say about …

1. Canberra? ______
2. the animals in Australia? ______
3. Aboriginal people? ______
4. tourists? ______

4P

p. 18/1

Ziel 2: I can discuss respectful behaviour.

→ ⊙ i82h7b → ⊙ ht6c27

Look at the picture and describe the situation. What is disrespectful?

The picture ______

4P

p. 18/2

Ziel 3: I can write a job application.

→ ⊙ a6ix7k → ⊙ nj26s6

Look at the job ad. Write an e-mail application.

Waiter/waitress wanted!

- Busy city centre coffee shop
- Saturdays only
- Must be friendly and have good customer service skills.
- Needs to be good at maths and hard-working
- No experience needed; on-the-job training will be given

Please contact gillian.ford@coffeetime.au

E-MAIL

Dear Ms Ford,

5P

→ p. 19/3

Ziel 4: I can understand a text about dangers to the environment.

→ ⊙ 72k3fw

Read the text on pages 20–21 in your book again. Answer the questions.

1. Why is the future of the Great Barrier Reef uncertain?
2. What are the greatest threats to the reef today?
3. What happens when the algae die?
4. Name two other things that damage the reef.
5. What does the Australian government do to stop the decline?

7P

→ p. 19/4

Ziel 5: I can pass on information about signs.

a) Du reist durch Australien und siehst unterwegs diese Schilder. Worauf weisen sie hin?

1. ______________________________

2. ______________________________

3. ______________________________

4. ______________________________

5. ______________________________

b) Du bist mit deinen Eltern bei einer Autovermietung. Vermittle zwischen deiner Mutter und dem Mitarbeiter der Autovermietung.

Your mum: Kannst du fragen, wie schnell man in Australien fahren darf?

You: ______________________________

Man: That depends on the road. It's always best to check the road signs.

You: ______________________________

Your mum: Sag ihm, dass wir ins Outback fahren wollen. Ist das gefährlich?

You: ______________________________

Man: Not really. But don't drive when it's dark because there can be animals on the road. And make sure you have enough water and gas. And pay attention to the road signs.

You: ______________________________

____

____

9P
p. 19/5

Lösungen online z8n354

○ Ziel 1: I can understand information about Australia.

About 30 million years ago the Australian continent broke away from Antarctica. Several animal species developed there that only exist in Australia, for example the koala and the kangaroo. The Aboriginal people have lived in Australia for over 50,000 years. When British settlers arrived in the 18th century, they killed a lot of the Aboriginal people. Australia is famous for its coasts and countryside, but there are also a lot of big cities. Australians like to spend a lot of time outside. They love the beach, where they have parties and do sports. The centre of Australia is known as the outback. There are huge farms in the outback, but few people actually live there. The distances are so great that there are often no schools or hospitals near the farms.

Right or wrong? Tick the right box.

	right	wrong
1. The Australian continent broke away from Africa.	☐	☐
2. The koala and the kangaroo only exist in Australia.	☐	☐
3. The British settlers killed a lot of the Aboriginal people.	☐	☐
4. Australia is famous for its big mountains.	☐	☐
5. There are a lot of big cities in Australia.	☐	☐
6. The distances in the outback are so great that there are no farms.	☐	☐

○ Ziel 2: I can discuss respectful behaviour.

Look at the picture. What is happening? Who is disrespectful? Write three sentences.

○ **Ziel 3: I can write a job application.**

Read the job ad and complete the application.

find attached my CV	worked at a coffee shop	I am … years
friendly and enjoy working	forward to hearing from you	excellent computer skills
well-qualified for	apply for the job as	a student at …

E-MAIL

Dear Cindy ______,

I would like to ______ a receptionist at HairCut. I am ______ ______ and ______ old.

I believe that I am ______ this job. I have already ______ for two months and I have ______ ______.

I am also very ______ with people. Please ______. I look forward ______.

Yours sincerely,

Receptionist at HairCut Hairdressers

Are you friendly and hard-working? Do you have good computer skills? Do you enjoy working with people?

We are looking for a receptionist. Friday afternoons and Saturdays only.

Please send your application to: cindy@haircut.au

○ **Ziel 4: I can understand a text about dangers to the environment.**

Read the text on pages 20–21 in your book again. Choose the right answer.

1. You can see the Great Barrier Reef from …	a) the moon.	☐	b) the UK.	☐
2. Visitors come to the reef to see …	a) whales and turtles.	☐	b) the ocean.	☐
3. Coral bleaching is caused by …	a) animals.	☐	b) climate change.	☐
4. The water is polluted by …	a) waste and oil spills.	☐	b) algae.	☐
5. Climate change has to be solved …	a) by Australia.	☐	b) globally.	☐

○ **Ziel 5: I can pass on information about signs.**

1

2

Beantworte die Fragen auf Deutsch.

1. Welches Schild ist für Autofahrer? ______
2. Für wen ist Schild Nr. 1? ______ ______
3. Welches Schild warnt vor Tieren? ______

A LISTENING

You will hear two Australian teenagers talking about their lives. You will hear the recordings twice.

Lauren

Damien

3 **1 Listen. Who says what? Write the names next to the sentences.**

1. I live with my parents and sister on a cattle station. ________________
2. We all use the School of the Air, but we often meet to study together. ________________
3. My favourite thing to do is to go to the beach and surf. ________________
4. The families nearby often get together to have a barbecue. ________________
5. At the weekend I often go to the city centre with my friends. ________________
6. I was bitten by a spider when I was little. ________________

3 **2 Listen again and complete the sentences.**

1. Lauren's family is lucky because they live near a ________________ .
2. When Lauren and her friends aren't at school, they spend most of their time ________________ .
3. The cows need water and trees that can protect them from the ________________ .
4. Damien thinks school is pretty ________________ .
5. His mum says he has to start surfing less because he has ________________ .
6. Sydney is a really cool ________________ .

B READING

The Royal Flying Doctor Service

What happens when you live in the outback and you have a medical emergency? Or you need some medicine? Well, you call the Royal Flying Doctors Service. One man's idea in 1928 to help people who lived far away from medical services has now grown to a service that has 68 planes, which fly over 15 million kilometres every year and cover an area of 7.13 million square kilometres. The service can reach any place in the country, no matter how far, in a few hours.

The Royal Flying Doctor Service became famous around the world in the 1980s with a TV drama called 'The Flying Doctors'. However, Mia Jefferies, who has worked as a 'flying doctor' for over ten years, explains that the doctor's job is not always as exciting as shown on TV. "Most people, when they think of the flying doctors, imagine people are rescued because they fell down a mountain or were attacked by a dangerous snake," she says. "But actually most of the time the doctors work in small hospitals in one of the towns of the outback. There we deal with normal, everyday complaints, do check-ups and give out medicine. Of course, some people have more serious problems and we regularly fly patients to bigger hospitals. And if there is an emergency, we fly out to the people who need help. But often we can give people medical advice on the phone, and most farms have medicine available which they can use in these cases."

Kenny Murray says the flying doctors saved his life after a fishing trip last year. "I tried to catch some fish in my boat when the engine stopped working. I tried to repair it, but I cut my hand really badly. I got back to land, but I had lost a lot of blood. My neighbour found me and called the doctors. They came by plane and took me to hospital within an hour. If the doctors hadn't come to help me so quickly I would be dead now."

The Royal Flying Doctors are very important in Australia and the service is used in every part of the country today.

1 True, false or not in the text?

1. The Royal Flying Doctor Service is over 150 years old. ______________
2. The flying doctors can reach any place in the country in a few hours. ______________
3. The service was founded by John Flynn. ________________________
4. Most of the time the doctors work in small hospitals in the towns of the outback. ______________
5. If there is an emergency, they fly out to the people who need help. ______________
6. The flying doctors couldn't help Kenny Murray. ______________

2 Answer the questions.

1. Why was the Flying Doctor Service created?

____

2. How many planes does the service have now? ______________________________
3. What made flying doctors famous around the world?

____

4. What do the doctors normally do?

____

5. What does Kenny Murray say about the flying doctors?

____

C LANGUAGE

A, B, C or D? Fill in the gaps.

Tasmania

A lot of tourists come to Australia every year, but only a few also ____________ (1) Tasmania, the island south of the country. Those who take the trip ____________ (2) the sea to Tasmania will find a place which is quite different to Australia. The ____________ (3) of the island is only 500,000 and there aren't many big cities. Tasmania has interesting countryside with ____________ (4) and beautiful beaches, many national parks and spectacular mountains. The most famous ____________ (5) on the island is the Tasmanian devil. It is a small animal which only lives in Tasmania. The island grows and produces some amazing food and wine and in Hobart, the state capital, you ____________ (6) visit a famous modern art museum, the MONA.

	A	B	C	D
1.	visited	visits	visit	have visited
2.	under	on	towards	across
3.	population	people	place	plant
4.	wildly	wild	wildlife	wilderness
5.	and	angry	animal	after
6.	could	may	have	can

D WRITING

Choose one of the following tasks:

1 You want to spend one year as an exchange student in Australia. Write a text about yourself for your host family. Include the following information:

- Name
- Age
- Where you go to school and what you like / dislike about it
- What you do in your free time
- What you are interested in
- What you like to eat / allergies …

2 Write an e-mail to apply for a job.

You are an Australian teenager who is looking for a part-time job. Read the job ad and write an e-mail to apply for the job. Include the following information:

- Name
- Age
- What you are looking for
- What you are good at
- Why you are a good candidate for the job

Burger Restaurant – Help wanted!

Working hours:
11 a.m. – 5 p.m. (Friday and Saturday only)
Sell food and clean tables.
Wage: AU$ 10 per hour
Work with a friendly and busy team.

Contact: paul@burgerfast.au

E-MAIL

E MEDIATION

INTERNET

Immigration to Australia

Australia has one of the largest immigrant populations in the Western world. There are now about 5.3 million immigrants living in the country, about a quarter of the population. Around 150,000 immigrants arrive to live in Australia every year.

Nowadays, most people move from New Zealand, India, China and the UK. New Zealand and the UK have a long history of people moving between the two countries and people from China and India move to Australia because they are looking for a better education and good work opportunities. Because there are so many immigrants in Australia, the country is very multicultural.

People from different countries bring their own cultures with them, so Australians enjoy celebrating lots of different festivals. Food from all over the world is available in Australian shops and restaurants. Immigrants to the country have contributed to the success of the country by working hard and starting up new businesses in the country.

Du recherchierst für ein Schulprojekt zur Einwanderungspolitik in verschiedenen Staaten. Du hast diese Seite gefunden und möchtest die Informationen für dein Projekt verwenden. Fasse die wichtigsten Punkte des Textes auf Deutsch zusammen:

- Wie viele Einwanderer leben in Australien?
- Woher kommen sie?
- Warum kommen sie nach Australien?
- Welche Auswirkungen hat das auf das Leben der Australier?

F SPEAKING

1 Information gap activity

a) Partner A asks questions and partner B gives the answers.

Partner A

- Name of the Day?
- When is it?
- Why is it celebrated?
- How is it celebrated?
- What else happens on this day?

Partner B

INTERNET

Australia Day
26th January

Every year the country comes together to celebrate the day the first British ships arrived in Sydney Harbour in 1788.

Around the country there are concerts, barbecues, sports competitions, festivals and fireworks.
A lot of immigrants choose this day to become Australian citizens, and prizes are given to important Australians. One person is chosen as 'Australian of the Year'.

b) Now change roles. Partner B asks questions and partner A gives the answers.

Partner B

- Name of the Day?
- When is it?
- What do people remember?
- What happens on this day?
- What do schools do?

Partner A

INTERNET

National Sorry Day
26th May

On National Sorry Day people remember the bad things that happened to Aboriginal people. For example many Aboriginal children were taken away from their families because the government wanted them to live like white Australians. There are concerts and people go on marches and make speeches about Aboriginal rights. The Aboriginal flag is flown and schools take part in special activities and watch films about Aboriginal rights and history.

Unit 2
Colourful Caribbean

4 28/2

1 (LISTENING) Listen to the travel report on the radio.

a) Put the pictures in the right order.
b) Listen again and write one sentence for each picture.

28/2

2 (WRITING) Describe the picture of a beach in the Caribbean.

This is a picture of

30/1

1 Find the words.

a) Write the words for the pictures.

1. ______ 2. ______ 3. ______ 4. ______

5. ______ 6. ______ 7. ______ 8. ______

b) Choose five words and write definitions for them in your exercise book.

31/4

2 Collect holiday words.

a) Complete the table. Write as many words as you can.

places you can visit	things you pack in your suitcase	holiday activities
beach,	sunglasses,	diving,

b) Compare your table with your partner.

31/5

3 Put a circle around the correct word.

1. Before you can go on a flight, you must buy a gate • ticket • delay.
2. You can pack all your things in a survey • stamp • suitcase.
3. When your plane is late, there is a delay • departure • boarding.
4. When you want to leave the European Union, the police checks your port • passport • photo.
5. Before you can get on the plane, you must go to the right gas • game • gate.
6. Getting on the plane is called boarding • bridge • bargain.

5 31/5

4 (LISTENING) Listen to the family at the airport.

a) Tick the right box.

	right	wrong
1. Mrs Adams is travelling with three children.	☐	☐
2. One of her suitcases is too heavy.	☐	☐
3. Mrs Adams has to pay extra.	☐	☐
4. She can move some things from one suitcase to another.	☐	☐
5. Her daughter is a vegetarian and wants a special meal on the plane.	☐	☐
6. There is an announcement that the flight is on time.	☐	☐

b) Listen again. Complete Mrs Adams' boarding pass.

Name of passenger		Flight No.	Date	Seat
Jennifer Adams		______	27th Dec 2018	______
From:	London			
To:	______			
Gate		Boarding time		
______		______		

32/6

5 Use who or which to make one sentence out of two.

1. We went to the island. It attracts the most tourists.
   We went to the island which attracts the most tourists.
2. I called my friend. She spends all her holidays in the Caribbean.
   ______
3. We met an old man. He knew Bob Marley.
   ______
4. I just heard a band. It played great reggae music.
   ______
5. I read about some pirates. They attacked ships in the Caribbean.
   ______
6. We had a young guide. She came from Jamaica.
   ______

6 Make contact clauses.

2/7a)

a) Which sentences can you say without who or which? Cross out the words.

1. The holiday ~~which~~ we had in the Bahamas was great.
2. Here's a photo of the beach **which** we loved the most.
3. We stayed in a hotel **which** had a beautiful view of the sea.
4. There were also day trips **which** we could book in the hotel.
5. People **who** liked diving could discover the beautiful sea life.
6. I saw amazing corals **which** I had never seen before.
7. We met a lot of tourists **who** came from the USA.
8. The teenagers **who** we met there enjoyed the parties on the beach.
9. We also booked a horse riding trip **which** was very expensive.

Folgt nach who oder which ein Personalpronomen (I, you, he, …) oder eine Person, kannst du who oder which weglassen.

2/7b)

b) Complete the sentences with who or which where necessary.

1. The resort ______________ I stayed in had three swimming pools and a diving school.
2. The receptionist ______________ checked us in was really friendly.
3. The beach ______________ was near the hotel had beautiful white sand.
4. The coconuts ______________ we drank were the freshest I have ever tasted.

7 Write relative clauses.

3/8a)

a) Rewrite the travel report. Make relative clauses for the underlined words.
b) Go through your sentences again. Leave out who or which where possible.

During our holiday in Cuba we stayed in a (1) hotel. It was awful. A (2) receptionist greeted us. She was very unfriendly. (3) Some other people stayed at the hotel. They complained about the dirty rooms. We ate (4) a meal in the hotel restaurant. It was terrible. We called the travel agency. The (5) lady there was very helpful. She showed us a new (6) hotel. The new hotel was fantastic. The (7) beach was wonderful. The beach was near the hotel. We booked a (7) jungle tour. It was very interesting. We saw a lot of (8) birds. They were very colourful. There were a lot of (9) insects. They attacked us the whole time.

During our holiday in Cuba we stayed in a hotel which was awful. The receptionist

____

____

____

____

____

____

____

8 (WRITING) Write a Caribbean story.

33/9

a) Write a story that takes place in the Caribbean. First, choose something you want to write about. You can use one of these posters from the tourist information centre or use your own ideas.

Adventure diving trip. Discover a shipwreck and look for the hidden treasure.

Come to the carnival party in Trinidad. Win a prize for the best costume.

Explore the jungle in Dominica. You will see snakes, bats and butterflies.

b) Collect ideas for your story. Answer the questions.

Who is telling the story?	
When does it happen?	
Where does it happen?	
Who is in the story?	
What happened (plot)?	beginning: parts of the story: ending:

c) Collect words for your story in a mind map.

d) Add adjectives, adverbs and connectives to your mind map.

e) Write a draft of your story in your exercise book.

f) Check your text. Use the list below.

Rechtschreibung
Hast du alle Wörter richtig geschrieben? Achte besonders auf:

- Buchstaben, die geschrieben, aber nicht gesprochen werden (z. B. walk)
- gleiche Aussprache, aber unterschiedliche Schreibung (z. B. see ⟷ sea)
- die Verdoppelung der Endkonsonanten (z. B. stop → stopping, stopped; plan → planning, planned)
- ‚y' wird zu ‚ie' (z. B. carry → he carried; city → cities; happy → happier, (the) happiest; aber buy → she buys; boy → boys)
- die Wortendung ‚-le' (z. B. simple, title)
- den Apostroph (z. B. she is → she's, Brad's bike, the Browns' house)
- Wenn du dir nicht sicher bist, schau hinten in deinem Buch oder in einem Wörterbuch nach.

Groß- und Kleinschreibung
- Hast du jeden Satz mit einem Großbuchstaben begonnen?
- Immer groß schreiben muss du: Monatsnamen, Wochentage, Eigennamen, geografische Namen

Zeichensetzung
- Endet jeder Satz mit einem Punkt? Endet jede Frage mit einem Fragezeichen?
- Denke an die Anführungszeichen bei der wörtlichen Rede.

Grammatik
- Hast du überall die richtige Zeitform verwendet?
- Hast du, wo es nötig ist, die Mehrzahl verwendet?

34/1

1 Complete the the comment on Tara's blog.

complicated | marry | struggles | disadvantaged
privileges | values | lucky | religion

BLOG

I have decided that I want to leave Jamaica. I have ________________ feelings about Jamaica, and I have different ____________ than most members of my family. ____________ is very important to them and they go to church every week. They think I should ____________ my boyfriend and start a family, but I want to experience more things. A lot of people here are ________________ and I don't want my own family to have so many ______________. My boyfriend is ___________ because he has family in the USA so maybe we will go there together. I think people there have more _______________ than we do here in Jamaica.

35/3

2 Find the words.

1. When you believe in something, you have ___________.
2. When someone is very close to you, you have a strong ___________.
3. When you have a lot of money, you can ____________ expensive things.
4. When you are never ill, you are in good ____________.
5. When you are happy to be part of a group, you ___________.

6
35/3

3 (LISTENING) Listen to three teenagers from Jamaica talking about values.

a) What is most important to these teenagers?

Linda
____

Tyler
____

Olivia
____

b) Answer the questions.

1. Why wasn't life easy for Linda and her family? ____________
2. How did Tyler feel as a child? ____________
3. Why did things get better for Tyler when he was older? ____________
4. What job does Olivia want to do when she is older? ____________
5. Why aren't some of Olivia's friends successful? ____________

36/5

4 Look at the picture. Write sentences in the present progressive.

shine | not sit | steal
sell | not wear | eat

1. The man ______.
2. Two girls ______.
3. The woman ______.
4. The children ______.
5. The dog ______.
6. The sun ______.

37/6

5 Complete the comment on Tara's blog with the past progressive.

Hi Tara. Thanks for the blog post. While I ______ (read) it, I thought about my own life here in Jamaica. My father ______ (work) at the local factory when he had an accident and lost his job. When that happened, I ______ (study) to become a nurse, but I had to give it up and move back home. We ______ (live) in a very poor area when my brother joined a street gang. A few years ago we ______ (eat) dinner when my brother came home. He was covered in blood. We were really afraid, so we decided to move to a new area. Life is better now. – Linda

37/7a)

6 Read Linda's notes about the area where she used to live. Complete her report. Use the past progressive.

- *local groups try to solve the problems*
- *members of street gangs talk to police*
- *police officers walk around the area*
- *churches collect food*
- *local businessmen create jobs*
- *teachers encourage young people to stay in school*
- *community offer job application training*
- *sports clubs organize activities*

Local groups in Kingston *were trying to* ______ in the area. Members ______. Police officers ______ at night. The churches ______. Local ______. The teachers ______. The community ______. Sports clubs ______.

7 Complete the news report. Put in the simple past or the past progressive.

37/7b)

1. Last night street gangs ________________ in Kingtson when the police ___________ . (fight, arrive)
2. The police ____________ several men while the other gang members _________________ .
   (arrest, escape)
3. The police ________________ for them when they __________ the sound of guns. (look, hear)
4. Some gang members _______________ at each other when the police ________ them. (shoot, find)
5. While the police officers ______________ to stop the fight, the gang leader _______ away. (try, run)
6. Later that night street the police ________ him while he _____________ to steal a car. (find, try)

8 (WRITING) Prepare a speech.

37/8

a) Give a speech on the following statement: “Money can buy you happiness.”
Do you agree? Why (not)? Try to find as many reasons as you can and write them in the list.

yes, because …	no, because …

b) Look at the phrases and sort them in the table.

Let me give you an example. | To sum up, … | My name is … | Thank you for listening. | First I'd like to talk about … | Good morning. | The reason is … | Do you have any questions? | That's the end of my speech. | Hello everyone. | Finally I think … | Another interesting point is …

introduction	main part	conclusion

c) Write a draft of your speech in your exercise book.

d) Give your speech to the class.

37/8

1 (SPEAKING) Act a dialogue at the travel agent's.

a) Work with a partner. One of you is a travel agent; the other one is a customer. Read your role cards and act a dialogue.

Travel Agent
- Say hello and ask how you can help.
- Offer different kinds of holidays: beach holiday, diving and hiking.
- Tell your customer more about these holidays:

Diving holiday in the Bahamas
two weeks, hotel near the beach
diving school next to the hotel
diving trips to different reefs

Hiking holiday in Dominica
one week, hotel in the jungle with swimming pool
hiking trips in the jungle

- Inform you customer about the prices:
  Diving holiday: £3,200 per person
  Hiking holiday: £1,800 per person

Customer
- Say hello and ask for information about holidays in the Caribbean.
- Ask for information about diving and hiking holidays.
- Say you want to travel with your friend.
- Ask for prices.
- Say that you want to talk to your friend first. Say thank you and goodbye.

b) Collect information about other holidays in the Caribbean and act another dialogue. Change roles.

37/8

2 (SPEAKING) Talk about values.

Read the comment on Tara's blog. Do you agree with Jade? Why (not)? Discuss with your partner.

BLOG

Jade: 19/02/2017 at 10:02 p.m.

I think it's important to be successful in life. If there aren't enough jobs in your country, you should try to leave and move to another country. It's sad if you have to leave family and friends behind, but I think it's more important to have the best opportunities in life.

In my opinion …	I think …	If you ask me, …
I'm sorry, but I don't think so.	I agree. / I don't agree.	That's true, but …
That's a good point.	Don't you think that …	I see what you mean, but …
Could you explain that, please?	I'm sorry, but I'm not sure what you mean.	

41/4

1 (READING) Read the story.

21st century pirates

"I'm so jealous!" said Sarah, Adam's little sister. "You're going to spend two weeks on a yacht[1] in the Caribbean and I'm going to spend three weeks in a caravan in rainy Wales. It's not fair!"
Adam laughed and checked his passport and ticket again. He couldn't believe it. His best friend Greg had invited him to spend two weeks on his family's yacht. Greg's dad was a successful businessman who worked really hard. His only chance to relax was on the family yacht, and this time Adam was invited! He was meeting Greg and his dad at the airport in Barbados and was a little nervous.
"Make sure you text us," said Adam's mum. "Greg's father told us there is wifi[2] on the yacht, and he has just bought a satellite phone, so no excuses!"
"Yes, Mum, don't worry," said Adam.

Greg and his father picked Adam up from the airport and then they took a taxi to the port. "We don't want to waste any time!" said Greg's dad. He loved sailing and was really funny when he wasn't thinking about work. Adam stopped feeling nervous. His excitement grew as he saw the yacht in the sun. He couldn't believe this was his home for the next two weeks!
Adam really enjoyed his first week on the yacht. They drove to different islands in the Caribbean and Adam helped Greg's dad on the boat and learned something new every day. After a few days Adam felt totally relaxed.

Then one evening, while Adam was doing the washing up below deck, he heard shouts above him and the sound of heavy boots or shoes. 'That's strange,' he thought because one of the first things Greg's dad had told him was to take his shoes off when he was on the yacht. He was walking up the stairs when he heard Greg's dad shouting, "Please, don't hurt us! Look, all the money I have is downstairs. Come with me and you can have it!" Adam's heart began to beat faster. Were there pirates on board? Was Greg's dad going to bring them downstairs? What would they do if they saw him? He quickly hid behind the kitchen door.

Greg and his father came down the stairs, followed by the three men, who were carrying long knives. They had masks[3] over their faces and he could only see their eyes. "Who else is on board?" shouted one of the pirates.
"No one, just my son and I," replied Greg's father. Greg looked around the kitchen, looking for Adam.
"Don't try to escape. We have broken your radio[4] so you can't call for help. Just show us where the money is."

Adam felt sick. What could he do? Even if he got to the radio, he couldn't call for help. Then he remembered – the wifi! He took out his phone – no signal! Of course, they were too far out in the ocean. The only other option was the satellite phone. But where was it? Adam looked around the kitchen. It wasn't there. The pirates had taken Greg and his father into the bedroom where the money and documents were kept. He couldn't go and look in there. His only chance was to try and sneak[5] up onto the deck and try and find the phone. He slowly opened the kitchen door and looked along the short corridor. The bedroom door wasn't completely closed, and he could see Greg sitting on the floor, his hands tied together. He tried to get his attention and when Greg saw him his eyes grew round and shocked. Adam pointed his finger upstairs.

1 yacht [jɒt] – *Yacht;* 2 wifi ['waɪfaɪ] – *WLAN;* 3 mask [mɑːsk] – *Maske;* 4 radio ['reɪdiəʊ] *hier: Funkgerät;* 5 to sneak [sniːk] – *schleichen*

Greg suddenly started shouting, “HELP! HELP! PIRATES!”. The pirates jumped on him to keep him quiet and Adam took his chance. He ran quickly up the stairs, hoping Greg’s shouts would hide any noises he made. He hoped the pirates wouldn’t hurt Greg or his father. And there it was! The satellite phone was on the table where they had had dinner. Of course, he had used it to call his mum. He grabbed the phone, but who could he call? He didn’t know the number for the police or coastguard. The only number in the phone was his mum’s. So he called it ….

Later that day, Adam called his mum again.
“Yes, mum, we are all fine, thanks to you! Two hours after I had called you, three boats full of police came and rescued us.”
“Oh, Adam! I’m so glad you’re all OK! But you were really lucky. We’ve only got one solar charger while we are camping and I put my phone away after you had called earlier. Luckily your sister used my phone to play games while hers was charging[6], so she saw you were calling!”

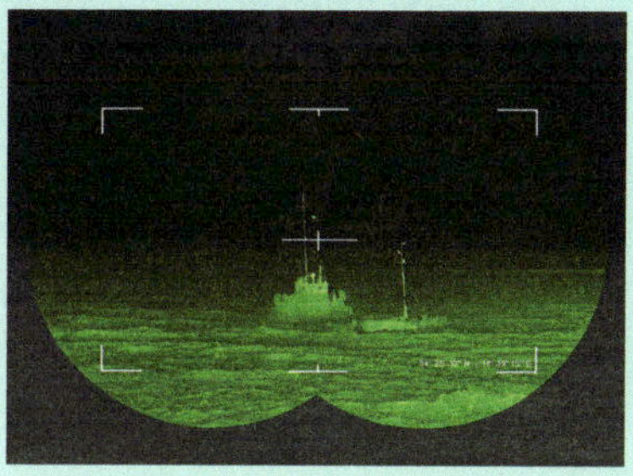

6 to charge [tʃɑːdʒ] – *aufladen*

2 Answer the questions.

41/4

1. Why did Adam fly to Barbados?

____

2. What did Adam hear while he was doing the washing up one evening?

____

3. Why was Adam afraid? ______________________________
4. Where did Adam hide? ______________________________
5. Why couldn’t Adam call for help on the radio? ______________________________
6. What was the only option to call for help? ______________________________
7. Why didn’t the pirates hear Adam when he ran up the stairs?

____

8. Who did Adam call and who rescued them? ______________________________

____

3 (WRITING) Write another part of the story.

41/4

a) What do you think happened between Adam’s phone call and the time the police arrived? Write notes.

b) Use your notes to write that part of the story in your exercise book.

Dominica – Welcome to Nature Island

Trafalgar Falls

Dominica has the nickname 'Nature Island' for some very good reasons. If you are bored with sunbathing, Dominica is the perfect island for you because there are lots of activities for active people.

Dominica has some of the most beautiful hiking trails in the Caribbean, which pass through mountains and forests. You can spend a day at the famous waterfall Trafalgar Falls, and even go swimming under it. Or you can hike to the world's second largest hot lake, the Boiling Lake in Morne Trois Pitons National Park. Dominica is one of the top five places in the world for diving. The island is also one of the few places in the Caribbean where you can dive around underwater volcanoes.

You can also go canoeing, horse riding and even whale watching. There is a great population of whales around Dominica, so you have a great chance to see some.

42/1

1 (MEDIATION) Fasse die wichtigsten Informationen zusammen.

Du hast beim Aufräumen eines Bücherregals zu Hause diese Broschüre über die Karibikinsel Dominica gefunden. Berichte deinem jüngeren Bruder, was man in Dominica alles sehen kann.

____

____

____

42/1

2 (MEDIATION) At the tourist information centre.

Du machst mit deiner Familie einen Ausflug zu den Walgebieten auf Dominica. Die Mitarbeiterin auf dem Boot gibt einige Anweisungen. Dein Vater versteht nicht alles. Vermittle zwischen den beiden.

Woman: Good morning. Welcome to our whale watching tour. Our boat leaves in ten minutes. Please make sure you're all wearing your life jackets now.

Your dad: Was hat sie gesagt?

You: ________________________________

Your dad: Kannst du sie fragen, wo genau wir hinfahren?

You: ________________________________

Woman: We will go around the coast. The deep water there is a feeding ground for whales.

You: ________________________________

Your dad: Können wir nahe genug an die Wale ran, um Fotos zu machen?

You: ________________________________

Woman: You'll be able to take photos, but we never to try to attract the whales with food.

You: ________________________________

Ziel 1: I can understand information about the Caribbean.

→ ⦾ a5k4rd

Rose Great Hall, Jamaica

Tourists who are bored of the beach can visit one of the many historic houses in Jamaica. These were mostly built in the 18th century by rich Europeans who owned sugar plantations. Perhaps the most famous of these houses is Rose Great Hall in Montego Bay. This house was built in 1770 and was owned by John Palmer, but it was his wife Annie who made this house very famous. Annie Palmer is also known as the 'White Witch of Rose Hall' and people say her ghost can be seen in the house at night. Annie's nursery teacher taught her how to do magic, and the legend says that Annie used her magic skills so that John Palmer would marry her. John Palmer was very rich and owned one of the largest plantations in Jamaica. People say Annie killed him so that she could control the plantation, and then killed her next two husbands too. Later she was killed by a slave who worked on the plantation.
We know today that the story is not true, but people still visit the house to see if they can see the famous ghost.

Answer the questions.

1. What is the name of the most famous historic house in Jamaica? ____________
2. What is the house famous for? ____________
3. Why did John Palmer marry Annie? ____________
4. What happened to Annie's husbands? ____________
5. How did Annie die? ____________
6. Is this story true? ____________

4P

→p. 42/1

Ziel 2: I can write a fictional story.

→ ⦾ 4y69vd → ⦾ 6d9r8u

Use these words to write a short story about the Caribbean.

holiday in Dominica
hiking tour jungle
insects
snake
not dangerous
smells bad when scared

____

6P

→p. 42/2

Ziel 3: I can talk about standards and values.

→ ⦾ 9pq5cw → ⦾ un3i33

Who gives better advice – friends or parents?

a) Collect reasons.

parents	friends

b) Write your opinion.

8P

→ p. 43/3

Ziel 4: I can understand a pirate story.

→ ⦾ ar2wy2

Read the text on pages 38–41 in your book again. Put the sentences in the right order.

- ☐ Eliza tried to protect Carol from the pirate.
- ☐ Eliza's journey from Bristol to the Caribbean was quiet and peaceful.
- ☐ Eliza and Carol were taken away and put in a cabin with the other prisoners.
- ☐ Pirates attacked the Lady Margaret.
- ☐ Captain Blackheart chose a punishment for Eliza.
- ☐ Eliza was offered a job as governess to Lord Winton's children.
- ☐ A ship of the Royal Navy arrived.
- ☐ Eliza put on men's clothes.

8P

→ p. 43/4

Ziel 5: I can pass on information about tourist attractions.

BLOG

Reiseabenteuer

Kuba – meine Highlights und die besten Tipps

Ich habe drei aufregende und spannende Wochen auf dieser karibischen Trauminsel verbracht und möchte meine tollsten Erlebnisse und Tipps heute mit euch teilen. Vielleicht bekommt ihr ja auch Lust auf einen Urlaub auf Kuba.

Für die Einreise nach Kuba benötigt ihr einen Reisepass, der noch mindestens sechs Monate gültig ist. Zusätzlich braucht man eine Touristenkarte (tourist card), die man vor der Einreise kaufen muss. Man erhält sie normalerweise in deutschen Reisebüros. Man kann die Insel gut mit dem Bus erkunden oder ein Auto mieten. Die Straßen sind aber meistens schlecht, also solltet ihr vorsichtig fahren. Die beste Reisezeit für Kuba ist von November bis April. Das ganze Jahr über liegt die Temperatur um die 28 Grad, aber von Mai bis Dezember kann es öfter regnen. Von Juli bis Oktober kann es auch Wirbelstürme geben. Die Landessprache auf Kuba ist Spanisch. Englisch wird kaum gesprochen, deshalb solltest du vorher unbedingt einige wichtige spanische Wörter lernen und ein Wörterbuch mitnehmen. Das Internet ist auf Kuba nicht sehr gut ausgebaut. In Hotels kann man meistens WLAN nutzen, aber es ist oft überlastet und sehr langsam. Es gibt auf Kuba sehr schöne Hotels, aber am besten lernt man Land und Leute kennen, wenn man in Gästehäusern übernachtet. Alle Unterkünfte, die eine Lizenz haben, sind an der Haustür mit einem blauen Anker gekennzeichnet. Buchen könnt ihr über das Internet.

Das waren die Highlights meiner Kubareise:

- Ein Bummel durch die Hauptstadt Havanna mit ihrer wunderschönen Altstadt und Uferpromenade.
- Die Strände im Norden der Insel. Dort kann man auch hervorragend tauchen.
- Der Baconao Park in der Nähe von Santiago de Cuba. Um die Aussicht zu genießen, müsst ihr auf den "großen Stein" klettern. Bei Santiago de Cuba könnt ihr auch Kaffeeplantagen besichtigen.

You are preparing a presentation about Cuba for your English class. You have found this blog entry on the internet. What tips does the text give you about travelling to Cuba?

6P

→p. 43/5

Lösungen online dz4p2r

○ Ziel 1: I can understand information about the Caribbean.

There are thousands of islands in the Caribbean. Some are large and have a lot of inhabitants and others are small and not inhabited. The islands are a true paradise for tourists, but not everything is perfect. A lot of people in the Caribbean are unemployed and some emigrate to other countries like the US, the UK or Canada. They work there and send money home to their families. The people who live in the Caribbean have different roots because most islands used to be British, Spanish or French colonies.

A lot of people are descendants of slaves who were brought from Africa and had to work in awful conditions on the plantations. As a result there have been many influences on Caribbean culture. There are different music styles like reggae, calypso and salsa and dishes which are made from African recipes.

Tick the right box.

	right	wrong
1. All islands in the Caribbean are inhabited.	☐	☐
2. Everything is perfect in the Caribbean.	☐	☐
3. A lot of people are unemployed.	☐	☐
4. Some people emigrate and send money home to their families.	☐	☐
5. There are no descendants of slaves from Africa.	☐	☐
6. There have been many influences on Caribbean culture.	☐	☐

○ Ziel 2: I can write a fictional story.

Use the words to write a story that takes place in the Caribbean.

holiday in Jamaica with family | go on a diving trip | pick up at hotel | go to harbour | small boat | mum feel sick and afraid | feel sorry for her | stay with mum | look around harbour and have lunch | have a great time | later feel sad | dad see whale shark

○ **Ziel 3: I can talk about standards and values.**

Who gives better advice – friends or parents? Choose phrases from below and write your opinion.

parents love you and want to help you | friends know you best | parents are older and have more experience in life | friends often have the same problems | parents had the same problems when they were young | listen to your friends and your parents | friends are young and understand you better | both give great advice

The question is ______________________ On the one hand, ______

____

______________________ On the other hand, ______________

____

In my opinion ______________________ because ______

____

○ **Ziel 4: I can understand a pirate story.**

Read the text on pages 38–41 in your book again. Find the information and write the lines.

1. Eliza's home town and her family: ______________
2. The pirates attack: ______________
3. Eliza puts on some men's clothes: ______________
4. Eliza protects Carol: ______________
5. Carol and Eliza are prisoners: ______________
6. HMS Revenge arrives: ______________

○ **Ziel 5: I can pass on information about tourist attractions.**

SEA TURTLE NEST

DO NOT DISTURB!

- Do not use lights on the beach at night.
- Never disturb a sea turtle that is crawling to or from the ocean.
- Only watch from a distance.
- Do not take photos with a flash.
- Do not touch or disturb nests or turtle babies.

Report all sightings if you see a dead or injured turtle.

Du hast im Urlaub dieses Schild am Strand gesehen. Worauf muss man achten, wenn man ein Nest von Meeresschildkröten sieht?

____

____

____

____

____

____

____

A LISTENING

You will hear five airport announcements. You will hear the recordings twice.

7 **1 Listen to the announcements. Write the correct numbers.**

1. Which announcement is for parents with small children and people who need assistance? ____________
2. Which announcement tells you about a delay in boarding? ____________________
3. Which announcement is for Mr Miller? ____________________
4. Which announcement tells you that a gate number has been changed? ____________________
5. Which announcement asks passengers to show their passports? ____________________

7 **2 Listen again. Choose the correct answer.**

1. There is priority boarding for the flight to …
   a) Miami. ☐
   b) London. ☐
   c) Havana. ☐
2. The new gate number for the flight to London is …
   a) A54. ☐
   b) A45. ☐
   c) B45. ☐
3. Boarding for the flight to Havana begins at …
   a) 11:30. ☐
   b) 9:30. ☐
   c) 10:30. ☐
4. Priority boarding is for …
   a) passengers with small children and passengers who need assistance. ☐
   b) passengers with small children and passengers with bags. ☐
   c) passengers with babies and small children. ☐
5. Passengers for the flight to New York are asked to …
   a) show their boarding passes and bags. ☐
   b) show their boarding passes and passports. ☐
   c) show their tickets and boarding passes. ☐
6. Mr Miller has to go to …
   a) Gate B39. ☐
   b) Gate B29. ☐
   c) Gate C39. ☐

B READING

Irma: A hurricane for the history books

Hurricanes and tropical storms are not unusual in the Caribbean. The hurricane season runs from June to November each year, but the most dangerous storms arrive in August and September. Each storm is given a name and a number between 1 and 5 according to how dangerous it is. A dangerous category 5 hurricane usually happens only once every three years. In 2017 category 5 hurricane Irma hit the Caribbean and the USA with winds of 180 mph and caused extreme damage. It was one of the worst hurricanes that have hit this area so far.

Hurricane experts were able to say the exact path the storm would take so people could prepare. Hundreds of public buildings such as churches and schools were set up as emergency shelters that offered food and water and a place to stay during the storm. Some hotels even allowed people to take shelter there. However, a lot of people were afraid to leave their homes because they were worried that their things might be stolen. They tried to protect their homes by taking everything inside and covering windows with wood. Inside their houses people hid in bathrooms until they could be evacuated. The winds were so powerful that people had difficulties keeping the doors closed. Even some shelters were destroyed.

Cara Delin, who lives on the Caribbean island of Barbuda, described the storm: "It was like something you see in a horror movie. I was staying in the local community center and we were all listening to the local radio and trying to stay calm. Outside we could hear the wind which was so strong that cars and parts of buildings flew around. Afterwards, when we went outside, we could see huge trees which had fallen over and blocked the roads. Most of the houses were destroyed. We're glad to be alive."

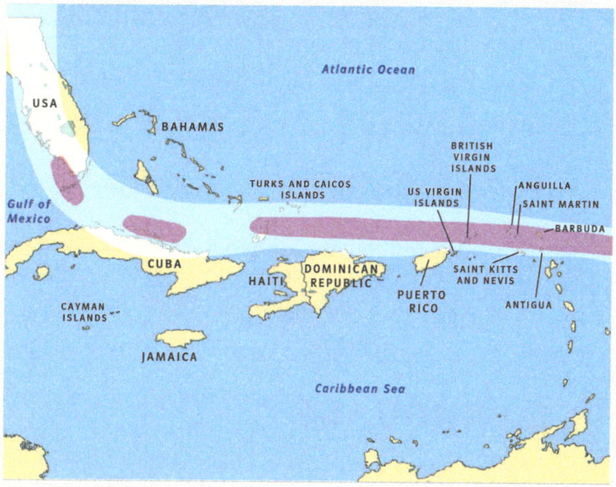

The islands in the Caribbean which suffered the most damage are Barbuda, St Martin, Anguilla, St Barts, the US and British Virgin Islands, Turks and Caicos and Cuba. 95% of the buildings on Barbuda were destroyed and all inhabitants had to leave the island because it was impossible to live there any longer. There was also a lot of damage in the US state of Florida, especially on the small islands called the Florida Keys. Thousands of people are now homeless and the hurricane has caused 134 deaths. It will take years to repair the damage and rebuild everything that has been destroyed.

Irma also brought great economic damages. Most Caribbean islands need tourists to make money, but a lot of tourists had to cancel their holidays because of the hurricane and the damage to hotels, ports and airports.

1 Right or wrong? Tick the right box.

	right	wrong
1. The most dangerous hurricanes arrive in August and September.	☐	☐
2. Hurricane Irma hit the Caribbean in 2017.	☐	☐
3. Hundreds of buildings were set up as emergency shelters.	☐	☐
4. People tried to protect their houses.	☐	☐
5. Only some houses on Barbuda were destroyed.	☐	☐
6. Thousands of people are homeless.	☐	☐
7. The hurricane caused 145 deaths.	☐	☐
8. A lot of tourists cancelled their holidays.	☐	☐

2 Find sentences in the text which mean the same. Write down the line number(s).

1. Hurricane Irma was one of the most dangerous storms in history. ____________
2. People could go to shelters in public buildings and get food and water there. ____________
3. The winds were so strong that they blew doors open. ____________
4. We're happy that we didn't die. ____________
5. The hurricane destroyed most of the buildings on Barbuda. ____________
6. 134 people died because of the storm. ____________

C LANGUAGE

1 Find words in the text which mean the same.

1. way → ____________
2. film → ____________
3. to be afraid → ____________
4. happy → ____________

2 Find words in the text which mean the opposite.

1. dead ⟷ ____________
2. stay ⟷ ____________
3. inside ⟷ ____________
4. sad ⟷ ____________
5. dead ⟷ ____________
6. destroy ⟷ ____________

3 Complete the sentences using words from the text.

1. It is not a good idea to travel to the Caribbean during the hurricane ______________ .
2. If there is a hurricane, it is important to find ______________ in a strong building.
3. Pay attention to ______________ radio and weather reports.
4. ______________ your windows with wood.
5. Hurricanes can cause a lot of ______________ to roads and buildings.
6. It can take years to ______________ the damage and rebuild the houses.

D WRITING

Choose one of the following tasks. Write in your exercise book.

1 Write a story.

Use the pictures below and write a story.
Plan your story. (Who? When? Where? What?)
Collect words for your story.
Write your story.
Check your story.

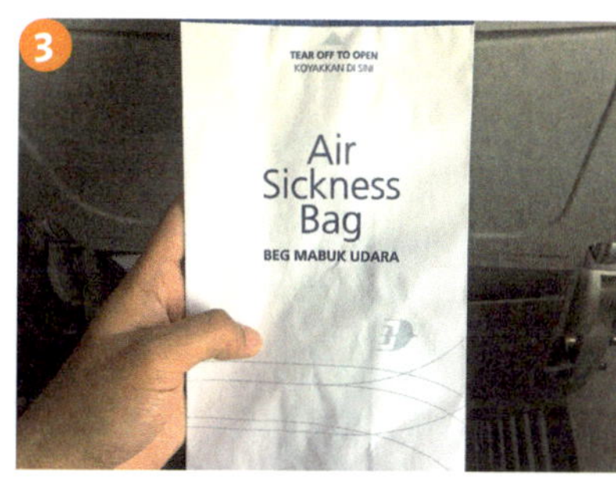

Write about 120 words.

2 Write your opinion.

'Teenagers should be allowed to go on holiday without their parents.'
Do you agree with the statement? Why (not)?
Write your opinion.
Give reasons and examples.

Write about 120 words.

E MEDIATION

INTERNET

Die Karibik – eine Geschichte mit dunklen Kapiteln

Der älteste Fund einer menschlichen Besiedelung in der Karibik wurde auf der Insel Trinidad gefunden und ist ca. 7000 Jahre alt. Im Laufe der Zeit wurden die Inseln von verschiedenen Völkern besiedelt, die vom südamerikanischen Festland auf die Inseln kamen. Die Taíno besiedelten die Inseln, um dort Ackerbau zu betreiben. Sie waren die einzigen Einwohner bis zum 8. Jahrhundert. Dann wurden die Inseln von den Kariben besiedelt. Sie lebten hauptsächlich vom Fischfang und bildeten die größte Bevölkerungsgruppe. Nach ihnen wurde die Karibik benannt.

Die Europäer erreichten die Karibik 1492, als Christoph Kolumbus im Auftrag der Spanier mit seinem Schiff auf den Bahamas anlegte. Die Spanier besiedelten die Karibik und versklavten die einheimische Bevölkerung. Die Menschen mussten auf den Zuckerrohrplantagen der Spanier arbeiten und die meisten starben aufgrund der schlechten Bedingungen oder an Krankheiten, die die Europäer einschleppten. Daraufhin wurden Sklaven aus Afrika in die Karibik gebracht.

Die Herrschaft der Spanier endete im 16. Jahrhundert als die Franzosen und Engländer und andere europäische Länder ihre Gebiete übernahmen. Sie führten die Plantagen weiter. Erst 1848 wurde die Sklaverei in der Karibik verboten.

Einige Inseln der Karibik sind heute unabhängige Staaten, aber es gibt noch viele, die zu europäischen Staaten gehören. Dementsprechend wird auf den Inseln entweder Englisch, Französisch, Holländisch oder Spanisch gesprochen. Die Karibik hat heutzutage ungefähr 35 Millionen Einwohner und viele sind Nachkommen der Sklaven, die einst aus Afrika in die Karibik verschleppt wurden.

You are on holiday with your family in the Caribbean and have made a friend from Italy. He sees this text in your guide book and is interested in what it says. Summarize the text in English and explain:
- where the word 'Caribbean' comes from
- who the first people to settle in the Caribbean were
- what the Spanish settlers did
- why slaves were brought from Africa
- which languages are spoken in the Caribbean and why

G1 Mit G sind die Grammatikkapitel gekennzeichnet und der Reihe nach durchnummeriert.

G5 Language tip: Die Seiten kennzeichnen zusätzliche Grammatikkapitel. Du kannst dir die neuen Formen dort wie neue Vokabeln merken oder – wenn du es genau wissen willst – ein paar Regeln dazu lernen.

G1 R: Modale Hilfsverben und ihre Ersatzformen

Revision: Modal auxiliaries and their substitutes

Modale Hilfsverben kannst du nur im **simple present** verwenden. Für alle anderen Zeiten benötigst du **Ersatzformen**. Ausnahme **can**: Für **can** kannst du im **simple past** auch **could** verwenden.

Mit **can / could** und der Ersatzform **be able to** sagst du, was du **kannst** (Fähigkeit).

Simple present	Simple past	Will-future
The guide **can / is able to** speak German. … kann …	He **could / was able to** read the text. … konnte …	I'm sure Tom **will be able to** help you. … kann …
She **can't / isn't able to** drive a truck. … kann nicht …	When he was seven, he **couldn't / wasn't able to** swim. … konnte … nicht …	He **won't be able to** repair his car himself. … kann … nicht …

Mit **can / could** und der Ersatzform **be allowed to** sagst du, was du tun **darfst** (Erlaubnis).

Tourists **can / are allowed to** visit Uluru. … dürfen …	We **could / were allowed to** take photos. … durften …	You'll **be allowed to** take photos. … darfst …
Tourists **can't / aren't allowed to / mustn't** go up Uluru. … dürfen nicht …	We **couldn't / weren't allowed to** catch fish. … durften keine …	You **won't be allowed to** make a fire. … darfst kein …

Mit **must** und der Ersatzform **have to** sagst du, was du tun **musst** (Verpflichtung).

You **must / have to** write an application. … musst …	I **had to** write an application. … musste …	You'll **have to** write an application. … musst …
You **don't have to** take part in the course. … musst nicht …	I **didn't have to** make breakfast. … musste nicht …	You **won't have to** wait for me. … musst nicht …

Eine **Empfehlung** ausdrücken:

Tourists **should / shouldn't** go by car.	Touristen **sollten / sollten** nicht mit dem Auto fahren.

Sagen, dass etwas nicht notwendig ist:

You **needn't** pay for the course.	Du **brauchst** den Kurs **nicht** zu bezahlen.

G2 R: Steigerung und Vergleich von Adjektiven und Adverbien

Revision: Comparison of adjectives and adverbs

Ein **Adjektiv** beschreibt eine **Person** oder eine **Sache**, z. B.: Rob is a **good** surfer.

Adjektive mit **einer Silbe** oder **zweisilbige** mit der Endung **-y** steigerst du mit **-er / -est.**
Adjektive mit **zwei und mehr Silben** steigerst du, indem du **more** und the **most** davor setzt.

cheap	cheap**er**	the cheap**est**
easy	eas**ier**	the eas**iest**
expensive	**more** expensive	the **most** expensive

Unregelmäßig gesteigert werden z. B.: good, **better**, the **best** und: bad, **worse**, the **worst**

So kannst du **Personen** oder **Dinge** miteinander vergleichen:

New York is **bigger than** Berlin.	New York ist **größer als** Berlin.
My friend is **as** old **as** you.	Mein Freund ist **so** alt **wie** du.
Mobiles are **not as** expensive **as** laptops.	Handys sind **nicht so** teuer **wie** Laptops.
Mobiles are **less** expensive **than** laptops.	Handys sind **nicht so** teuer **wie** Laptops.
Nick's new laptop was **the most expensive**.	Nicks neues Laptop war **das teuerste**.

Ein **Adverb** dagegen beschreibt, **wie** jemand etwas **tut** oder **wie** etwas **geschieht**. Man erkennt Adverbien im Englischen durch ein angehängtes **-ly**, z. B.: The actor spoke slow**ly** and clear**ly**.

Ein **Adverb** steigerst du mit **more** und the **most**.

slowly	**more** slowly	(the) **most** slowly	langsam, langsamer, der / die / das langsamste

Einige unregelmäßige Adverbien wie **fast** und **hard** steigerst du wie einsilbige Adjektive:
You work **fast / hard**, she works **faster / harder**, he works (the) **fastest** / (the) **hardest**.

Achtung! **good**, better, the best (Adjektiv) wird zu: **well**, **better**, (the) **best** (Adverb).

So vergleichst du **Handlungen** miteinander:

You speak **more clearly than** Colin.	Du sprichst **deutlicher als** Colin.
Kate works **as carefully as** Kim.	Kate arbeitet **so sorgfältig wie** Kim.
Ben doesn't write **as nicely as** Nora.	Ben schreibt **nicht so schön wie** Nora.
Amy dances (the) **most beautifully**.	Amy tanzt **am schönsten**.

G3 R: Relativsätze mit und ohne Relativpronomen

Revision: Relative clauses with and without relative pronouns (contact clauses)

Wenn du eine Person oder Sache genauer beschreiben willst, verwendest du die Relativpronomen **who** (für Personen), **which** (für Dinge) oder **that** (für Personen oder Dinge).

He is the man **who / that** showed us the reef.	Er ist der Mann, **der** uns das Riff zeigte.
Look, that's the seafood **which / that** is sold on the Caribbean islands.	Schau, das sind die Meeresfrüchte, **die** auf den karibischen Inseln verkauft werden.

Um Besitz und Zugehörigkeit auszudrücken, verwendest du **whose**.

Bob Marley is a singer **whose** music is very famous.	Bob Marley ist ein Sänger, **dessen** Musik sehr berühmt ist.

Folgt nach **who**, **which** oder **that** ein Personalpronomen wie **I**, **you**, **he**, **she**, **it**, **we**, **they** oder **eine Person**, kannst du **who**, **which** oder **that** auch weglassen. Diesen Satz nennt man **contact clause**.

The dancer **(who) we** saw last night taught us a few moves.	Der Tänzer, **den wir** gestern Abend sahen, brachte uns ein paar Schritte bei.
The ferry **(which) the guide** chose was very slow.	Die Fähre, **die der Reiseleiter** auswählte, war sehr langsam.

G4 Verlaufsform der Vergangenheit

The past progressive

Mit dem **past progressive** drückst du aus, dass etwas in der Vergangenheit über einen längeren Zeitraum passierte. So bildest du Aussagen im **past progressive**: **was / were + Verb + -ing**

On Monday afternoon I **was visiting** Grandad.	Am Montagnachmittag **habe** ich Opa **besucht**.
What **were** you **doing** then?	Was **hast** du dann **gemacht**?
I **wasn't working** last Saturday.	Ich **habe** am letzten Samstag **nicht gearbeitet**.

Das **past progressive** verwendest du auch, um eine Handlung zu beschreiben, die andauerte, als plötzlich eine neue eintrat. Das neue Ereignis wird mit dem **simple past** ausgedrückt.

While she **was watching** a film, her mum suddenly **came** into the room.	**Während** sie (gerade) einen Film **anschaute**, **kam** plötzlich ihre Mutter ins Zimmer.
Tom **was painting** the walls **when** his friend **called** him.	Tom **strich** (gerade) die Wände, **als** sein Freund **anrief**.

Liefen in der Vergangenheit zwei Handlungen zur gleichen Zeit und gleich lange, wird für beide Handlungen **past progressive** benutzt.

While I **was repairing** my bike, Sue **was working** in the garden.	**Während** ich mein Fahrrad **reparierte**, **arbeitete** Sue im Garten.

G5 Das Partizip Präsens

The present participle (after verbs of perception and instead of adverbial clauses)

Partizip Präsens nach Verben der Wahrnehmung (after verbs of perception)

Verben wie **see**, **watch**, **notice**, **hear**, **feel** usw. drücken eine Wahrnehmung der Sinne aus. Wenn eine längere Handlung wahrgenommen wird, verwendest du nach diesen Verben das **present participle**: **verb + -ing**

I **saw** the car **driving** towards the bus.	Ich sah, wie das Auto auf den Bus zufuhr. Oder: Ich sah das Auto auf den Bus zufahren.

Partizip Präsens anstelle von adverbialen Nebensätzen (instead of adverbial clauses)

Sätze, die mit Partizipien (having / being … etc.) beginnen, findest du überwiegend in der Schriftsprache. Da die einleitenden Adverbialen (because, as, if, when usw.) fehlen, musst du versuchen, den Sinn aus dem Zusammenhang zu erschließen.

Being poor and black, it's hard to get a job.	**Wenn** man arm und dunkelhäutig ist, ist es schwer, einen Job zu bekommen.
Not knowing the way to the station, she asked a policeman.	**Da** sie den Weg zum Bahnhof nicht kannte, fragte sie einen Polizisten.

G6 R: Die Vorvergangenheit

Revision: The past perfect

Um über Ereignisse zu sprechen, die noch **vor** einem vergangenen Ereignis stattfanden, verwendest du die Vorvergangenheit, das **past perfect**: **had / hadn't + 3. Form** des Verbs (past participle)

Signalwörter	
after	nachdem
before	bevor
when	als

Bei den regelmäßigen Verben hängst du für die 3. Form ein **-ed** an das Verb: visit → **visited**
Achte auf unregelmäßige Verben, z. B. go → **gone**; see → **seen**; be → **been** etc.

Eine Liste der unregelmäßigen Verben findest du auf Seite 213.

After we **had lived** in Cape Town for two years, we moved to Pretoria.	**Nachdem** wir zwei Jahre in Kapstadt **gelebt hatten**, zogen wir nach Pretoria um.
Before school started, she **had heard** some bad news.	**Bevor** die Schule anfing, **hatte** sie schlechte Nachrichten **gehört**.
When the accident happened, the bus **had not arrived** yet.	**Als** der Unfall passierte, **war** der Bus noch **nicht angekommen**.

Und so kannst du im **past perfect** Fragen stellen:

Had you ever **been** to South Africa before you left the USA?	Yes, I **had**. No, I **hadn't**.
Which countries **had** you **visited** before you went to South Africa?	I **hadn't visited** any other countries.

G7 R: Das Passiv (einfache Vergangenheit)

Revision: Passive voice (simple past)

English is important.
It is spoken all over the world.

Mit dem Passiv kannst du über eine Handlung Auskunft geben, ohne zu sagen, wer die Handlung ausführt. Im Vordergrund steht dabei die Sache.
So bildest du das Passiv im **simple present:**
am / are / is + 3. Form des Verbs (past participle)
English **is spoken** in a lot of countries. A lot of photos **are taken** in the park every day.

So bildest du das Passiv im **simple past:**
was / were + 3. Form des Verbs (past participle)

Eine Liste der unregelmäßigen Verben findest du auf Seite 213.

The park **was named** after Paul Kruger.	Der Park **wurde** nach Paul Kruger **benannt**.
Roads and visitor centres **were built.**	Straßen und Besucherzentren **wurden gebaut**.
The park **wasn't opened** in 1910.	Der Park **wurde nicht** 1910 **eröffnet**.

Was the park **created** in 1926?	**Yes**, it **was**.
Was the park **named** after a singer?	**No**, it **wasn't**.

So kannst du aus einem Aktivsatz einen Passivsatz machen. Die handelnden Personen müssen nicht immer genannt werden. Wenn doch, dann werden sie mit **by** angehängt.
Das Verb im Aktiv wird in der gleichen Zeit im Passiv gebildet.

Aktiv: South African workers built a new road.
Passiv: A new road was built (**by** South African workers).

Aktiv: Hunters killed elephants for their ivory.
Passiv: Elephants were killed for their ivory (**by** hunters).

G8 Indirekte Rede I (mit Zeitverschiebung → simple past)

Reported speech (with backshift → simple past)

Wenn du berichten willst, was jemand **vor einiger Zeit** gesagt hat, benutzt du die indirekte Rede. Du beginnst mit **He said that … / She told me that** … . usw. Das Wort **that** kann man auch weglassen.
Das **Verb** des Satzes wird vom **simple present** in das **simple past** zurückgesetzt (**backshift**).

Direkte Rede	Indirekte Rede
Kenneth: "I **work** a lot."	Kenneth told me (that) he **worked** a lot.
"Sneakerheads **are** a group of people with the same interest."	He added (that) sneakerheads **were** a group of people with the same interest.
"I **hate** kids who **don't care** about their shoes."	He said (that) he **hated** kids who **didn't care** about their shoes.

Und so kannst du **Fragen** in der indirekten Rede wiedergeben:
Ohne Fragewort: **He asked if** … Er fragte, **ob** …
Mit Fragewort: **She asked why / when / where** … Sie fragte, **warum / wann / wo** …

Cindy: "**Do** you **wear** the shoes?"	She asked **if** he **wore** the shoes.
"**How many** pairs **do** you **own**?"	She asked him **how many** pairs he **owned**.

In der indirekten Rede ändern sich auch **Personalpronomen** und **Possessivbegleiter**!

"I want to meet **my** friend Tom."	He said (that) **he** wanted to meet **his** friend Tom.
"**We** often help **our** neighbours in the garden."	She told me (that) **they** often helped **their** neighbours in the garden.

G9 Indirekte Rede II (mit Zeitverschiebung → past perfect)

Reported speech (with backshift → past perfect)

Wenn du berichten willst, was jemand über **Vergangenes** erzählt hat, benutzt du die indirekte Rede so: Das **Verb** wird vom **simple past** in das **past perfect** (**had / hadn't + 3. Form**) zurückgesetzt.

Direkte Rede	Indirekte Rede
Bob: "I **moved** to Hong Kong in 2010."	He told me (that) he **had moved** to Hong Kong in 2010.
"I **didn't like** Chinese food."	He added (that) he **hadn't liked** Chinese food.
"**Did** you **visit** New York in the spring?"	He asked **if** I **had visited** New York in the spring.
"**Where did** you **buy** the tickets?"	He asked **where** I **had bought** the tickets.

Steht in der Aussage der direkten Rede **present perfect**, so wird das Verb in der indirekten Rede ebenfalls in das **past perfect** zurückgesetzt:

"I **have been** to Sneakers Street only once."	She said (that) she **had been** to Sneakers Street only once.
"I **haven't seen** the new shopping centre yet."	She said (that) she **hadn't seen** the new shopping centre yet.
"**Have** you **been** to Hong Kong before?"	She asked **if** I **had been** to Hong Kong before.

G10 R: Zukunftszeiten will und going to

Revision: Future tenses: Will-future and going to-future

Wenn du über etwas sprechen möchtest, das in der Zukunft geschieht, kannst du das im Englischen auf verschiedene Weise tun. Die beiden häufigsten Zukunftszeiten sind das **will-future** und das **going to-future**. Zu weiteren Zeiten für die Zukunft siehe **G11**.

Will-future

Das **will-future** verwendest du
- allgemein für Zukünftiges
- für **Wünsche**, **Hoffnungen**, **Vorhersagen** (nach I hope, I think, I'm sure, probably, maybe etc.)
- für **spontane Entscheidungen**
- in **if-Sätzen Typ I**

Im Deutschen kann man über Zukünftiges mit der Zukunft oder der Gegenwart sprechen.

I'**ll call** an ambulance.	Ich **rufe** einen Krankenwagen. (spontan)
I hope Rachel **will call** me soon.	Ich hoffe, Rachel **ruft** mich bald **an**. (Hoffnung)
Maybe we'**ll meet** the boys at the club.	Vielleicht **treffen** wir die Jungen im Klub. (Wunsch)
Don't worry, it **won't take** long.	Mach dir keine Sorgen, es **wird nicht** lange **dauern**. (spontan)
When **will** you **be** back from Hong Kong?	Wann **bist** du wieder zurück aus Hongkong? (Hoffnung)
If I meet Peter Lai, I **will talk** to him.	Wenn ich Peter Lai treffe, **werde** ich mit ihm **reden**. (if-Satz Typ I)

Going to-future

Das **going to-future** verwendest du, wenn du beschreiben willst, was du in der Zukunft vorhast. Es drückt eine bestimmte **Absicht** oder einen **Plan** aus. Mit dem **going to-future** kannst du aber auch ausdrücken, dass etwas sicher eintreten wird, weil es schon **Anzeichen** dafür gibt.

I'**m going to talk** to the boss tomorrow.	Ich **habe vor**, morgen mit dem Chef **zu sprechen**. (Absicht, Plan)
Are you **going to visit** Hong Kong?	**Habt** ihr **vor**, Hongkong **zu besuchen**? (Plan)
No, we **aren't going to travel** to Asia this year.	Nein, wir **haben** dieses Jahr **nicht vor**, nach Asien **zu reisen**. (Plan)
Look at those black clouds. It'**s going to rain** in a few minutes.	Schau dir diese schwarzen Wolken an. Es **wird** in ein paar Minuten **regnen**. (Anzeichen)

G11 Zukunftszeiten (einfache Gegenwart und Verlaufsform der Gegenwart)

Future tenses (simple present and present progressive with future meaning)

The party starts at 7 p.m.
Are you coming?
Sorry, but I'm working until late.

Simple present

Wenn du über feste Termine in der Zukunft sprechen willst, kannst du das **simple present** verwenden. Dabei geht es meistens um genaue Zeitangaben aus Fahrplänen, Programmen, Stundenplänen usw.

The next train from Fort Lauderdale to Miami Airport **leaves** at 6:08 p.m.	Der nächste Zug von Fort Lauderdale zum Flughafen Miami **fährt** um 18:08 Uhr.
Most shops in Miami **don't close** before 12 o'clock today.	In Miami **schließen** die meisten Geschäfte heute **nicht** vor 0 Uhr.
When **does** the flight to New York **leave**?	Wann **geht** der Flug nach New York?

Present progressive

Wenn du für die Zukunft etwas fest geplant oder vereinbart hast, kannst du das **present progressive** verwenden.

Tomorrow I'**m watching** a film at the cinema.	Morgen **schaue** ich mir einen Film im Kino **an**.
On Sunday we **are visiting** Liz in hospital.	Am Sonntag **besuchen** wir Liz im Krankenhaus.
I'**m not doing** anything special on Friday.	Am Freitag **mache** ich **nichts** Besonderes.
What **are** you **doing** at the weekend?	Was **machst** du am Wochenende?

Achtung! Mit dem **present progressive** kann man sowohl eine **gegenwärtige** als auch eine **zukünftige** Handlung ausdrücken. Die Signalwörter zeigen den Unterschied!

I'**m talking** to a blogger **at the moment**.	Ich **spreche gerade** mit einem Blogger.
I'**m talking** to a blogger **tomorrow**.	Ich **spreche morgen** mit einem Blogger.

F SPEAKING

1 Describe the photo. What can you see? What are the people doing?

2 Write a dialogue for two of the people in the photo.

Unit 3

Around South Africa

1 (WRITING) Write about South Africa.

48/2

a) What do you know about South Africa? Write notes for the pictures. You can also look on pages 48–49 in your book for help.

b) Use your notes to write a text about South Africa in your exercise book.

1 Read the newspaper article about the accident. Put in the right words.

51/3

questioning	construction	flashbacks	guilty
private	victims	consequences	crash
health insurance	equal	suffered	

On Saturday, 9th January at 1 p.m. there was a ______________ between a car and a bus with students from the ______________ Redhill School. The driver of the bus died and one student was taken to hospital. The driver of the car ______________ back injuries.

A worker from the Umlazi township was taken to the police station for ______________. The man, who lives in a township and works in ______________, told the police that he saw the car go out of control and drive towards the bus. Several people have written to our newspaper and complained about crazy drivers and the ______________ of accidents. A lot of ______________ have ______________ and nightmares after their accidents and only those with good ______________ get treatment. Drivers who cause accidents also often feel ______________. Everyone who is involved in an accident should get ______________ treatment

2 Use the present participle to rewrite the sentences.

51/3

1. I heard a noise. It was coming from the back of the bus.
   I heard a noise coming from the back of the bus.
2. We felt the car when it was crashing into the bus.
   ____
3. I noticed some people. They were running to the bus.
   ____
4. I saw the driver. He was lying on the road.
   ____
5. Because I live in a big city, I'm used to car accicents.
   ____
6. When you have an injury, it's hard to have a normal life.
   ____

Du kannst das Partizip verwenden, um zwei Sätze zu verbinden oder um einen Nebensatz zu verkürzen.

8 51/3

3 (LISTENING) Lefa and Cebila met at the police station where they were for questioning. Listen to their conversation and tick the right box.

	right	wrong
1. At the police station Lefa was treated like a guilty person.	☐	☐
2. Lefa was allowed to make a phone call.	☐	☐
3. Lefa thinks he was treated unfairly.	☐	☐
4. Cebile's mum can't work and they can't afford treatment for her injury.	☐	☐
5. Cebile and her mum had to leave their home.	☐	☐
6. Cebile's mum is in prison.	☐	☐

52/4a)

4 Do the word search and complete the sentences.

1. Gated communities have a lot of _________.
2. Rich people are _______________.
3. A _______________ writes for newspapers.
4. A ___________ watches over something.
5. In democratic states there are ______________.
6. The opposite of war is ___________.
7. A synonym for the word same is ___________.
8. When something is in the middle, it is ___________.

Q	W	T	F	P	T	F	H	S	G	J	B
H	J	O	U	R	N	A	L	I	S	T	F
C	H	D	H	I	S	J	S	W	V	B	E
E	J	D	B	V	E	V	G	B	E	B	Q
N	D	P	W	I	E	G	U	E	E	F	U
T	B	E	V	L	N	M	A	W	D	E	A
R	B	A	S	E	C	U	R	I	T	Y	L
A	M	C	W	G	C	B	D	E	N	X	N
L	F	E	L	E	C	T	I	O	N	S	F
G	S	G	W	D	C	H	U	R	Z	Z	E

5 Put in the right word.

52/4a)

a) Find nouns for these adjectives.

1. social → _______________
2. natural → _______________
3. different → _______________
4. informative → _______________
5. interested → _______________
6. experienced → _______________

52/4b)

b) Put in the correct form of the word.

1. The government made the _______________ to end apartheid in 1991. (decide)
2. A lot of black people still live in _______________. (poor)
3. Black people often live in townships and white people live in _______________ communities. (guard)
4. Nelson Mandela said everyone should be treated _______________. (equal)
5. Most South Africans _______________ the country has a bright future. (believe)

6 (WRITING) Do you think there are social differences where you live (e. g. schools, job opportunities, health insurance)? Write about 60 words.

52/5

____
____
____
____
____
____
____
____

7 Complete the police report from the accident. Put in the past perfect.

53/7

Before the accident happened, the weather ________ (be) good. The traffic ________ (not be) too bad and the road was in good condition. A witness told us that the car ________ (not go) too fast and that the bus ________ (not move) too fast either. Other witnesses confirmed that the students ________ (not leave) their seats. The driver of the car told us that she was driving home after she ________ (pick up) her daughter from school. She said she had been worried because she ________ (lose) her job that day.

8 Read the text about Nelson Mandela and put in the right tense.

53/7

a) Underline the signal words for the simple past and the past perfect.

b) Put in the simple past or the past perfect.

Before he *became* (become) president, Nelson Mandela *had fought* (fight) for the rights of black people. After he ________ (help) students to complain about bad food, he ________ leave university. (have to). After he ________ (find) a place at another university, he ________ (join) the African National Congress. After he ________ (start) to work, the government ________ (introduce) the system of apartheid. Before he ________ (have to) go to prison, his protest group ________ (use) violence. Before the president ________ (release) him in 1990, Nelson Mandela ________(spend) 27 years in prison. After apartheid had ________ (end), there ________ (be) free elections in South Africa. Before Nelson Mandela ________ (become) president, South Africa ________ never ________ (have) a black president.

9 (WRITING) Compare the photos.

53/8

1

2

a) Talk to your partner and describe one of the photos. What can you see? What are the people doing? Take turns.

- This photo shows …
- In this photo you can see …
- This photo was taken in / at …
- In the foreground / middle / background …
- On the right / left …
- At the top / bottom …
- In the upper / lower left / right corner …
- He / she is / has …
- He / she is wearing / holding / …
- The person looks happy / sad / relaxed / …
- Maybe he / she is thinking / saying …

b) What do you think the people in the photos are saying? Act a dialogue with your partner.

c) Compare the two photos.

- In the first photo there is … but in the other one …
- Both photos show …
- One of the photos shows …
- The first / second photo is …
- I think the people in the first / second photo are …
- rich / poor / …

54/1

1 Find the words.

1. a person whose job it is to protect a park
2. to control something
3. to protect something from damage or change
4. catching and killing animals where it is forbidden
5. something that needs a lot of effort
6. when you act carefully, you act with …
7. reasons for believing something is true (or not true)
8. a place on the internet where you can talk to other people

The animal is an: ______________

9
55/3

2 (LISTENING) Listen to the radio interview about an attack at Kruger National Park.

a) Before you listen, look at the two photos. What do you think happened at Kruger National Park? Talk to a partner.

b) Listen to the interview and answer the questions.

1. Where did Dawn and Michael see the group of zebras? ______________
2. What happened when the zebras started drinking?
____
3. Where was the rhino? ______________
4. What did the rhino do after the crocodile had attacked the zebra?
____
5. What happened to the zebra? ______________
6. Did the rhino really try to help the zebra? ______________
7. Will the zebra survive with a broken leg? ______________

3 Find words to describe landscapes.

55/3

a) Add as many words as you can to the mind map.

b) Compare your mind map with your partner's. Who has written more words?

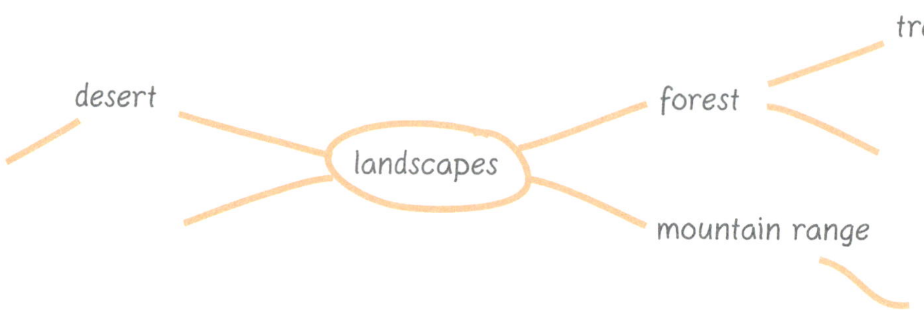

c) Write a short text in your exercise book. Use the mind map and describe the landscape where you live. Check each other's texts for spelling mistakes.

4 Put in the right words.

55/4

ivory | poaching | conserve | value | nature reserve | rangers

1. Kruger National Park is a ______________________ .
2. The goal of nature reserves is to ________________ the wildlife.
3. People hunt elephants because they want ____________ .
4. Forbidden hunting is called ________________ .
5. ________________ are there to watch over the park and the wildlife.
6. We must recognise the _____________ of the wild animals.

5 Put the verbs into the passive. Use the simple past.

56/6

1. The zebra *was caught* (catch) by a crocodile.
2. The zebra __________________ (pull) into the water.
3. The other zebras ________________________ (not attack).
4. A rhino ________________ (see) as it ran towards the zebra.
5. The zebra's leg ___________________ (break).
6. A film of the scene ___________________ (share) on social media.
7. The tourists who filmed the scene _________________________ (interiew) on the radio.

6 Write questions and give short answers.

56/7

a) Write questions in the passive.

born in Germany | bring to school today | house build a long time ago | lunch make your mum | give much homework yesterday

Your questions: | Your partner's answers:

1. Were you born in Germany? ______
2. ______ ______
3. ______ ______
4. ______ ______
5. ______ ______

b) Your partner answers your questions and writes short answers in your workbook.

7 Rewrite the sentences about South Africa's history. Use the passive.

57/8a)

a) Start with the underlined words and write passive sentences.

1. People discovered very old rock art in a cave.
   Very old rock art was discovered in a cave.
2. They found diamonds in the 19th century.
   ______
3. The British government gave South Africa independence in 1931.
   ______
4. They made the country a republic in 1961.
   ______
5. They ended apartheid in 1991.
   ______
6. South Africa organized the Football World Cup in 2010.
   ______

57/8b)

b) Rewrite the sentences. Use by to say who did it.

1. The Dutch controlled South Africa in the 17th century.
   ______
2. The British invaded South Africa in the 19th century.
   ______
3. South Africa won the Rugby World Cup in 2007.
   ______

8 (WRITING) Write a magazine article.

57/9

a) Read the notes a journalist made about shark diving in South Africa.

Shark cage diving
- location: Atlantic ocean (2 hours from Cape Town)
- price: 100 dollars per person
- trip takes 4–5 hours (depending on shark activity)
- full safety advice before the tour starts
- diving equipment offered for each person
- no diving experience necessary
- 8 people per cage (cage fully under water)
- tour guides throw fish food into the water to attract sharks
- take photos from the boat or under water
- cage is attached to the boat, sharks cannot hurt you
- more shark attacks because of cage diving?
- possible that sharks have changed their behaviour
- not animal friendly

b) Plan your text. Fill in the table.

introduction:	
main part:	
conclusion:	

c) Write your article in your exercise book.

When you are in South Africa, you can ... | For example ... | This trip is ... | Some people say ... | Therefore... | It is possible that ... | In addition ... | However, ... | because

d) Check your article. Swap your text with a partner and check each other's articles for spelling, punctuation and grammar mistakes.

1 (SPEAKING) Compare the two photos.

57/9

a) Choose one picture and describe it to your partner. What can you see in the picture? What are the people doing? Your partner describes the other picture.

b) Compare the two pictures and talk about social differences.

- In the first photo there is … but in the other one …
- Both photos show …
- One of the photos shows …
- The first / second photo is …
- I think the people in the first / second photo are …
- relaxed / busy / …
- privileged / underprivileged / rich / poor / …
- equal / unequal / fair / unfair / …

2 (SPEAKING) Tell a story.

57/9

a) Work with a partner. Look at the pictures. What can you see in each picture? Describe the pictures to your partner. Take turns.

b) Think of a story for the pictures.

c) Tell your story to the class.

61/5

1 (READING) Read the story.

Amahle's story

Apartheid was a way of life for me; it was all I had ever known. My dad, a teacher, was killed by a police officer while he was taking part in a protest when I was a baby. I don't remember him. I just know that it meant we didn't talk about politics, and we tried to stay out of trouble. Despite this, our house was still searched by the police in the middle of the night every few months, and we were forced from our beds, crying and confused.

Our house was in a black township. We had no electricity, no bathroom. My mum went to work every day, and my grandma and aunts helped to look after me and my brother and sister. We all had to leave school and work as soon as we turned 13 because we needed the money to support our family. Mum found it hard to look after three children. I dreamt of going to university and getting an office job, but as soon as I left school I started working in the kitchen for the white family mum worked for. I was angry at the world, I thought all my problems were caused by white people; they had taken my dad, they had killed my dreams and they treated us like animals.

It was early February in 1990 when we heard that there was going to be an announcement on TV. We thought they were going to say that Nelson Mandela was going to be released (a man whose name we couldn't even say in public for fear of arrest). Actually, they told us apartheid was going to end. We partied all night. But in real life, nothing much changed quickly; it took a lot of time to take apart the system of apartheid . I left working for the white family as soon as I could because I hated feeling like a slave. My mum stayed there and worked until she died at the age of 55 of a disease that we couldn't afford to treat.

The only thing I was good at was cooking, so I found a job in a small restaurant in a nice part of town. One day, when I looked out from the kitchen window, I saw an old, white man come in. He was tall with grey hair. I recognised his face from TV – he had been a well known police officer in the apartheid system. He was the man who had ordered the attack on the protesters when my dad was killed. I felt the anger[1] of many years coming up inside me. How dare[2] he sit there, eating in a restaurant when he had been responsible for so many deaths? When his food was ready, I decided to take it to him myself. I placed the dish in front of him, stared straight into his grey eyes and said, "You killed my father." I didn't wait for an answer; I just turned and returned to the kitchen.

When the restaurant closed nearly two hours later, I noticed he was still there, sitting alone in the corner. He looked at me. "Can I talk to you?" he asked. I sat down opposite him. I wanted to feel equal. He didn't speak for a moment but when he did I saw tears in his eyes. "I'm sorry," he said. We spoke for an hour. I told him about my mum, about my life. He told me how he had rejected violence, how he was campaigning against police violence towards black people. As he spoke, I thought of Nelson Mandela's words, "I knew if I didn't leave my bitterness[3] and hatred[4] behind I'd still be in prison." If Mandela could forgive[5], then I knew I had to try too.

He stood to leave, holding out his hand to me. I took it in mine and looked him in the eye again. "I forgive you," I told him. I felt relief[6]. I don't know if my mum or dad would have done the same, but I knew it was what I needed to do to stop living my life with anger and hate.

1 anger ['æŋgə] – *Wut;* 2 to dare [deə] – *wagen;* 3 bitterness ['bɪtənes] – *Bitterkeit;* 4 hatred ['heɪtrɪd] – *Hass;* 5 to forgive, forgave, forgiven [fə'gɪv] – *vergeben;* 6 relief [rɪ'li:f] – *Erleichterung*

61/5

2 Right or wrong? Tick the right box.

	right	wrong
1. Amahle's dad was killed by a police officer.	☐	☐
2. Amahle's family was treated badly by the police.	☐	☐
3. Amahle went to university after school.	☐	☐
4. Amahle's family celebrated when Nelson Mandela was released.	☐	☐
5. Things quickly improved for black people after apartheid had ended.	☐	☐
6. The police officer was looking for Amahle.	☐	☐
7. The police officer was proud of everything he had done.	☐	☐
8. Amahle felt better after she had talked to the police officer.	☐	☐

61/5

3 Complete the character profiles with information from the text.

Amahle

has one brother and ______

Amahle's dad

has three children ______

Amahle's mum

______

police officer

______

61/5

4 (WRITING) Do an interview.

a) Work with a partner. One of you is a reporter for the school magazine. You are going to interview the police officer from the story. Write down questions you would like to ask him.

b) Your partner thinks of answers to the questions and writes notes.

c) Act the interview.

English in South Africa

Most people in South Africa speak more than one language. English is understood nearly everywhere, but you may hear some unfamiliar words because some words from other languages are used in South African English. Many words have been taken from Afrikaans, a language which has its origins in Dutch dialects. Almost everywhere you will hear people say 'ja' instead of 'yes'. If you are invited to a 'braai' (barbecue) you might describe the food as 'lekker' (nice or good) or maybe even 'vrot' (no good)! If someone calls you 'dof' (stupid) you might be upset, but if someone calls you 'kwaai' (cool) you should be pleased. Most people's first language is an African language, so many African words have found their way into the English language. This word comes from the Xhosa language. Many words have also been taken from Zulu, such as 'bonsella' for a present or bonus, 'gogo' for grandmother and 'muti' to mean traditional African medicine. Some English words have a different meaning in South Africa. For example, 'robot' means 'traffic light' and 'café' is a corner shop. A common phrase that confuses visitors is 'just now' because it means 'later' rather than 'now'. Even when South Africans say 'now now' it still doesn't mean now but 'just as soon as they can'.

62/1

1 (MEDIATION) Du bist mit deiner Familie in Südafrika und hast diesen Text in deinem Reiseführer gefunden. Fasse für sie den Text auf Deutsch zusammen.

____

____

____

____

62/1

2 (MEDIATION) Du hast im Urlaub einen Jungen aus Südafrika kennengelernt. Deine Mutter versteht nicht alles, was er sagt. Vermittle zwischen den beiden.

Your friend: My gogo wants to invite you to a braai just now. Would you like to come?

Your mum: Ich verstehe nur, dass er uns zu etwas einladen will. Hast du mehr verstanden?

You: ______________________________

Your mum: Thank you for the invitation. Of course we'd like to come. When is the party?

Your friend: Tonight at eight o'clock. I'll pick you up just now.

Your mum: Now? But you said at eight o'clock?

You: ______________________________

Your mum: Ach so. Frag ihn mal bitte, was wir seiner Großmutter schenken können.

You: ______________________________

Your friend: You needn't bring a bonsella. Just come and enjoy her lekker food.

You: ______________________________

____

Ziel 1: I can understand information about South Africa.

→ ⦾ q2pg53

Hang out with the penguins

There aren't many places in the world where you can get close to penguins and even swim with them. But you can at Boulders Beach, just 45 minutes away from Cape Town. The penguin colony at Boulders Beach is one of only a few in the world, and it has become a famous and popular tourist destination. You can sit on the beach with the penguins or swim with them. You might even have to share your beach towel with one of them, but you should not touch of feed them. You can also see whales, sharks or dolphins in the bay. Boulders Beach is part of the Table Mountain National Park where you can go hiking, take a cable car trip to the top of the mountain or visit an old silver mine.

Answer the questions.

1. What type of text is this? a) an e-mail ☐ b) an ad ☐ c) a magazine article ☐
2. Where is Boulders Beach? ____________________
3. Why is the beach so popular and what can you do there? ____________________
____
4. What else can you see in the bay? ____________________
5. Where does the cable car go? ____________________
6. What can you visit if you are interested in history? ____________________

4P
→ p. 66/1

Ziel 2: I can talk about social differences.

→ ⦾ g9dj9p → ⦾ fz8q3d

Describe the photo. Then write your opinion of it.

____
____
____
____
____
____
____
____
____

6P
→ p. 66/2

Ziel 3: I can write an article about a nature reserve.

→ ⦾ h37j6b → ⦾ b7td6j

a) Read the information about the Table Mountain National Park.

Table Mountain National Park

- Table Mountain, most famous mountain in South Africa
- height 1,084 m (60 other mountains in South Africa are higher)
- most famous tourist attraction
- millions of tourists every year, take cable cars to the top
- national park founded 1998
- 2,200 different plants, 1,470 different flowers, only grow in the area
- one of the New Seven Wonders of Nature
- baboons, zebras, penguins at Boulders Beach
- Cape of Good Hope, old silver mine

b) Write a magazine article about the park.

8P

→ p. 67/4

Ziel 4: I can understand a story about apartheid.

→ ⊙ 2xi5es

Read the story on pages 58–60 in your book again Put the events in the right chronological order.

Rosa walks to Oranje Primary School and is afraid of the protesters. ☐	Hennie saves Rose from a group of children. ☐	Nelson Mandela is free from prison. ☐
The girl takes Rosa to a dark, quiet part of the school. ☐	Hennie's dad gets angry and they aren't allowed to play together any longer. ☐	Rosa's mama buys a newspaper. ☐
Rosa plays with Hennie. ☐	A girl tells Rosa the headmaster wants to see her. ☐	When Rosa's mama goes to vote, she stands in the same queue as Hennie's parents. ☐

9P
→p. 67/4

Ziel 5: I can pass on information about languages in South Africa.

Die Sprachen Südafrikas

Südafrika wurde ca. 2200 v. Chr. zum ersten Mal von Menschen verschiedener Stämme besiedelt und vor ungefähr 2000 Jahren ließen sich die ersten schwarzen Nguni-Stämme an der Südspitze Afrikas nieder. 1652 richtete der Niederländer Jan van Riebeeck die erste Versorgungsstation für Schiffe auf dem Kap der Guten Hoffnung und brachte die holländische Sprache nach Südafrika. Aus ihr entwickelte sich das Afrikaans. Mit der Zeit siedelten sich Menschen aus verschiedenen Ländern rund um das Kap an, aus Portugal, Holland, Großbritannien und Deutschland. Sie importierten Sklaven aus Ostafrika, die ebenfalls ihre eigenen Sprachen mitbrachten. Als Südafrika 1902 zur britischen Kolonie wurde, wurde Englisch zur meist genutzten Sprache in den Medien und in der Politik. Die meisten Südafrikaner verstehen Englisch, obwohl nur ca. 9,6 % Englisch als Erstsprache sprechen. Die meisten Einwohner Südafrikas sprechen isiZulu (22,7 %), isiXhosa (16 %) oder Afrikaans (13,5 %) Heute gibt es Zeitungen, Radiosendungen und Fernsehprogramme in allen 11 offiziellen Sprachen des Landes.

You have found this information about the languages of South Africa in a history book. You would like to use this text for a presentation in your English lesson. Write down the most important information in English.

6P
→p. 67/5

○ **Ziel 1: I can understand information about South Africa.**

INTERNET

The Rainbow Nation

South Africa is the most southern country in Africa. It has a coast that stretches along the South Atlantic and Indian Oceans and has borders with six other African countries, including Lesotho, which is in the middle of South Africa.
Since apartheid ended, South Africa has been known as the Rainbow Nation because South Africa has a multicultural society where people from different nations are able to live together peacefully. The people of South Africa still remember their difficult history and there are a lot of social differences, but the people are proud of their country. They love sports and celebrate their national teams' successes, and they are also proud of their amazing wildlife. Many tourists come to take part in safaris in one of the many national parks and look for the 'Big Five' or to relax on the country's beautiful beaches.

Read the text and complete the sentences.

1. South Africa has ____________ with six other African ____________.
2. Since ____________ ended, South Africa has been known as ____________.
3. There are still a lot of social ____________, but the people are proud of their ____________.
4. Many tourists take part in ____________ in one of the many ____________.
5. They look for the 'Big Five' or relax on ____________.

○ **Ziel 2: I can talk about social differences.**

Describe the photo. Then write your opinion of it.

expensive | homeless | ask for money | social differences | help each other | rich | poor

____

____

____

____

____

____

____

____

____

____

____

○ **Ziel 3: I can write an article about a nature reserve.**

Read the information about Addo Elephant Park and complete the magazine article.

Addo Elephant Park is ______________________________
______________________. It is in ______________________
______________________ covers an area ______________________.
The park ______________________________
______________. In 1931 ______________________________
______________. Now ______________________________
____
each year.

Addo Elephant Park

- third biggest national park in South Africa
- in the southeast
- 1,640 km^2
- opened in 1931 to protect elephants
- in 1931: eleven elephants
- now more than 600 elephants
- about 120,000 visitors each year

○ **Ziel 4: I can understand a story about apartheid.**

	right	wrong
1. Hennie's dad was happy that he and Rosa were friends.	☐	☐
2. Rosa's family was happy when apartheid ended.	☐	☐
3. Rosa's mum sent her to a school with white children.	☐	☐
4. Rosa was afraid of the protesters in front of the school.	☐	☐
5. The other children at the school were friendly.	☐	☐
6. Hennie helped Rosa when she was afraid of the other children.	☐	☐

○ **Ziel 5: I can pass on information about languages in South Africa.**

Did you know?

South Africa holds the record for having the most official languages in the world – 11!
There are over 15 more languages spoken unofficially, including Arabic, German, Hindi and Portuguese.
English is the most spoken language in official and public life – but only the fifth most spoken at home.
Most South Africans are multilingual; they speak and understand more than one language.

Lies den Text und fasse die wichtigsten Punkte auf Deutsch zusammen.

____
____
____
____
____
____
____
____
____
____

A LISTENING

You will hear a teenager from South Africa talking about his life. You will hear the recording twice.

Akani

10 **1 True or false? Listen and tick the right box.**

	true	false
1. Nearly two million people live in Soweto.	☐	☐
2. There are often negative reports about townships.	☐	☐
3. Akani lives close to his family.	☐	☐
4. Akani's mum has a restaurant.	☐	☐
5. Akani's house has a bathroom.	☐	☐
6. The buses are always crowded.	☐	☐
7. There are problems with gangs and guns in the township.	☐	☐
8. Akani wants to be a football player.	☐	☐

10 **2 Listen again. Answer the questions with 1–5 words / numbers.**

1. How many Nobel Peace Prize winners come from Soweto? ______________
2. Why don't the rich people leave Soweto? ______________________________________
3. What does Akani do to get a free dinner at the restaurant? ______________________________
4. What job does everyone hate doing? ______________________________________
5. Where does Akani's dad work? ______________________
6. How does Akani go to school? __________________
7. What are they going to do at Akani's school? ____

B READING

1

Robben Island Trip

Boats depart three times a day from Cape Town to famous Robben Island.
See the prison where Nelson Mandela was kept for over 18 years and visit the room of Africa's great president.
A look into the past you will never forget.

2

Two Oceans Aquarium

Located near the ocean in Cape Town. See thousands of types of fish, sharks, penguins and much more.
Visit the cafe and children's play area.
Open 365 days a year from 9.30–18.00

3

Blyde River Canyon

Take a boat trip down the canyon. Our guide will introduce you to the local wildlife and the history of the area before we visit the famous Kadishi Tufa waterfall.

Contact us at info@canyontours.za

4

Victoria and Alfred Waterfront

The best shopping destination in the heart of Cape Town.
Visit over 450 shops.
When you need a rest, try one of the many restuarants or coffee shops and enjoy watching the fishing boats.Bring a picnic and enjoy the beautiful lakes.

1 Read the adverts. Write the correct number of the advert.

1. Which advert is for people who want to learn more about sealife? ______
2. Where can you go if you like shopping? ______
3. Go there if you are interested in history. ______
4. This is open every day. ______
5. Which activity involves taking a boat? ______
6. Where can you find different restaurants? ______

2 Read the reviews on page 70. Match the reviews with the places described in the adverts. There are more reviews than adverts.

Advert 1	
Advert 2	
Advert 3	
Advert 4	

INTERNET ×

A ★★★★★ If you want to go on a safari, I really suggest you use this company! We had a small group with a really friendly driver and guide. The bus was comfortable and the accommodation was really lovely, small hotels in the local community. I felt like we had a chance to see the real South Africa! The scenery along the road was so beautiful, and we saw so many more animals than I thought we would. I hope to come back and go on a longer tour one day!

B ★★★★ The boat trip was quite rough and the boat was small. I suggest taking medicine to stop being seasick before leaving! The tour was really amazing and the guide was excellent. It helps you to understand modern South Africa and how the country has developed. The tour was about three hours long. Although a bit of a sad thing to do on holiday, I would say it is important to visit this place. Leave some time to explore the island. It is best to book trips early as they often sell out.

C ★★ This is a beautiful place to visit, but if you go, I advise you to use a different company! First, they couldn't find our reservation (even though we made it a week ago and had an e-mail confirming it). This made us late for on the tour so they said there wasn't enough time to visit the waterfall. Our guide didn't seem to know that much, or wasn't interested in telling us a lot. He seemed to be in a bad mood. We were looking forward to our trip, but we felt it was a bit ruined.

D ★★★★★ Such a lovely place to visit! It is always busy but not too crowded. It is clean, tidy and feels safe. Most of the shops are quite expensive, but there is a nice market, and it is a good place to eat with many different types of restaurants and coffee shops. It is also one of the best places to book tours and there is also a museum, art gallery and cinema too. It is easy to spend the whole day enjoying yourself there, and it has a beautiful setting too.

E ★★★ We did enjoy our trip but it was a lot shorter than we thought it would be, and there wasn't that much to see really. I didn't think it was very good value for money either. Even the food in the café cost a lot. It would be OK for small children (the play area looked nice) but our teenagers were bored after an hour or so. The shark area was the best part. They swam over your head.

3 True or false? Give evidence from the text. Write the number of the line(s).

1. The tour guide on Robben Island was very good. ______
2. Blyde River Canyon is not worth visiting. ______
3. The people who went on a safari saw lots of wild animals. ______
4. The Victoria and Alfred Waterfront doesn't have many visitors. ______
5. Two Oceans Aquarium is good for young children. ______
6. The waterfall was great. ______

C LANGUAGE

1 Complete the sentences using words from the text.

1. The tourists enjoyed staying in the ____________________ with local people.
2. The sea was ______________ that day so some people felt sick.
3. The ____________________ for the boat trip was made the week before.
4. The tour guide's attitude and no time for the waterfall _______________ the canyon trip.
5. Two Oceans Aquarium was so small that is wasn't good ______________ for the money.

2 Rewrite the underlined sentence parts using your own words.

1. We had a great vacation in South Africa.

____

2. We visited some family members in Johannesburg.

____

3. The train journey lasted over 26 hours.

____

4. In Johannesburg we couldn't find our way so we asked a police officer for help.

____

5. When we got to our family, they had already prepared a great meal for us.

____

D WRITING

Choose one of the following tasks:

1 Write an e-mail.

Write an e-mail to Canyon Tours and ask for more information about the Blyde River Canyon tour on page 69. Ask about prices, dates, activities, food and drink.
Write about 100 words.

2 Write an essay.

'Beach holidays or adventure holidays?'
Write about the pros and cons of each kind of holiday and give your opinion.
Write about 100 words.

E MEDIATION

BOEREWORS

A traditional, long sausage that is rolled up. It is normally made of beef mixed with pork or lamb and spices. It is delicious cooked on the barbecue!

BOBOTIE

This dish is thought to have been brought to South Africa by Asian slaves but is now the country's national dish. Made of meat, spices and dried fruit, it is topped with eggs and milk and then cooked in the oven.

CHAKALAKA

Chakalaka is a vegetable dish made with onions, cabbage, peppers, carrots, beans and spices. It can also be served as a side dish.

MALVA PUDDING

Originally made by the Dutch, this is a sweet dessert made with jam, and covered with a hot cream sauce.

1 Du bist mit deiner Mutter in einem Restaurant in Südafrika. Sie kann nur schlecht Englisch und versteht die Speisekarte nicht. Hilf ihr, ein Gericht auszuwählen.

Your mum: Die Speisekarte sieht interessant aus, aber ich verstehe kaum, was da steht. Kannst du mir helfen? Woraus besteht die Wurst im ersten Gericht?

You: ______________________________

Your mum: Ich darf ja nichts mit Milchprodukten essen. Welche Gerichte könnte ich dann nehmen?

You: ______________________________

Your mum: Gibt es auch vegetarische Hauptgerichte?

You: ______________________________

Your mum: Was bedeutet "side dish"?

You: ______________________________

Your mum: Was ist in dem Malva Pudding? Malven?

You: ______________________________

Your mum: Oh, Sahne kann ich nicht essen. Vielleicht kann man die Soße ja weglassen.

F SPEAKING

1 Look at the photo and prepare a three-minute talk about it.

First describe the picture:
- What can you see in the picture?
- Where are the students?
- What are they doing?

Then give your opinion:
- What do you think the biggest differences are between this school and your school?
- What things do you need for a good school?
- Do you think wearing a uniform is important?
- How does poverty and inequality affect school life?

Unit 4

Living in Hong Kong

68/2 1 (WRITING) **Make a brochure for tourists in Hong Kong.**

a) Complete the sentences. Use the pictures and the information on pages 68–69 in your book for help.

History of Hong Kong

For many years Hong Kong was ____________________.
Today it is ____________________ ____________________ and a lot of signs ____________________ ____________________. Hong Kong is one of the biggest ____________________ ____________________ ____________________.

Shopping

Hong Kong is a great place ____________________. There are ____________________ ____________________. Many stalls ____________________.

Media scene

Hong Kong has a busy ____________________. There is a large ____________________ ____________________ ____________________ newspapers.

Pollution

Hong Kong has a lot of problems ____________________ ____________________ can cause health problems. The city also ____________________.
But Hong Kong ____________________ ____________________.

b) What else can you put in your brochure? Search the internet. Find another picture and write two sentences about it in your exercise book.

70/2

1 Write definitions for these words.

1. must-have: ______
2. fashionable: ______
3. brand-new: ______
4. pocket money: ______
5. grown-up: ______
6. rare: ______

1/5a)

2 Put in the right words.

browse | try on | major | save | afford | swap | special offers | district | shopping malls | floor | favourite | mixture

BLOG

Shopping is one of my ______ hobbies! At the weekend my friends and I like to go to Mong Kok, which is a ______ in Hong Kong. Mong Kok is one of the ______ shopping areas in Hong Kong. There are huge ______, restaurants and entertainment centres there. Some of the shopping malls are so huge that there is a whole ______ for mobile phones. We always look for ______ because we are trying to ______ some money. We often ______ in the luxury shops and ______ clothes that we hope we can ______ one day! Sometimes we ______ our clothes so we have something different to wear without spending more money.

1/5b)

3 Talk to your partner. Write down your partner's answers.

1. When was the last time you found a bargain?
______
2. What was the last piece of clothing you purchased?
______
3. Why do you think people return things?
______
4. Which shops stock your favourite brands?
______

11 71/6

4 (LISTENING) **Listen to the radio report. What do the teenagers think about buying fake products[1]? Write notes.**

 Jenny	
 Lee	
 Carl	

1 fake (product) [feɪk] – *gefälscht(es Produkt)*

72/7

5 What else did Lee tell the reporter? Make sentences in reported speech.

1. I buy most of my clothes in department stores.
2. I often go to Sneakers Street.
3. The shops in Sneakers Street are the best.
4. I have 25 pairs of sneakers at home.
5. Most of my friends have even more sneakers.
6. My best friend owns an extra cupboard for his sneakers.
7. He keeps his favourite sneakers on a shelf over his bed.

You can start your sentences with these words:

say | add | claim | explain | tell

1. Lee said that he bought most of his clothes in department stores.
2. He added that ______
3. ______
4. ______
5. ______
6. ______
7. ______

6 The reporter also asked the teenagers about their shopping habits. Report what she asked them.

72/8

1. How often do you go shopping?
2. Do you buy fake products?
3. What do you buy at the street markets?
4. Where did you get your sneakers?
5. Do you own a lot of luxury goods?
6. How much money do you spend on clothes?

1. *She asked the teenagers how often they went shopping.*
2. *She asked them* ____________________
3. ____________________
4. ____________________
5. ____________________
6. ____________________

7 Report what Jenny answered.

73/9

"I've never bought a fake product. I've just bought some snacks at the market. I got my sneakers in a shop on Sneakers Street. I only have one luxury bag. My mum gave it to me for my birthday. Last week I spent all my pocket money on clothes."

____

____

____

____

____

8 (WRITING) Read these comments in an online forum. Write a reply in your exercise book. Write about 100 words.

73/10

INTERNET

RosieLee98
I don't like the idea of buying fake goods at all. The people who make them are stealing from the designers. And these cheap goods are made in factories with really bad working conditions.

34HKBoy
People who buy fake goods can't afford luxury products! I think designer goods are too expensive.If the prices were lower, people wouldn't buy so many fake products!

1 Complete the crossword.

74/1

1. the waste from a car is called … fumes
2. a factory that makes electricity
3. if you watch a TV show, you … in
4. a group of people who are watching a show
5. to change into
6. the person who presents a TV show
7. it covers your face
8. to take something in

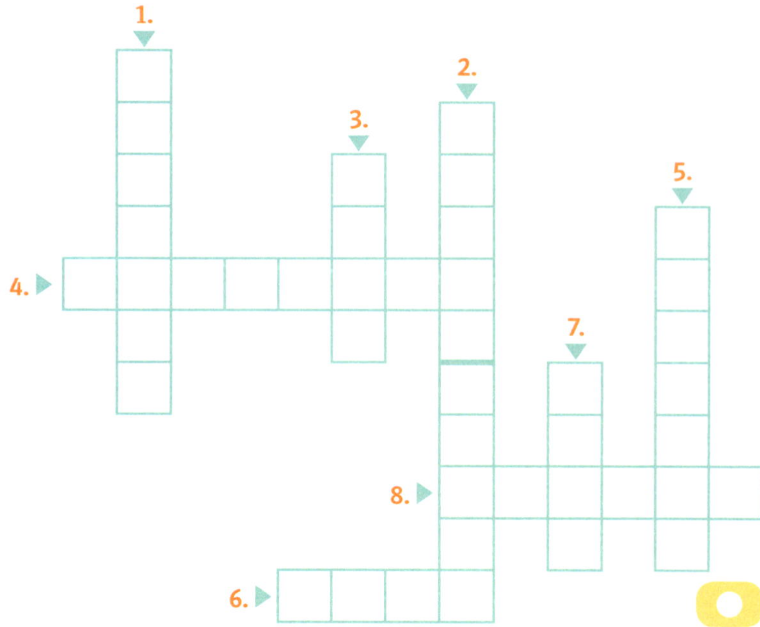

2 Rewrite the underlined sentence parts.

75/4a)

a) Use the words in the boxes.

install | improve | produce | suggest | create | travel | convert

1. Peter came to the studio to explain how we can make the environment of the city better.

   Peter travelled to the studio to explain how we can

2. He said that if we used less electricity, then the power plants would make less.

3. He also said that we should put in more solar panels to change the sun's energy into electricity.

4. Finally, he said we should build Personal Rapid Transport pods.

75/4b)

b) Rewrite the sentence parts using your own words.

1. Pollutions generates health problems.

2. It is important to reduce the number of cars and buses in Hong Kong.

3. Hong Kong should conserve enough green areas.

75/4

3 Find the opposites.

1. to increase ⟷ ______ 4. host ⟷ ______
2. to install ⟷ ______ 5. luxurious ⟷ ______
3. future ⟷ ______ 6. clean ⟷ ______

12
76/5

4 (LISTENING) Listen to Jenny talking about her life in Hong Kong.

a) Complete the table.

pros of living in Hong Kong	cons of living in Hong Kong

b) Answer the questions.

1. What is Jenny's opinion of living in Hong Kong as a teenager?

______

2. What percentage of Hong Kong is still green?

______

3. What are Jenny's dreams and ambitions?

______

______

76/5

5 (SPEAKING) Analyse the chart. What does it tell you about how teenagers live in Hong Kong?

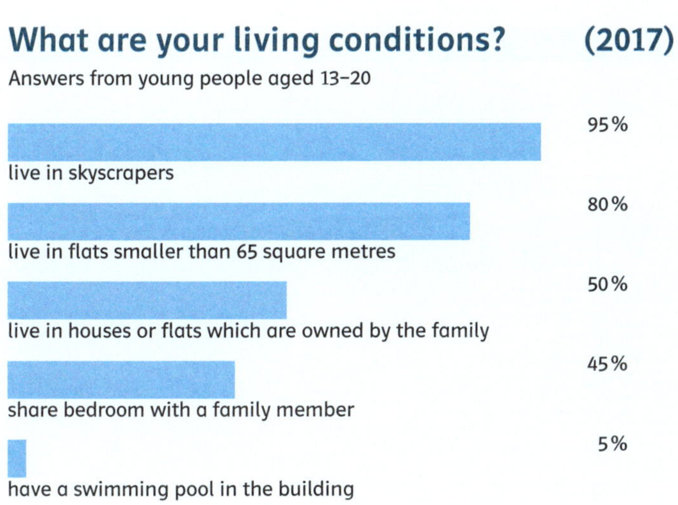

- This is a chart about …
- The chart shows …
- 95% of the teenagers …
- The majority …
- The minority …
- Most of …
- More than …
- Half of …
- … percent of …
- We can draw the conclusion that …

6 Complete Jenny's sentences. Put in the will-future or going to-future.

77/7a)

a) Underline the signal words.
b) Put in the right tense.

1. I ________________ to a concert next week. (go)
2. I hope we ________________ to a bigger flat soon. (move)
3. I ________________ my friends after school today because I have too much homework. (not meet)
4. Next weekend we ________________ at the beach. (swim)
5. There's a lot of smog today. I think I ________________ a mask. (wear)
6. I hope the pollution ________________ any worse. (not get)
7. I ________________ my exams next year. (take)

7 Will-future or going to-future? Put in the verbs in the right tense.

77/7a)

spend | go (2 x) | write | send | do | watch

Archie: Hi Jenny, what ________________ about for your history project?

Jenny: I think I ________________ my project on the history of Hong Kong. What about you?

Archie: I don't know. I can't find where I wrote the details of what we need to do!

Jenny: Don't worry, I ________________ you my copy.

Archie: Thank you, that would be great. On Saturday I ________________ all day on it and if I finish it, I ________________ skateboarding in the park on Sunday. Do you want to come?

Jenny: Ah thanks, but I ________________ that new martial arts film at the cinema with my sister and then I think we ________________ to the shopping mall.

8 Write four questions for your partner about his / her plans for the weekend. Ask your questions and then write three answers.

77/7b)

What are you … ? | If you … ? | Are you … ?

1. What are you ________________?

____

____

2. If you ________________, will you ________________?

____

____

3. Are you ________________?

____

____

❀ 77/8

1 (SPEAKING) **Imagine you are going to visit Hong Kong with your partner. Try to agree on three sights that you would both like to visit. Give reasons for your choices.**

Visit Hong Kong!

Where east meets west and ancient meets modern.

Visit the ancient Man Mo Temple.

Take a trip on the Star Ferry.

Ride the Peak Tram for amazing views of the city.

Enjoy the rides on the rollercoasters at Ocean Park.

Experience the future at the Space Museum.

Sho and eat at Temple Street Market.

❀ 77/8

2 (SPEAKING) **How can you live more eco-friendly? Collect ideas and discuss them with your partner.**

What can you do to …
- save water?
- save energy?
- produce less rubbish?
- use more public transport?

I could use an alarm to help me take shorter showers.

We could collect rain water and give it to our plants.

79/6

1 (READING) Read the e-mails from three friends.

E-MAIL

Lina

Henry

Jin

Hi Jin,
How are things back at home? Is it strange to be back in Hong Kong after your exchange year in England? How is your family? I'm sure they were happy to see you! Is your new school OK? We miss you here. I'm busy at school. Everyone is studying for exams and waiting for the holidays. I got top grades in the maths challenge last week ☺.
Send us news soon!
Love, Lina xxx

Hi Jin!
How are you? We lost our basketball game 65-52 at the weekend – we need you back! Is there a basketball team at your new school? The house is quiet without you here. Mum and Dad send their love.
Henry

Hi Lina and Henry,
It was good to hear from you both! It's great to be back with my family but I still have to get used to living in a big city again after the English countryside!
After spending a year in England, I'm much more aware[1] of the way the government controls our life here in Hong Kong. I want to fight for more freedom and democracy, so I've joined a pro-democracy student group and I'm helping create a blog. It has caused some arguments with my parents. They are worried I might get into trouble and won't be allowed to go to university. But I believe in justice and freedom, and I think it's important to not just stand by and do nothing.

Anyway, say hi to everyone at school for me, and love to your mum and dad, Henry. And good luck with your next basketball games and your exams.
Miss you guys! Jin

Hello Jin,
It's so good to hear from you. ☺ I'm glad you are well, and I think it's great you are getting involved in student politics. My exams went well and I'm looking forward to the holidays. I hope what you're doing is not dangerous. Didn't you once tell us that some protesters in Hong Kong were sent to prison? Got to go - I'm going to the cinema with some friends. Keep in touch!
Lina xxx

Hi Lina,
Thanks for your e-mail. I just wanted to send you a link to our <u>pro-democracy blog</u> (it's in English and Cantonese[2]). My first entry is about trying to get political prisoners free. The blog is anonymous[3], but the headmaster of our school had a 'chat' with us the other day and I fear they are watching us.
Jin

1 to be aware [bi͜ əˈweə] – *sich bewusst sein*; 2 Cantonese [ˌkæntəˈniːz] – *Kantonesisch*; 3 anonymous [əˈnɑːnɪməs] – *anonym*

E-MAIL

Hi Jin!

How are you? Lina sent me the link to your blog. I like the design. It looks really professional. I like your article too. What are you going to write about next? I'm leaving for basketball summer camp tomorrow. Take care!

Henry

Hey Jin,

Are you OK? We haven't heard from you since last month. Is everything alright, or are you just busy? Please write soon!

Lina xxx

Dear Lina and Henry,

My name is Kelly and I'm a friend of Jin's. Sorry to contact you like this, but I found your e-mail address in Jin's room, and he often spoke about you. I wanted to ask if you'd had any contact with him in the last few days? We're really worried because he hasn't been home for two days and no one has heard from him. His parents are very upset, and the police haven't been helpful. He told me he thought someone was following him the other day. Jin was organizing a big protest through the blog so I'm worried he got in trouble because of that. Please contact me if you know ANYTHING.

Thank you! Kelly

2 Answer the questions.

79/6

1. What did Jin do in England? ______
2. Where did Jin live in England? ______
3. Why does Jin feel it's important to fight for more freedom and democracy in Hong Kong? ______
4. Why are Jin's parents worried? ______
5. Why does Lina think Jin's work on the blog might be dangerous? ______
6. What is Jin's first blog entry about? ______
7. Who is Kelly and why does she write to Lina and Henry? ______
8. Why does Kelly think Jin might be in trouble? ______

3 (WRITING) What do you think has happened to Jin? Write an e-mail from Jin in your exercise book.

79/6

INTERNET

Cyberbullying at Hong Kong School

When Angie Chen got a place at a top international school in Hong Kong, she and her family were very excited. However, her dream soon turned into a nightmare. The happy, confident, intelligent girl she was disappeared into a shy, stressed and sad teenager. At first, Angie didn't want to talk about what was happening, but one day her mum looked through her phone to see if she could find any clues to what had changed in her life. She found hundreds of messages and posts cyberbullying Angie. Most of them were laughing at the fact that she was 'poor', that she didn't have the latest phone, that her shoes were cheap and her glasses weren't a designer brand. "It broke my heart as a parent," said Angie's mum. "She was too embarrassed to tell us because she didn't want us to be sad that we couldn't afford these things. We explained to her that yes, we were poor, but she was at the school because she was clever and not because we had paid for her to be there and, secondly, that having expensive things does not make you a better person, as the people cyberbullying her have shown."

Once Angie's parents told the school what was happening, they moved quickly to stop the cyberbullying and teach the students why it was wrong. Angie says things have improved, and that she is glad she spoke up about the problem in the end.

"It was horrible because I was unhappy at school but couldn't even escape at home. Now, I talk to other students about cyberbullying and what to do about it. I wish I had told someone sooner."

STOP CYBERBULLYING

1 DO NOT RESPOND
Don't answer or comment to the message.

2 SAVE IT
Save, copy or print the bullying message.

3 CLOSE IT
Close the message or website and don't look at it again.

4 TELL SOMEONE
Talk to someone you trust (e.g. friends, teachers, parents) and show them the bullying message.

80/1

1 (MEDIATION) **Du willst für die Schülerzeitung einen Artikel zum Thema Cyber-Mobbing schreiben und hast bei Recherchen im Internet diesen Artikel gefunden. Fasse die wichtigsten Punkte auf Deutsch zusammen. Was ist der Schülerin in Hongkong passiert und was kann man gegen Cyber-Mobbing tun?**

Ziel 1: I can understand information about Hong Kong. → ◎ cs4gi8

Hong Kong – Where east meets west

Hong Kong is a territory in the south of China. Over 7.2 million people live there, including a large number of people from other countries. It has created a multicultural society with many different religions, festivals and languages. Hong Kong used to be a British colony but in 1997 it became a part of China again, but it has kept a separate political and financial system.
It describes itself as a place where 'East meets West' due to its mixture of Chinese and Western influences. Hong Kong is famous for its financial centre and it has its own money, the Hong Kong Dollar. It has the most skyscrapers of any city in the world. It also has a busy port which is an important business place in Asia. It is also a popular destination for tourists.
Even though most people in the city use its excellent public transport system, Hong Kong still has a big problem with air pollution, much of which is caused by industry in China. It is one of the most densely populated cities in the world, and there are great differences between the rich and the poor of the city.

Answer the questions.

1. Why is Hong Kong so multicultural? ______
2. What is different in Hong Kong compared to China and why? ______
3. What is the city famous for? ______
4. What problems does the city have? ______

4P
p. 88/1

Ziel 2: I can write an online comment. → ◎ tm5h6y → ◎ u55sk6

Write a reply to this comment on an online forum.

FORUM

Rex8

People spend too much money on clothes. They want all the latest designs, but I think they are wasting money which they could save for more important things.

______

4P
p. 88/2

Ziel 3: I can talk about how to make a place more eco-friendly.

→ ⦾ g7nt9h → ⦾ q9i6yp

a) You are going to give a presentation at school about how the school could be more eco-friendly. Collect ideas in a mind map.

b) Write down your presentation.

____

____

____

____

____

____

____

____

____

____

____

8P

→ p. 89/3

Ziel 4: I can understand a text about the media.

→ ⦾ a5y9pi

Read the text on pages 78–79 in your book again. Where can you find the following information? Write the line number(s).

1. The way we see the world is influenced by the media. ____________
2. In a democratic society people are free to publish facts or give their opinions. ____________
3. The situation in Hong Kong is different compared to the rest of China. ____________
4. Journalists and publishers in Hong Kong are facing problems. ____________
5. The Chinese government censors internet sites. ____________
6. It's difficult to control the huge flood of information. ____________
7. You should always be critical of the information that is presented in the media. ____________

7P

→ p. 89/4

Ziel 5: I can pass on information about cyberbullying.

INTERNET

Please share your experiences with cyberbullying in the comments below.

+ LittleM: Don't respond! I was being cyberbullied and I kept replying but as soon as I stopped, the person got bored.

+ D1Love Keep copies of all the mean things they say. I did this and then showed them to my aunty who went with me to speak to the person's parents.

+ Polly34 Block, block, block! A group of girls kept sending me horrible messages so I blocked them all so they couldn't contact me anymore.

+ KeitaKC Tell someone about it. I was so sad about being cyberbullied all the time that I eventually couldn't take it anymore. I broke down crying in front of my mum and as soon as I had someone to talk to about it, everything seemed better. We worked out how to deal with it together. Don't suffer alone. ☹

Dein Freund hat Probleme mit Cyber-Mobbing. Ihr überlegt zusammen, was ihr dagegen tun könnt, und habt diese Kommentare in einem Online-Forum gefunden. Hilf deinem Freund, die Informationen besser zu verstehen.

Dein Freund: Ich habe dieses Onlineforum gefunden. Da geht es auch um Cyber-Mobbing, aber ich verstehe nicht alles. Warum schreiben die Leute da rein?

Du: ______________________________

Dein Freund: Da schreibt jemand, man soll nicht auf solche Nachrichten anworten. Warum?

Du: ______________________________

Dein Freund: Und wenn das nicht reicht? Man soll die Nachrichten kopieren und jemandem zeigen. Und was hat D1Love dann gemacht?

Du: ______________________________

____

Dein Freund: Das ist gut. Und wie kann man dafür sorgen, dass man solche Nachrichten nicht mehr bekommt?

Du: ______________________________

____

Dein Freund: Trotzdem fühlt man sich schlecht. Was haben die Opfer sonst noch gemacht?

Du: ______________________________

____

____

6P

p. 89/5

Lösungen online c2g5zz

○ **Ziel 1: I can understand information about Hong Kong.**

Join us on an open-top bus sightseeing tour of the most famous places in Hong Kong. The tour starts on Hong Kong Island and will pick you up at your hotel. First we will visit the beautiful and historic Man Mo Temple and the HSBC skyscraper, which has 52 floors and was the world's most expensive building when it was built in 1985. We will then stop at the Hong Kong Zoo and Gardens for some tea before taking the Star Ferry across the harbour.
We will have a lunch of noodles and dumplings by the water and enjoy the spectacular view before taking a walk along the Avenue of Stars to the Hong Kong Museum of Art. The bus will then take you north, where you can choose to either visit Temple Street Market for some shopping or go to Kowloon Park to learn about the history of the area.

Right or wrong? Tick the right box.

	right	wrong
1. The tour starts on Hong Kong Island.	☐	☐
2. The HBSC skyscraper is still the world's most expensive building.	☐	☐
3. Tourists will have lunch at the Hong Kong Zoo.	☐	☐
4. There will be noodles and dumplings for lunch.	☐	☐
5. The tour finishes at the Hong Kong Museum of Art.	☐	☐
6. Tourists who like shopping can visit a market.	☐	☐

○ **Ziel 2: I can write an online comment.**

Write a reply to this comment on an online forum.

FORUM ×

Louis9

I wouldn't visit Hong Kong in my holidays. I think it's a big, dirty city with too many people and the smog is terrible! I would hate to go there.

I think Hong Kong ... | I would / wouldn't go there because ... | interesting / boring / traditional / modern ... | tourist destination | museums / parks / markets

____

____

____

____

____

○ **Ziel 3: I can talk about how to make a place more eco-friendly.**

Use these ideas to prepare a talk about making your school more eco-friendly.

- *recycle all our waste*
- *different bins for waste*
- *use public transport*
- *throw away less food*
- *save toilet water*
- *save energy with solar panels*

____

____

____

____

____

____

○ **Ziel 4: I can understand a text about the media.**

Read the text on pages 78–79 in your book again. Which sentences are correct? Tick the boxes.

1. The media in Hong Kong is becoming less free. ☐
2. Without free media governments can abuse their power and oppress people. ☐
3. The journalists in Hong Kong write and publish whatever they want. ☐
4. China is starting to control the media in Hong Kong. ☐
5. People who live in China have free access to the internet. ☐
6. You should always be critical, but too many restrictions keep people from communicating. ☐

○ **Ziel 5: I can pass on information about cyberbullying.**

Cyberbullying

- Nearly 43 % of kids have been cyberbullied.
- 70 % of students say they often see cyberbullying online.
- 63 % of teenagers say cyberbullying is a serious problem.
- Only one in ten victims of cyberbullying tell an adult.
- Girls are victims twice as often as boys.

Lies dir die Umfrage an einer Schule in Hongkong durch und beanworte die Fragen auf Deutsch.

1. Was sagt die Mehrheit der Schüler? ______________________

____

____

____

2. Wieviele Opfer sprechen mit einem Erwachsenen?

____

3. Wer wird öfter Opfer von Cyber-Mobbing, Jungs oder Mädchen? ______________________

A LISTENING

You will hear a woman from Indonesia talking about her job as a helper in Hong Kong.
You will hear the recording twice.

13 ### 1 Listen and choose the best summary.

1. A helper in Hong Kong fights for more rights. ☐
2. A helper in Hong Kong describes her life. ☐
3. A helper in Hong Kong explains why people come to work in the city. ☐

13 ### 2 Listen again and choose the right answer.

1. In Indonesia Rika trained as a …
   a) teacher. ☐ b) doctor. ☐ c) cook. ☐
2. In Indonesia Rika didn't have any …
   a) family. ☐ b) friends. ☐ c) opportunities. ☐
3. In Hong Kong Rika was shocked when she …
   a) met the family. ☐ b) saw the skyscrapers. ☐ c) started work. ☐
4. Rika works …
   a) 16 hours a day. ☐ b) 16 hours a week. ☐ c) 6 hours a day. ☐
5. A lot of helpers in Hong Kong …
   a) are sent home. ☐ b) are treated badly. ☐ c) become rich. ☐
6. The helpers in Hong Kong want to …
   a) have their own place to live. ☐ b) earn more money. ☐ c) have more days off. ☐

B READING

Living in Hong Kong

Julie Chen is the host of a TV morning show in Hong Kong. Today she is talking to Steven Taylor, who moved from England to Hong Kong three years ago.

Julie: Today in our series about expats[1], we are talking to Steven from London.
Hi Steven! Can you tell us when and why you moved to Hong Kong?

Steven: Yes, of course. I've been here for three years now. I was in my twenties and working for an international bank in the City of London when an opportunity became available to transfer to Hong Kong and I just thought it would be a big adventure and be good for my career.

Julie: And was it difficult to settle in to life here?

Steven: It wasn't too bad. About 50% of the workers at my company are expats, so there are lots of people in the same situation as me and it was easy to make friends. The other 50% are local workers who are really helpful if you need advice or help.

Julie: Was Hong Kong like you expected it to be?

Steven: Yes and no. I knew it was a big, busy city but I wasn't expecting it to be so green. There are so many parks and there are islands you can visit and lots of countryside for hiking. I also didn't think there would be so many temples and traditional buildings. It really is a place where traditional and modern buildings sit side by side. I wasn't prepared for the inequality though. You think of Hong Kong as a rich place with all the skyscrapers and with it being a financial centre, but next to this there is real poverty. You see homes falling down and people with nothing. Another thing that surprised me was how clean and orderly everything is here. Even though there are a lot of people, everyone seems to respect the rules. There are people cleaning everywhere, it all seems very organised.

Julie: What were the things that you found most difficult to adapt to?

Steven: The weather is hard. The summers are so hot and humid and the smog is so bad you feel like you can't breathe. I try to stay inside in the air-conditioning as much as possible. The winters are beautiful though! The weather is cooler and the air is clean.

Julie: What about the food?

Steven: Well, it is a very international city and people like their food here so you can buy almost anything. The supermarkets are quite expensive and there is not much choice. It's better to buy fruit and vegetables at the market; I would never have done this before. There are British supermarkets so you can buy familiar things there if you don't mind paying more for them. People eat out a lot though; you can get everything from cheap bowls of noodles to really expensive food. The one thing I can't understand is why people in Hong Kong like eating chicken feet so much, they love them! And they drink tea all the time. I mean the British drink a lot of tea, but people in Hong Kong are on another level!

Julie: Hong Kong has a reputation for very small, expensive homes. Is that your experience?

Steven: Well, I lived in London before which is also very expensive so I didn't find the rents to be too different. The flats are tiny, especially if you want to live on Hong Kong Island. I live a little out of the centre and yes, my flat is small, but I have a swimming pool and a gym in my building, which is nice. It makes you tidy when you don't have much space and the flats are very well designed. Also, Hong Kong has a work hard, play hard lifestyle so I'm not at home very much!

Julie: Thanks so much for telling us about your life in Hong Kong, Steven!

1 expat [eks'pæt] – *im Ausland Lebende(r)*

1 Read the interview. Which of these things does Steven talk about? Tick the boxes.

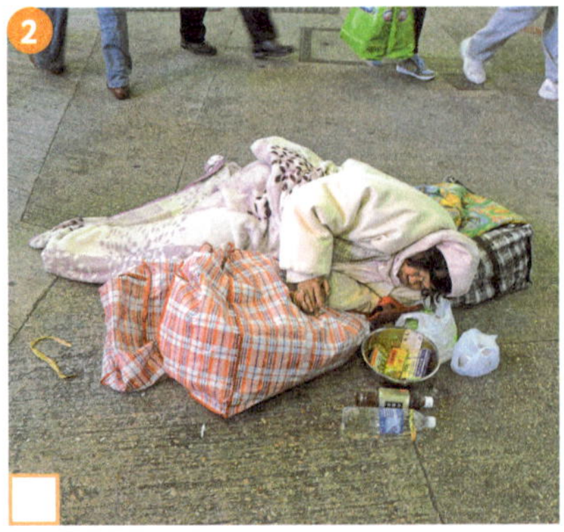

2 Complete the sentences with information from the text.

1. Steven moved to Hong Kong because he thought it would be ______________________
2. His company in Hong Kong has half local workers and ______________________
3. There are lots of green spaces in Hong Kong, for example ______________________
4. Steven thinks people in Hong Kong have a lot of respect ______________________
5. Summers in Hong Kong are hot, humid and ______________________
6. Steven didn't expect people to drink ______________________
7. Compared to London, rents in Hong Kong ______________________
8. It doesn't matter that Steven's flat is so tiny because ______________________

C LANGUAGE

1 Find suitable words to fill in the gaps.

1. A lot of people move to another country because of a job ______________________.
2. In Hong Kong ______________________ are next to poor houses and temples.
3. People in Hong Kong like to follow rules and life there is very ____________________.
4. It is good to stay inside places with ___________________________ in the summer.
5. When you live in a foreign country, it can be difficult to find __________________ food.
6. There is often a different __________________ which you have to get used to.

D WRITING

Choose one of the following tasks:

1 Write an online comment.

Read this comment on an online forum. Write a reply and give your opinion.

FORUM

ED_G11

I think the problem nowadays is everyone is so busy with their lives and their phones that they have forgotten about respect. No one helps each other or pays attention to other people's lives. People often behave disrespectfully towards others.

Write about 150 words.

2 Write an essay.

'Why is it important to be eco-friendly?'
Write about the things you do to be more eco-friendly and the reasons why you think it is important.

Write about 150 words.

E MEDIATION

Religion in Hong Kong

Although many citizens of Hong Kong wouldn't describe themselves as religious, most people take part in some of the traditions associated with Chinese religions such as Buddhism or Taoism. These religions believe in respecting and remembering local gods and ancestors. Around the city there are many temples and statues where people can come to remember and show respect.

An important part of religion in the city is the the practice of making offerings. People try to please the gods by leaving fresh fruit and vegetables for them. People also burn incense, sticks that release a nice smelling smoke, which they believe cleans the area of bad spirits. Another common practice is the burning of paper money. People believe their ancestors can spend it in the spirit world. Some people even burn pictures of things like as cars or TVs so that their dead relatives can use them.

Tin Hau is the goddess of the city of Hong Kong. She is also the goddess of the sea. As the city used to be a fishing village, the inhabitants believed that she would protect the fisherman at sea and make sure they caught lots of fish. There are over 60 temples for Tin Hau in the city.

There are also Christians and Muslims in the city. Many people also believe in fortune tellers and are superstitious. In the city people often mix together elements of different religions. Almost everyone uses feng shui to protect themselves from bad luck. No building in Hong Kong is built without using feng shui to design it.

Du recherchierst für ein Referat über die verschiedenen Weltreligionen und hast diesen Artikel über die unterschiedlichen Religionen in Hongkong gefunden. Fasse die wichtigsten Punkte auf Deutsch zusammen.

F SPEAKING

Partner A: Look at card A. Explain to partner B how you can get to the top of Victoria Peak.
Partner B: Look at card B. Explain to partner A what you can visit at the top of Victoria Peak.
Partner A + B: Discuss if you would like to visit Victoria Peak and which part of trip you would find the most interesting.

A Victoria Peak Tram

Times: 7 a.m. to midnight, Monday to Sunday.
How often: every 10–15 minutes
Fares: HK$45 adult return, HK$18 children
Journey time: 8–10 minutes
Distance: 1.4 km
Height: The tram travels from 28 metres to 396 metres above sea level.

Tip! Sit on the right side of the tram for the best views.

B Peak Tower

Visit the most unusual building in the city, which is also the top station for the Peak Tram. There are viewing platforms for spectacular views of Hong Kong.

Height: 396 metres above sea level
Sights: Level 2: Visit Madame Tussauds and see over 100 models of stars.
Level 3: Sky Terrace 428. Hong Kong's highest viewing area at 428 metres above sea level.
Open 10 a.m. – 11 p.m., Monday to Friday.
8 a.m. – 11 p.m., Saturday & Sunday.

Audios zum Hörverstehen

Aufnahmeleitung: Ernst Klett Verlag
Redaktion: Lisa Poeira
Sprecherinnen und Sprecher: Sophie Aldred, Eilidh Beaton, Brian Bowles, Harriet Carmichael, Polly Edsell, James Goode, John Green, John Hasler, Eve Karpf, Harriet Kershaw, Daniel Koek, Sarah Lam, Nneke Okeye, Rebecca Perfect, Nigel Pilkington, Caitlin Shannon, David Way

Textvertonung (Schülerbuch MP3-Dateien): Track 10 – 12: from OUT OF BOUNDS by Beverley Naidoo. Copyright © Beverley Naidoo, 1999; **Track 14:** © 2007, Jill Townsend; **Track 15 – 18:** © 2004, Lynne Reid Banks, Stealing Stacey, first published by Harper Collins Children's Books.
Produktion: John Green, TEFL Audio, London
Tontechnik: Tim Woolf
Gesamtzeit: 39' 32''

Inhaltsverzeichnis der Audios zum Hörverstehen
Hörverstehenstexte aus dem Workbook

Track	Titel	Seite/Übung
1	Listen to Merindah talking about respect.	4/4
2	Listen to Sonya and Barry.	7/4
3	You will hear two Australian teenagers talking about their lives.	20/1–2
4	Listen to the travel report on the radio.	26/1
5	Listen to the family at the airport.	28/4
6	Listen to three teenagers from Jamaica talking about values.	32/3
7	You will hear five airport announcements.	44/1–2
8	Lefa and Cebile have met at the police station where they were for questioning.	52/3
9	Listen to the radio interview about an attack at Kruger National Park.	55/2
10	You will hear a teenager from South Africa talking about his life.	68/1–2
11	Listen to the radio report. What do the teenagers think about buying fake products?	76/4
12	Listen to Jenny talking about her life in Hong Kong.	79/4
13	You will hear a woman from Indonesia talking about her job as a helper in Hong Kong.	90/1–2

Zusätzlich:
- Alle Tracks des Workbooks als MP3-Dateien
- Lesetexte des Schülerbuchs als MP3-Dateien

Weitere Übungsmöglichkeiten zu Orange Line 5:

Klassenarbeitstraining aktiv
978-3-12-548105-3

Vokabellernheft
978-3-12-548095-7

Grammatiktraining aktiv
978-3-12-548305-7

Vokabeltraining aktiv
978-3-12-548245-6

Vokabelübungssoftware
978-3-12-548645-4

Die Hörtexte gibt es auch online als MP3-Dateien zum Herunterladen. Dazu den Code **i8ce82** ins Suchfeld auf www.klett.de eingeben.

Liebe Schülerinnen und Schüler!

Zuerst meinen **herzlichen Glückwunsch** zum Bestehen der 7. Jahrgangsstufe! Ihr habt nun die Unterstufe erfolgreich durchlaufen und seid in der 8. Klasse, in der **Mittelstufe,** angekommen.

Damit ändert sich für euch einiges: Eure Klasse wurde neu zusammengestellt, ihr lernt neue Mitschülerinnen und Mitschüler kennen. Ihr habt euch bereits am Ende der 7. Klasse für eine besondere **Ausbildungsrichtung** entschieden, in der ihr euch nun bis Ende der 10. Klasse befindet (ab der 11. Klasse spielen die Ausbildungsrichtungen dann keine entscheidende Rolle mehr). Das bedeutet: **Neue Fächer** kommen dazu, in denen ihr von Anfang an gut mitarbeiten müsst. Dabei dürft ihr aber die bisherigen Fächer nicht vernachlässigen. Die Anforderungen, die eure Lehrerinnen und Lehrer an euch stellen, steigen. Doch ihr habt es bis hierher geschafft und es wäre doch gelacht, wenn ihr den Weg bis zum Abitur nicht erfolgreich meistern würdet!

Wenn ihr gute Noten haben wollt (und wer will das nicht?), solltet ihr eure **Hausaufgaben** ordentlich erledigen. Hausaufgaben sind keine Schikane, die extra für Schüler erfunden wurden, **sie helfen euch**, das anzuwenden und zu vertiefen, was ihr in der Schule gelernt habt. Habt ihr bei den Hausaufgaben Probleme, müsst ihr das unbedingt euren Lehrern sagen. Diese erkennen dann, was ihr wirklich könnt oder bei welchen Themen sie mit euch noch üben müssen bzw. was sie euch noch einmal erklären müssen, weil ihr es nicht verstanden habt. **Darum bringt auch das Abschreiben von Hausaufgaben nichts** – außer dass ihr ein Ergebnis vorweisen könnt, das aber nicht euer eigenes ist und außerdem vielleicht gar nicht stimmt.

Eure Freundinnen und Freunde und die gemeinsamen Unternehmungen werden für euch immer wichtiger. Das ist richtig und gut so. Umso genauer müsst ihr aber das **Lernen planen**: für die nächsten Tage und für die Schulaufgaben. Am besten, ihr führt einen **Terminplan**, in den ihr eintragt, wann die Schulaufgaben anstehen. Dann könnt ihr rechtzeitig, also mindestens eine Woche vorher, mit dem konzentrierten Lernen beginnen und die Schulaufgaben in diesem Heft zur Übung bearbeiten. **Fragt rechtzeitig bei euren Lehrerinnen und Lehrern nach, wenn euch etwas unklar ist.** Lasst es euch noch einmal erklären und geniert euch nicht – denn vermutlich haben das die Mitschüler auch nicht ganz genau verstanden und trauen sich oft nur nicht, danach zu fragen! Am Tag vor der Schulaufgabe solltet ihr das Gefühl haben: „Ich habe genug gelernt, mir kann nicht viel passieren!" **Geht ausgeschlafen und entspannt in die Prüfung.** Lasst euch auch nicht von euren Mitschülern nervös machen, die mit dem Lernen zu spät begonnen haben!

Wie hilft Dir GYM 8?

- Du kennst inzwischen die Anforderungen des Gymnasiums recht genau und weißt, was von dir verlangt wird. Deshalb findest du in diesem Heft nur noch **Kernfächer**, das sind die, in denen auch Schulaufgaben geschrieben werden.
- Die hier abgedruckten Schulaufgaben zeigen dir, **worauf es wirklich ankommt**: Verschaffe dir mit ihrer Hilfe einen Überblick, während du dich auf „deine" Schulaufgabe vorbereitest.
- Nimm dir dann die betreffende Schulaufgabe vor, bearbeite sie unter **„Echtbedingungen"** (in der angegebenen Zeit, ohne Hilfsmittel, mit Ruhe am Arbeitsplatz und ohne Unterbrechungen).
- Überprüfe danach im Lösungsheft dein Ergebnis – schummeln gilt nicht, denn schließlich willst du wissen, **wie gut du wirklich schon bist**!
- Für „Kurzeinsätze" eignen sich die **Stegreifaufgaben und Übungen**.
- **Jahrgangsstufentests** kannst du durchaus auch portionsweise bearbeiten.

Für die 8. Klasse am Gymnasium wünsche ich euch viel Freude und Erfolg!

Claus Gigl, Studiendirektor
Schulleiter am Burkhart-Gymnasium Mallersdorf-Pfaffenberg

AUFSATZ-TIPPS Inhaltsangabe

Mit der Inhaltsangabe sollst du den Leser über einen Text und seinen Inhalt **informieren**. Der Text kann ein literarischer Text sein, z. B. eine Fabel, eine Legende, eine Ballade oder eine Kurzgeschichte sein; es kann sich auch um einen Sachtext, z. B. aus einer Zeitschrift oder aus einem Jugendsachbuch, handeln.

Aufbau einer Inhaltsangabe

1. Einleitung: In der Einleitung musst du den **Verfasser**, den **Titel** des Textes und die **Textsorte** nennen. Außerdem nennst du die **Hauptpersonen**, **Ort** und **Zeit** des Geschehens sowie den **Handlungskern** bzw. die grundlegende Thematik des Textes.

2. Hauptteil: Hier gibst du den **Inhalt des Textes** wieder – nicht zu ausführlich (damit nicht die Gefahr der Nacherzählung besteht), aber doch so genau, dass der Leser weiß, um was es geht. Zusammenhänge musst du klar herausarbeiten, Ursachen und Folgen des Geschehens deutlich machen. Die zeitliche Reihenfolge des Geschehens musst du so vermitteln, dass keine Spannung entsteht (es handelt sich ja bei der Inhaltsangabe um eine sachliche, nicht um eine erzählende Aufsatzform).

3. Schluss: Nicht jede Inhaltsangabe braucht einen Schlussteil – kläre das mit deiner Deutschlehrerin oder deinem Deutschlehrer. Wenn dein Aufsatz einen Schluss haben soll, kannst du eine kurze, sachlich begründete **Bewertung des Textes** schreiben.

Folgende Vorarbeiten sind nötig

* **Lies den** zugrunde liegenden **Text mehrmals**, mindestens zweimal.
* **Streiche an**, was dir wichtig erscheint.
* **Gliedere den Text**, damit du ihn besser verstehst, **in Sinnabschnitte**.
* Verfasse einen **Schreibplan**.

Der Schreibplan

Meist wird zum Aufsatz ein Schreibplan, also eine kurze Gliederung, verlangt. Dieser Schreibplan hilft dir dann, dass du deinen Aufsatz in der **richtigen Reihenfolge** niederschreibst und **nichts Wichtiges vergisst**.

So sollte dein Schreibplan aufgebaut sein, den du dann je nach Textvorlage mit Inhalt füllen musst:

1. Einleitung: Autor, Titel, Textsorte. Hauptpersonen, Ort und Zeit der Handlung, Handlungskern
2. Hauptteil: Worum geht es?
3. Schluss: Abschließende Bewertung

Beim Schreiben musst du beachten

* Die Inhaltsangabe ist eine **sachliche Form**, du darfst also nicht wie in der Erzählung Spannung erzeugen.

* Verwende deshalb **Sachstil**: Satzgefüge (Hypotaxen), Konjunktionen; keine wörtliche Rede, keine Ausrufe; Gedanken und Gefühle werden nicht ausschmückend erzählt, sondern nur genannt; präzise Ausdrucksweise.

* Schreibe im **Präsens**.

In der 8. Klasse sollst du dich **argumentierend** mit Themen aus deinem eigenen Erfahrungsbereich auseinander setzen. Dies kann durch eine begründete Stellungnahme (siehe dazu GYM 7, dort ist die begründete Stellungnahme beschrieben) oder eine einfache, steigernde Erörterung geschehen. Die Aufgabenstellung kann auch an einen vorgegebenen Text anknüpfen.

Aufbau der Erörterung

1. Einleitung: In der Einleitung führst du z. B. durch ein **aktuelles Beispiel** oder eine **allgemeingültige Behauptung** zum Thema hin.

2. Hauptteil: Im Hauptteil schreibst du die **Argumente** nieder. Dabei musst du das Argumentationsschema der einfachen Erörterung beachten, das besagt, dass ein Argument aus folgenden vier Teilen besteht:

Behauptung
↓
Begründung
↓
Beispiel
↓
Rückführung zur Behauptung

Mehrere solcher Argumente bilden den Hauptteil deiner Erörterung.

3. Schluss: Der Schluss rundet die Erörterung ab. Dies kannst du erreichen, indem du **das Wichtigste noch einmal zusammenfasst** oder indem du **an die Einleitung anknüpfst**.

Folgende Vorarbeiten sind nötig

* **Kläre zuerst das Thema genau**, überlege, was du beweisen oder begründen sollst.
* Überlege, welche Argumente es gibt. Lege eine **Stoffsammlung** an.
* **Ordne deine Stoffsammlung**. Achte darauf, dass du jede Behauptung begründen kannst und suche nach einem passenden Beispiel.
* Verfasse nun eine steigernde **Gliederung**. Dabei sollte der wichtigste Gesichtspunkt am Schluss stehen.
* Suche nun nach **passenden Gedanken für die Einleitung und den Schluss**.

Die Gliederung

Die Gliederung **zeigt dem Lehrer, wie du argumentierst**, sie hilft dir auch bei der zielgerichteten Abfassung deines Aufsatzes, **damit du kein Argument vergisst**.

So sollte deine Gliederung aufgebaut sein, die du dann je nach Thema mit Inhalt füllen musst:

1. Einleitung: Hinführung zum Thema.
2. Hauptteil: Frage, die du in der Erörterung klären sollst (= Themafrage)
1. Behauptung (mit Begründung, Beispiel und Rückführung)
2. Behauptung (mit Begründung, Beispiel und Rückführung)
3. Behauptung (mit Begründung, Beispiel und Rückführung)
4. Behauptung (mit Begründung, Beispiel und Rückführung)
...
3. Schluss: Abschließende Stellungnahme

AUFSATZ-TIPPS Steigernde Erörterung

Beim Schreiben musst du beachten

* Die Erörterung ist eine **argumentative Form**, du musst also deine Meinung begründet darlegen, damit du überzeugen kannst.

* Achte auf den richtigen **Aufbau deiner Argumente**: **vom schwächsten zum stärksten.**

* Beginne bei jedem **neuen Argument** in einer **neuen Zeile**.

* Stelle **Zusammenhänge** klar heraus.

* Verwende dazu einen **sachlichen Schreibstil**: Satzgefüge (Hypotaxen), mit Gliedsätzen (und Konjunktionen) wie Kausalsatz (weil), Konzessivsatz (obwohl), Finalsatz (damit), Konditionalsatz (wenn), Konsekutivsatz (sodass); abwechslungsreicher Satzbau; stütze deine Argumentation auf Fakten oder erkläre deine Meinung so, dass sie nachvollziehbar ist; vermeide Floskeln und Allerweltsbegriffe wie „natürlich", „es ist bewiesen, dass..." und „wie jeder weiß".

* Achte auf **Anschaulichkeit** in deiner Darstellung: präzisiere deine Argumentation durch treffende Verben und Adjektive.

* Schreibe im **Präsens**.

AUFSATZ-TIPPS Protokoll

Das Protokoll ist in der 8. Klasse **keine verpflichtende Schulaufgabe**, manche Deutschlehrerinnen und Deutschlehrer verlangen es aber, weil es in höheren Jahrgangsstufen wichtig ist, Protokoll schreiben zu können.

Das Protokoll ist eine **sachliche Form**. Im Protokoll kannst du den Verlauf und die Ergebnisse einer Besprechung (z. B. eine Klassensprecherversammlung) oder einer Unterrichtsstunde so festhalten, dass man später oder wenn man nicht dabei war nachlesen kann, was geschehen ist oder was besprochen und vereinbart wurde.

Aufbau des Protokolls

1. Protokollkopf: Die Gestaltung des Protokollkopfs ist ziemlich starr festgelegt. Darin werden genannt: der **Titel der Veranstaltung**, das **Thema**, das **Datum**, **Uhrzeit und Ort**, die **Anwesenden** (evtl. auch die Abwesenden) und der **Protokollführer**.

2. Tagesordnung: In der Tagesordnung werden die Punkte **aufgelistet**, die bei der Besprechung oder Unterrichtsstunde von Bedeutung waren. Die einzelnen Tagesordnungspunkte werden durchnummeriert.

3. Hauptteil: Im Hauptteil **behandelst du die einzelnen Tagesordnungspunkte ausführlich**: Du schreibst auf, worum es dabei ging und hebst besonders wichtige Wortbeiträge hervor. Am Ende notierst du die **Ergebnisse** der Besprechung oder Abstimmung.

4. Schlusszeile: In der Schlusszeile **unterschreiben** der Vorsitzende der Veranstaltung und der Protokollführer.

Folgende Vorarbeiten sind nötig

* Du nimmst an der Veranstaltung (z. B. Besprechung oder Schulstunde) teil und **schreibst das Wichtigste** chronologisch, also in der Reihenfolge des Geschehens, **mit**.
* Nach dem Ende der Veranstaltung **liest du deine Mitschrift durch**, streichst, was dir inzwischen unwichtig erscheint, und ergänzt Wichtiges, das du noch im Gedächtnis hast, aber nicht mitnotiert hast.
* Dann machst du dich an die Niederschrift deines Protokolls.

Beim Schreiben musst du beachten

* Das Protokoll ist eine **sachliche Form**, bei der du Wichtiges **ohne eigene Wertung** niederschreibst.
* Schreibe zuerst den Protokollkopf. Achte auf **Vollständigkeit** und **Richtigkeit**.
* Achte auf die **chronologische Abfolge** der Tagesordnungspunkte.
* Beginne im Hauptteil bei jedem **neuen Tagesordnungspunkt** in einer **neuen Zeile** oder trenne die Tagesordnungspunkte durch **Leerzeilen** voneinander ab.
* **Schreibe sachlich, genau und objektiv**.
* Verwende statt wörtlicher Rede die **indirekte Rede** und den **Konjunktiv**.
* Schreibe je nach Absprache im **Präsens** oder **Präteritum**.

Beispiel für ein Unterrichtsprotokoll
So kann das Protokoll einer Unterrichtsstunde aufgebaut und gestaltet sein

Gymnasium ___________ Schuljahr ____________

Niederschrift über die Deutschstunde

vom ____________

Ort: _______________

Zeit: _______________

Anwesend:	alle Schülerinnen und Schüler der Klasse 8A, die Praktikantin Frau Bauer, der Deutschlehrer Herr Obermayer
Abwesend:	-
Leitung:	Herr Obermayer
Schriftführer:	Max Müller

Tagesordnung:

1. Einführung
2. Vorstellung der Arbeitsergebnisse zu den Gedichten „Hoffnung" und „Ende des Jahres"
3. Vorstellung der Arbeitsergebnisse zum Auszug aus dem Jugendbuch „Blueprint – Blaupause"
4. Vorstellung der Arbeitsergebnisse zum Romanauszug „Die Aufzeichnungen des Chemikers Leo Kall"
5. Vorstellung der Arbeitsergebnisse zu den Sachtexten „Alles wird ganz anders"
6. Stellung der Hausaufgabe

Zu TOP 1:

Herr Obermayer erklärt, dass die von den einzelnen Gruppen erarbeiteten Ergebnisse vorgestellt werden würden. Er erwähnt außerdem, dass von jedem Schüler eine Mitschrift über die Stunde anzufertigen sei, nach der als Hausaufgabe ein Protokoll anzufertigen ist.

Zu TOP 2:

Der Lehrer ruft nun die erste Gruppe, bestehend aus Karolina, Magdalena und Christian, auf. Zunächst wird das Gedicht „Hoffnung" von Friedrich Schiller vorgelesen, das im Lesebuch auf S. 95 abgedruckt ist. Die Gruppe veranschaulicht mit Hilfe einer Folie die im Gedicht beschriebene Hoffnung der Menschen auf Verbesserungen. Im Kontrast dazu wird das Gedicht „Ende des Jahres" von Sarah Kirsch betrachtet, in dem die Angst vor dem Neuen im Vordergrund steht. Herr Obermayer ruft nun zwei weitere Gruppen auf, die sich ebenfalls mit dem Gedicht beschäftigt haben. Es entsteht eine Diskussion über die Bedeutung der 2. Strophe, die schließlich Herr Obermayer klärt: Dabei handelt es sich um die alltägliche Normalität angesichts eines drohenden Krieges. Anschließend entlässt Herr Obermayer alle Schüler in die Pause.

Zu TOP 3:

Nach der Pause ruft Herr Obermayer die nächste Gruppe, bestehend aus Stefanie, Julia, Rebecca und Laura auf, die sich mit dem Text „Blueprint – Blaupause" beschäftigt hat. Es geht darin um die Komponistin Iris Sellin, die an MS, einer tödlichen Krankheit erkrankt ist, und sich, um ihr Talent der Nachwelt zu erhalten, von einem Wissenschaftler namens Fisher klonen lässt. Ihr Klon, aus dessen Sicht die Geschichte geschrieben ist, bringt auch Vorwürfe gegen die Mutter, wie Stefanie erklärt. Laura meint, dass einige Fragen noch völlig offen blieben, wie z. B. ob die Mutter an ihrer Krankheit stirbt. Zwei weitere Gruppen, die sich mit diesem Text beschäftigt haben, werden aufgerufen. Dabei wird festgestellt, dass bereits alle wesentlichen Fragen geklärt wurden.

Zu TOP 4:

Die nächste Gruppe wird aufgerufen. Martin, Christoph und Felix haben sich mit der Kurzgeschichte „Die Aufzeichnungen des Chemikers Leo Kall" beschäftigt. Sie erklären die Situation des Chemikers, der vom Militär gefangen gehalten wird und für dieses eine Droge entwickeln soll. Dennis und Daniel stellen fest, dass dem Chemiker die Verwendung der Droge gleichgültig ist. Elisabeth, Alexandra und Julia erklären sein Verhalten dadurch, dass sich Leo Kall nicht dafür verantwortlich fühlt, weil er selbst ein Gefangener ist.

Zu TOP 5:

Die nächste Gruppe, bestehend aus Fabian, Stefan und Dominik, stellt drei Texte unter dem Motto „Alles wird ganz anders" vor. Alle drei Texte befassen sich mit Vor- und Nachteilen neuer Techniken in den Bereichen Spionage, Biotechnik, Klima und Raumfahrt. Stets geht es dabei um ethische Fragen der Wissenschaft. Sophie, Elena, Kathrin, Johannes und Edgar, die sich ebenfalls mit diesem Thema befasst haben, klären einige restliche Fragen, die jedoch eher unwesentlich sind.

Zu TOP 6:

Da nun alle Gruppen ihr Thema vorgestellt haben, beendet Herr Obermayer die Stunde und erinnert noch einmal an die Hausaufgabe.

_________________________ _________________________

Der Schriftführer Der Lehrer

Arbeitsauftrag:

Verfasse zu der Erzählung (Aufgabe 1 und 2) oder zu dem Sachtext (Aufgabe 3 und 4) eine Inhaltsangabe. Achte auf einen stimmigen Basissatz. Fertige einen Schreibplan auf einem separaten Blatt.

Aufgabe 1: „Eine schöne Beziehung"

Grete Hehmke hatte das nordfriesische Dorf, in dem sie geboren und aufgewachsen war, nur einmal in ihrem Leben für längere Zeit verlassen: vor 50 Jahren, 1933, als eine dreiwöchige Hochzeitsreise ihr den unauslöschlichen Eindruck vermittelte, dass es im südlichen Harz immer regnet. Ihr Mann war ja nun tot. Aber Grete Hehmkes Lust zu leben war noch nicht erschöpft. Es gab mehr als nur den einen Edeka-Laden, das wusste sie genau.

Mit dem Autobus in die Kreisstadt - das war schon ein Erlebnis! Gierig nach neuen Eindrücken warf sie sich energisch ins Getümmel. Sie war aufgeregt, glücklich, neugierig. Futter für den alten Kopf. Wunderbar. Als Höhepunkt das Warenhaus. Nein, so was Schönes aber auch!

Hunger! Restaurant? Da!Ein frischer Tisch. Handtasche über die Stuhllehne hängen, Mantel an den Haken, in Blickrichtung. Hinsetzen, Erleichterung. Bedienung kommt nicht. Aha, es gibt gar keine Bedienung hier. Genau hinsehen, wie die anderen das machen. Kapiert.

Grete Hehmke verlässt ihren Tisch, reiht sich ein in die Schlange, greift sich das orangefarbene Tablett. Ordert selbstbewusst Kohlrouladen mit Salzkartoffeln und einen Karamelpudding, eine Brause dazu, bezahlt an der Kasse. Teuer ist es ja, muss man schon sagen. Trägt das Tablett zu ihrem Tisch, nimmt Platz. Die Kohlroulade sieht elend aus, man müsste ihr mal was zu futtern geben - Grete Hehmke ist voller Heiterkeit. Aber sie hat kein Besteck. Wo bekommt man hier denn Messer und Gabel? Einen kleinen Löffel braucht sie auch. Und eine Serviette. Aha, da neben den orangefarbenen Tabletts. Aufstehen, hingehen, holen. Grete Hehmke kommt an ihren Tisch zurück.

Sie stutzt, setzt sich. Auf ihrem Platz hockt ein Neger und isst von ihrem Teller. Ganz manierlich. Es schmeckt ihm. Grete Hehmke nimmt gegenüber von dem schwarzen Mann Platz. Der lächelt einladend. Grete Hehmke wundert sich über nichts mehr. Sie lächelt ebenfalls freundlich und zieht das orangefarbene Tablett behutsam, aber bestimmt in die Tischmitte. Die Portionen in diesem Kaufhaus sind ja reichlich bemessen, das reicht schon für zwei. Sie speisen. Teilen jede Kartoffel, er schiebt ihr ein besonders appetitliches Gürkchen zu, sie überlässt ihm ein größeres Stück Roulade. Er ist schließlich ein kräftiger junger Mann. Der Neger gießt gelbe Brause in sein Glas, bietet ihr zuvorkommend an, trinkt selbst aus der Flasche. Manchmal klappern ihre Teelöffel gegeneinander, wie sie sich den Pudding geschwisterlich teilen. Eine Unterhaltung findet darüber hinaus nicht statt. Nur gelegentlich ein Blick des Einverständnisses. Seele essen Angst auf. Mit den Papierservietten die Münder abwischen, ein liebenswürdiges Kopfnicken, der Neger steht auf und geht.

Na, dankeschön hätte er ja wenigstens sagen können. Grete Hehmke hat doch Grund, an den Umgangsformen der Schwarzen zu zweifeln. Ihre Handtasche ist weg. Sie hing über der Lehne des Stuhls, auf dem dieser Neger saß. Auf, auf! Hinterher! Haltet den Dieb! Eben geht er hinaus.

Grete Hehmke dreht sich um, stößt an den Stuhl in ihrem Rücken. Gott sei Dank! Da hängt ja die Handtasche. Es gibt auch anständige Neger. Die Kohlroulade auf dem orangefarbenen Tablett auf dem Nebentisch ist leider schon etwas kalt. Aber den Karamellpudding könnte sie noch essen. Na, und eine halbe Brause schafft sie wohl auch noch...

Henning Venske

aus: Svende Merian & Norbert Ney (Hg.): Nicht mit dir und nicht ohne dich. Rowohlt, Reinbek 1983.

Aufgabe 2: „Verliebt"

Seit ein paar Tagen kommt meine kleine Schwester mit bemalten und beschmierten Händen und Armen aus der Schule. Ich glaube: Sie ist verliebt. Denn genau wie sie jetzt kam auch ich vor einigen Jahren häufig mit Edding verziert nach Hause. Schuld daran hatte meistens Jan Ahlen. Sitzen geblieben, also ein Neuling in unserer siebten Klasse. Er war älter, cooler, dreckiger als die Jungs in unserer Klasse. Heute kann ich es zwar nicht mehr verstehen, aber mit seinen blonden, fast roten Haaren und den Sommersprossen sorgte er dafür, dass ich nicht mehr in fließenden Sätzen sprechen konnte, meine Bleistifte in kürzester Zeit auf wenige Zentimeter heruntergekaut waren und sein Name etwa 300 Mal in meinem Hausaufgabenheft auftauchte. Das alljährliche Ritual der Platzverlosung zu Beginn des Schuljahres brachte uns zusammen - oder an einen Tisch

Ab dem Zeitpunkt war mein Schulalltag nicht mehr traurig, öde und grau, sondern aufregend, lustig und rosa-rot. Die sonst quälenden Deutschlektüren waren plötzlich schöne Geschichten, in denen Jan und ich die Hauptrollen spielten. Selbst auf das langweiligste aller Fächer - Erdkunde - konnte ich mich freuen, wusste ich doch, dass Jan mich garantiert vor jeder Stunde zwecks Abschreibens um die Hausaufgabe bitten würde. Mit anderen Worten: Ich war verliebt.

Die erste Annäherung seinerseits bestand darin, seinen Filzstift auf mich loszulassen. Prima, er mag mich. Also griff ich zu Füller, Tintenkiller und allem anderen, was sich in meiner Federmappe befand, und dekorierte ihn mit bunten Strichen. Bei so viel Einsatz dauerte es nicht lange, bis ich auf Jans persönlicher „Mädchen-Hitparade" den vordersten Platz belegte. Bei mir war er sowieso schon lange Spitzenreiter und hatte Thomas, den ich schon seit Kindergartentagen kannte, und Daniel, für den fast alle Mädchen schwärmten, weit hinter sich gelassen.

Es klingt komisch, aber manchmal vermisse ich die Zeiten, in denen man einfach mit dem Stift aufeinander losgehen konnte. Überhaupt, die ersten Flirtversuche früher waren so viel einfacher, unschuldiger und irgendwie netter als heute. So unkompliziert kann man wahrscheinlich nur mit zwölf Jahren sein. Oft haben meine Freundinnen und ich kleine Zettel geschrieben, die während der Stunde unauffällig weitergegeben wurden. Darauf stand in schöner Mädchenschrift: „Hallo Jan, schreib bitte in Prozent." Darunter aufgelistet alle Mädchennamen aus der Klasse, Birgit und Yvonne waren die Beliebtesten. Hinter ihren Namen stand meistens eine 100 oder wenigstens eine 90. Eine andere Variante war: „Hallo Jan, wie findest du ...?" Hinter den Namen stand dann „nett", „doof" oder „super". „Super" war das Beste, was man kriegen konnte, „nett" recht nichtssagend, und „doof" konnte einen tagelang traurig stimmen.

Wenn so manches Mädchen in der großen Pause von mehreren Jungs gleichzeitig über den Schulhof gejagt wurde, war das als Kompliment zu verstehen. Und wenn einer mein Pausenbrot aus dem Fenster warf, fand er mich toll. Wenn Jan eine Damenbinde aus meinem Ranzen gefischt hatte, um sie dann vor allen Anwesenden sichtbar an die Tafel zu kleben, war das so peinlich, dass sich mein Gesicht dunkelrot verfärbte. Manche dieser Neckereien waren gemein, manchmal sogar schmerzhaft. Trotzdem habe ich es genossen. Heute fände ich es rührend, wenn mich jemand in der Vorlesung mit vollgelüllerten Papierkügelchen bewerfen oder mir beim Rausgehen ein Bein stellen würde. Es wäre schön, wenn ich meinen Freund dabei erwischen könnte, wie er mir die Luft aus den Fahrradreifen lässt und sich dabei totlacht. Vielleicht frage ich ihn einfach morgen, wer zur Zeit bei ihm Platz eins belegt.

aus: „Freistunde", hrsg. von Kerstin Gleba u. Rudolf Spindler

Aufgabe 3: „Sind Esel wirklich stur?"

Schon immer stand der Esel im Schatten seiner vierhufigen Verwandten - dem Zebra und dem Pferd. Sein schlechter Ruf, ein unverbesserlicher Dickkopf zu sein, eilt ihm überall voraus. Zu Unrecht! Denn Esel sind klug - und leisten dem Menschen viele gute Dienste

Zwei starke Kerle ziehen vorne am Halfter; zwei stemmen sich gegen das graue Hinterteil. Aber der Esel bewegt sich kein Stück. Das Langohr gilt allgemein als stur, widerspenstig und faul. Dabei lassen sich Esel schon seit über 6000 Jahren geduldig vor die Karren der Menschen spannen und schleppen in allen Weltgegenden ihre Lasten. Zeit, aufzuräumen mit alten Vorurteilen gegenüber einem der ältesten und doch ewig unverstandenen Haustiere des Menschen.

„Oh Schreck, eine Maus!" - Wittert ein Pferd Gefahr, so sucht es kopflos das Weite - wie alle Fluchttiere. In der ebenen Steppe, der ursprünglichen Heimat der Wildpferde, hat sich dieser Reflex bewährt. In einer Geröllwüste aber empfiehlt sich für ein staksiges Huftier etwas mehr Besonnenheit! Und so erklärt sich, dass Esel, die in den gebirgigen Teilen Nordafrikas beheimatet sind, bei Gefahr wie angewurzelt stehen bleiben. Besonders schnell könnten Esel ohnehin nicht fliehen: Ihre Höchstgeschwindigkeit liegt bei 50 Stundenkilometern. Damit sind sie gut 20 Stundenkilometer langsamer als Pferde - von nordafrikanischen Raubkatzen oder herabstürzenden Gesteinsbrocken gar nicht zu sprechen.

Ihren Reflex, bei Gefahr zu erstarren, haben die Esel auch nicht abgelegt, als die Etrusker sie vor etwa 3000 Jahren nach Europa brachten. Im Gegenteil: Zusätzlicher Stress, zum Beispiel durch Schläge oder Schreie der europäischen Eseltreiber, haben diesen Reflex nur verstärkt. Und so standen die Esel sehr schnell in Verruf, unverbesserliche Dickschädel zu sein. Als sie später von den schnelleren und größeren Pferden als Reittiere abgelöst wurden, sanken die Esel noch tiefer im Ansehen der Menschen. Während die Reichen hoch zu Ross ihren Jagd-Vergnügungen nachgingen, wurde der Esel zum Lastentier der ärmeren Bevölkerung. Im Ansehen standen Esel von da an ihren Besitzern gleich: „Du armer Packesel", sagt man noch heute zu einem Menschen, der von früh bis spät für andere arbeiten muss.

Dabei haben Esel den Pferden einiges Voraus: Zum Beispiel können sie viel länger ohne Wasser und Nahrung auskommen. Schließlich waren sie ursprünglich zähe Wüstenbewohner. Daher können Esel auch schwere Lasten über viele Kilometer hinweg durch trockenes Gebiet tragen. Ohne Probleme trägt ein Esel 20 Prozent seines eigenen Körpergewichts. Zudem kommt er in dem steinigen Gelände seiner Heimat viel sicherer voran als andere Huftiere. Und trotz der harten Arbeit benötigen Esel nur drei Stunden Schlaf am Tag. Mit ihrer Hilfe wurden zum Beispiel die Pyramiden in Ägypten gebaut.
Aber auch noch heute leisten Esel den Menschen in Afrika gute Dienste: Dort sind Esel sogar oft der kostbarste Besitz einer Familie. Auf ihrem starken Rücken können sie schwere Wasserkanister von weit entfernten Brunnen transportieren oder ein krankes Kind zu einem der wenigen Krankenhäuser in der Gegend bringen. Deshalb gründete eine Mitarbeiterin des Deutschen Umweltministeriums, Stefanie Christmann, vor elf Jahren eine Esel-Initiative für das Land Eritrea: Mit Spendengeldern hat sie seitdem schon 5500 Esel auf den Weg zu den Ärmsten der Armen geschickt.

Seit es in der Landwirtschaft Maschinen gibt, wurden Esel in den meisten Ländern als Lastenträger und Zugtiere in den Ruhestand geschickt. Packesel gibt es heute eigentlich nur noch in den ärmeren Mittelmeerländern und in Afrika. Aber Esel können viel mehr als Lasten schleppen: Sie besitzen nämlich ein hervorragendes Gedächtnis und lernen sogar schneller als Dressurpferde. Deshalb haben die Bauern in Amerika eine neue verantwortungsvolle Aufgabe für die Esel gefunden: Ihre angeborene Angst vor wilden Raubtieren gepaart mit einem feinen Gehör und Geruchssinn macht Esel zu idealen Viehhirten. Sobald der Herde Gefahr droht, legt ein Esel die Ohren an und ruft mit lautem Geschrei den Bauern herbei. Sein durchdringender Ruf ist auch aus weiter Ferne gut zu hören. Und noch etwas: Der Wachesel kann seine Stimmbänder auch beim Einatmen schließen. So muss er nicht einmal eine Pause machen, um Luft zu holen, während er „I-A" schreit.

Auch in Deutschland übernehmen Esel ehrenvolle Aufgaben. Zum Beispiel helfen sie in der Eseltherapie (man nennt das auch Asinotherapie, von lateinisch Asinus = Esel) behinderten Menschen dabei, sich in Geduld zu üben und mutiger zu werden. Ein besonderes Projekt hat die „Regens Wagner Einrichtung" in Absberg ins Leben gerufen: Dort lernen behinderte Menschen, wie man sich die Freundschaft der grauen Zottel Stück für Stück erarbeitet. Denn Esel gehorchen den Menschen nie blind. Wer ihr Vertrauen gewinnen möchte, muss zuerst ihre Körpersprache studieren: Sind die Ohren eines Esels aufmerksam nach vorne gerichtet, ist er neugierig. Dreht er aber die Ohren nach Außen und stellt sie auf, signalisiert er Angst. Während der Therapie erfahren die Patienten, dass Eselschnauzen weich sind und nicht zuschnappen. Am Ende trauen sich auch die Schreckhaftesten unter ihnen, eine kleine Runde auf dem Rücken der Esel zu drehen.
Und wer jetzt immer noch behauptet, Esel seien dumm und stur, ist selbst ein Dickschädel!

Text von Lena Ullrich
http://www.geo.de/GEOlino/natur/60572.html (ohne Zwischenüberschriften)

Aufgabe 4: „Die Geschichte der Gabel"

Seine Nahrung mit Messern zu zerteilen und per Löffel in den Mund zu schieben, beherrscht der Mensch seit Jahrtausenden. Dass auf einem gedeckten Tisch die Gabel nicht fehlen darf, ist dagegen vergleichsweise neumodisch.

Du sollst mit den Händen essen! Ja, richtig gelesen: Was klingt wie der Aufruf zum offenen Widerstand gegen alles, was euch eure Eltern jahrelang in Sachen Tischsitten beigebracht haben, ist für den Großteil der Weltbevölkerung gang und gäbe. Zwar nehmen wir an, dass bei euch zu Hause - wie bei rund 900 Millionen weiteren Menschen auf der Erde - Messer und Gabel ihren festen Platz auf dem gedeckten Tisch haben. Doch mehrheitsfähig ist das nicht.

Selbst zu Ess-Stäbchen wird, unter anderem in China und Japan, häufiger gegriffen als zum Besteck. Nämlich von deutlich mehr als einer Milliarde Erdenbürgern. Ganz zu schweigen vom großen Rest: Vermutlich um die vier Milliarden Menschen leben wortwörtlich von der Hand in den Mund - sie essen mit den Fingern.

Unappetitlich? Einen Moment! Bevor ihr die Nase rümpft, fassen wir uns lieber erst einmal an dieselbe - oder besser: an die unserer Vorfahren. Dass wir essen, wie wir essen, ist bei uns nämlich eine recht neue Errungenschaft. Zwar zerlegte schon der Urmensch seinen Mammutschinken mit Faustkeilen aus Stein - also der frühesten Form des Messers; und blieb nach dem Mahl ein passender Knochen übrig, schnitzte er sich vielleicht einen Löffel daraus. Aber die dritte im Bunde, die Gabel, ließ noch eine ganze Weile auf sich warten. Die frühesten Modelle, die Archäologen bis jetzt gefunden haben, stammen von den Ägyptern und sind rund 3200 Jahre alt. Auch bei den Griechen und Römern wurden wohl schon hier und dort Speisen aufgegabelt. Doch die Altertumsforscher sind sich einig: nur in Ausnahmefällen.
Der Großteil der Menschen lebte ohnehin von wenig mehr als Brot oder Brei, und für beides braucht man keine Gabel. Selbst die, deren Tisch reichhaltiger gedeckt war, griffen mit den Fingern zu. Im alten Rom ebenso wie bei den Rittern des Mittelalters - und weit darüber hinaus: Noch vor 300 Jahren, so berichtet ein Chronist vom Hofe Ludwigs XIV., des Königs von Frankreich, habe der Herrscher selbst „mit den Pfoten ins Ragout" gelangt.

Sicher, als König kann man sich manches erlauben, wofür andere schief angeguckt würden. Doch Ludwig tat nur, was den allgemeinen Regeln guter Erziehung entsprach. In einem italienischen Benimmbuch des 17. Jahrhunderts kann man dazu lesen: „Hat uns die Natur nicht fünf Finger an jeder Hand geschenkt? Warum wollen wir sie mit jenen dummen Werkzeugen beleidigen, die eher dazu geschaffen sind, Heu aufzuladen als das Essen?"
Mit einer Gabel auf dem Teller herumzustochern, galt bestenfalls als unnötig. Mancher wollte darin gar Gotteslästerung erkennen: Erinnern die Zinken nicht an des Teufels Dreizack? Mönchen war es daher ausdrücklich verboten, Gabeln zu gebrauchen! Die allermeisten aber sahen wohl schlicht mit Spott und Verachtung auf jene herab, die sich offensichtlich zu gut oder zu schade waren, die Finger am Essen schmutzig zu machen.
Doch dann muss irgendwem aufgefallen sein, dass es ja durchaus Vorteile hat, wenn die Hände sauber bleiben. Und wenn es nur dazu diente, sich von der Masse des Volkes abzuheben, die weiterhin mit groben Löffeln oder schmutzigen Pranken ihre Mahlzeiten einnahm, kaum kultivierter als die Schweine im Stall nebenan. Und so wurde, was lange als unmännlich und verweichlicht galt, plötzlich vornehm.

Wer also etwas auf sich hielt, spießte von nun an sein Essen auf. Aber bitte nicht mit einer x-beliebigen Gabel! Kunstschmiede überschlugen sich, immer prächtigere und kostspieligere Modelle zu ersinnen. Aus Silber und Gold, mit Elfenbein und Edelsteinen verziert. Bestens geeignet zum Angeben - und um sich abzugrenzen: So gern das Volk auch den Reichen und Mächtigen nachgeeifert hätte, es konnte sich derlei Luxusbesteck schlicht nicht leisten. Der Durchschnittsbürger musste bis ins späte 19. Jahrhundert Geduld haben. Da wurde die Gabel, aus billigem Stahl gefertigt, zum Massenprodukt.
Das ist keine 150 Jahre her. Seitdem ist sie von unseren Esstischen nicht mehr wegzudenken. Oder? Noch sind wir zu neunhundertmilliont. Doch manch Schwarzmaler der Tischkultur sieht etwa die Freunde des Fast Food bereits an das übermächtige Lager der Bestecklosen verloren: Wozu die Gabel bemühen, wo sich Burger, Pizza und Pommes doch prima „ungezinkt" verzehren lassen.

Text von Martin Verg
http://www.geo.de/GEOlino/mensch/60490.html (ohne Zwischenüberschriften)

⌛ 45 / 📖 14-18 Schulaufgabe 2: Steigernde Erörterung

Arbeitsauftrag:

Verfasse zu einem der Themen eine steigernde Erörterung.
Fertige eine Gliederung auf einem separaten Blatt.

1. Immer wenn große Fußballveranstaltungen – z. B. eine Europa- oder Weltmeisterschaft - stattfinden, ist das Interesse der Menschen daran groß. Auch am Wochenende trifft man viele Menschen in Fußballstadien oder auf Fußballplätzen an.
Warum hat gerade der Fußballsport so viele Anhänger?

2. Tausende Klassen fahren jedes Jahr ins Skilager.
Lege dar, warum du dies für richtig hältst.

3. In bayerischen Gymnasien gibt es in der 8. Klasse zwei Sportstunden. Dabei machen Mädchen und Buben getrennt voneinander Sport.
Zeige auf, warum du es für sinnvoll hältst, dass Mädchen und Jungen im Sport getrennt unterrichtet werden.

4. Viele Eltern beklagen den häufigen Ausfall von Unterricht, weil die Schülerinnen und Schüler im Schullandheim, bei religiösen Orientierungstagen oder auf Abschlussfahrt sind.
Begründe, warum du Schulfahrten für wichtig / für unnütz hältst.

Weitere mögliche Themen für eine steigernde Erörterung

1. Schon 10-jährige Mädchen und Jungen sitzen heutzutage oft 3 bis 5 Stunden täglich vor dem Fernseher. Lege dar, warum dieses Verhalten schädlich ist.

2. In manchen Ländern ist es üblich, dass Schülerinnen und Schüler eine Schuluniform tragen. Es stellt sich deshalb für viele die Frage, ob das auch an deinem Gymnasium so sein sollte.
Lege dar, warum du eine Schuluniform an deiner Schule befürwortest / warum du sie ablehnst.

3. Jeden Montag ist in den Tageszeitungen zu lesen, wie viele Menschen am voran gegangenen Wochenende im Straßenverkehr zu Tode gekommen sind. Viele Opfer sind Jugendliche, die oft auf dem nächtlichen Heimweg von der Disco ihr fahrerisches Können überschätzt oder aus Mangel an Routine in einfachsten Situationen falsch reagiert haben. Nun fordern aber immer mehr Jugendliche eine Senkung des Führerscheinalters; sie wollen mit dem Autofahren nicht mehr bis zum 18. Geburtstag warten, sondern schon mit 16 Jahren den Führerschein machen.
Wie stehst du zu dieser Forderung?

4. An deinem Gymnasium ist es üblich, dass Schülerinnen und Schüler aus 10. bis 12. Klassen als Tutoren den „Neuankömmlingen" aus der Grundschule den Einstieg ins Gymnasium erleichtern.
Lege in einem Brief an deine Brieffreundin / deinen Brieffreund dar, warum du ihr /ihm rätst, ebenfalls Tutor zu werden.

5. Warum lohnt es sich für ein Mädchen / einen Jungen acht Jahre aufs Gymnasium zu gehen, Abitur zu machen und dann zu studieren?
Lege dar, welche Vorteile du siehst.

6. Welche Vorteile bringt es Schülern, wenn sie mehrere Monate im Ausland verbringen und dort zur Schule gehen? Lege deine Meinung begründet dar.

7. Viele Schüler nehmen schon in der 9. Klasse einen Job an, den sie nachmittags oder am Samstag ausüben. Welche Vorteile (oder welche Nachteile) bringt so ein Nebenjob mit sich? Lege dar, warum du für (oder gegen) einen Nebenjob bist.

Teil 1: Texte lesen und verstehen ✓18 / ⏳15 / 📖 18/19

1. Lies den folgenden Text in zehn Minuten genau durch!

Auf der Spur der großen Jäger

Sie haben sie „Rasta" genannt. Weil ihr Verhalten an die Mitglieder der Rastafari-Sekte auf Jamaika erinnert und an den Reggaesänger Bob Marley; weil sie selbstbewusst wirkt, offen, dominant und in sich ruhend. Seit 1997 ist sie jedes Jahr im südafrikanischen Winter nach „Seal Island" gekommen, zur „Robbeninsel" bei Kapstadt, um dort auf Jagd zu gehen. Sie kam zusammen mit Dutzenden anderen Weißen Haien - von denen aber keiner so berühmt wurde wie Rasta. 1

Wenn die Forscher auf ihrem Beobachtungsboot standen, konnte es vorkommen, dass Rasta den Kopf aus dem Wasser reckte und die Menschen anschaute. Sie war so ruhig und zutraulich, dass sie stundenlang das Boot begleitete, anstatt schnell wieder zu verschwinden wie die meisten ihrer Artgenossen. Und sie war verspielt: Einmal schnappte sie einen Seevogel. Tauchte unter. Tauchte wieder auf; und ließ den Vogel frei. Bei alldem konnten die Forscher Rasta immer gut erkennen: an ihrer verkrüppelten Rückenflosse. Vermutlich war sie der Motorschraube eines Fischerbootes zu nahe gekommen. Weiße Haie: Das sind, wie die Biologen inzwischen wissen, Tiere, die über ein individuelles Wesen verfügen. Räuber, deren Charakter durch ihren Erfolg beim Jagen geprägt wird. 2

Mit ihrem grauen Rücken ist Rasta im Dämmerlicht des Morgens für Pelzrobben, die an der Oberfläche schwimmen, kaum zu erkennen. Von unten schießt sie plötzlich empor, 40 km/h schnell - mit solcher Gewalt, dass sie mitunter ihren etwa eine Tonne schweren Körper einige Meter weit in die Luft katapultiert. Weiße Haie sind vorsichtige Tiere, sie greifen immer aus dem Hinterhalt an. Mit genau geplanten Überraschungsattacken minimieren sie ihr Sicherheitsrisiko und steigern die Aussicht auf Erfolg. Gelingt es nicht, die Beute mit einem einzigen Biss zu erledigen, beginnt ein Todesballett. Die Robbe flieht im Zickzackkurs, wehrt sich mit Bissen. Irgendwann, spätestens nach zehn Minuten, geben die meisten Haie auf. Nicht aber Rasta. Sie ist eine geduldige Verfolgerin. Sie jagt weiter, so lange, bis sie den Feind zu fassen bekommt. Ja, sie sieht dessen Aktionen sogar voraus. Am 29. Juli 2003 greift Rasta, sie ist zu dieser Zeit knapp vier Meter lang, eine Robbe an. Diese versucht zu entkommen. Verschwindet für 15 Sekunden unter Wasser, springt plötzlich in die Luft, fällt herunter – ins geöffnete Maul von Rasta, die an der richtigen Stelle gewartet hat. Die Forscher haben errechnet, dass an der Robbeninsel 47 Prozent der Hai-Attacken tödlich enden; bei Rasta sind es fast 80 Prozent. 3

Als Rasta um das Jahr 1990 aus dem Mutterleib ins Meer entlassen wurde, war sie bereits eine fertige Beutegreiferin: vielleicht 1,40 Meter lang, etwa 25 Kilo schwer, mit den dreieckigen, extrem spitzen Zähnen des Weißen Hais und dessen typischer Stromlinienform. Schon als Embryo lernte sie zu fressen. Im Mutterleib verschlang sie - gemeinsam mit den Geschwistern - unbefruchtete Eier. In einer Hinsicht ähnelt die Fortpflanzung mancher Haie der von Säugern. Die Jungen von etwa zwei Dritteln aller Arten werden lebend geboren; denn die Entwicklung der Eier ist im Laufe der Evolution nach und nach in den schützenden Körper übergegangen. Die Eischale verschwand, die Versorgung erfolgte stattdessen über den Dottersack im Mutterleib – so auch beim Weißen Hai, dessen Weibchen nach 14 Monaten zwei bis zehn Minijäger zur Welt bringen. Bei anderen Arten bildete sich gar ein Plazenta-ähnliches Organ aus. Immer mehr Energie investierten die Muttertiere so in ihren Nachwuchs. 4

Solch eine evolutionäre Perfektionierung brauchte viel Zeit. Vor knapp 400 Millionen Jahren schwammen die ersten Urtypen der Haie im Meer. ... Und so sieht es aus, Rastas in Jahrmillionen entwickeltes Jagdinstrumentarium: Da sind zunächst die überscharfen Sinne. Weiße Haie können die Beute über Hunderte Meter hinweg erschnüffeln. Ein einziger Tropfen Blut in einem Schwimmbecken - Rasta käme ihr auf die Spur. Sogar rechts und links kann sie mit ihrem Geruchssinn unterscheiden und durch S-förmiges Schwimmen einem Duftgefälle präzise über mehr als 100 Meter folgen. Das Zappeln eines verletzten Tieres spürt sie noch in einigen Kilometern Entfernung. Ihre Augen sind empfindlicher als die einer Katze. Wenn Rasta zum Angriff ansetzt, lässt sie sich von Haarsinneszellen leiten, die unter der Haut angeordnet sind und auf Druckschwankungen reagieren - ausgelöst etwa durch Flossenschläge. Für präzise Ortung sorgen zudem die Lorenzinischen Ampullen am Maul, kleine Hautkanäle voller Nervenzellen. Mit ihnen ermitteln Haie das elektrische Feld, das Lebewesen umgibt. Schnappt Rasta schließlich zu, kann sie einen Beißdruck von drei Tonnen pro Quadratzentimeter entwickeln, doppelt so viel wie ein Königs- 5

tiger. Ihr Maul ist eine Art Munitionslager. Dort stehen mehrere Reihen Zähne; nur die vorderste wird gebraucht. Ist ein Zahn abgenutzt, fällt er aus, und von hinten rotiert Ersatz nach vorn.

6

Sogar beim Verfolgungsrennen gegen kleine, wendige Gegner hat die Evolution dem Superjäger der Meere Chancen eingeräumt. Dank ihres Knorpelskeletts kann Rasta fliehenden Robben auf der Spur bleiben, kann ihren massigen Körper krümmen und verdrehen; undenkbar bei Knochenfischen dieser Größe. Der zweite wichtige Unterschied zur Bauweise der Knochenfische: Haie haben keine Schwimmblase. Deren Aufgabe übernimmt die ölhaltige Leber - ein gigantischer Energiespeicher, der beim Weißen Hai 15 bis 20 Prozent des Körpergewichts ausmacht...

7

Sobald im Mai vor Seal Island die Jagdsaison beginnt, sind die Superjäger zur Stelle, denn ihr Zeit- und Raumgefühl funktioniert perfekt. Einige kommen fast auf den Tag genau Jahr für Jahr zur Robbeninsel. Kennen sie sich? Gehören sie einer Gruppe an, die gemeinsam die Insel erreicht und in den folgenden Monaten auch zusammenbleibt? Manche Forscher glauben, dass Weiße Haie Zweckbündnisse schließen, um ihre Nahrungsausbeute zu erhöhen, oder in bestimmten Entwicklungsphasen lockere Gruppen bilden. Vor der kalifornischen Küste haben Wissenschaftler fünf Weiße Haie mit Ultraschallsendern überwacht - und herausgefunden: Die Räuber griffen zwar nicht gemeinsam an; aber sie blieben stets nahe genug beieinander, um die Beute eines Artgenossen zu teilen. Ob es Verwandte waren, Angehörige vielleicht eines Familienclans, soll nun ein genetischer Abgleich klären. Noch stehen die Wissenschaftler erst am Anfang, noch haben sie nicht geklärt, ob sich die sozialen Kontakte der Weißen Haie auf Extremsituationen wie die Beutejagd beschränken; ob sie lediglich dazu dienen, Konflikte zu entschärfen, oder ob sie darüber hinaus Beziehungen aufbauen.

8

Auch wenn Rasta in den Jahren nach 1997 auffällig oft mit einem männlichen, ebenfalls noch nicht geschlechtsreifen Begleiter gesehen wurde: Permanent scheint kein Weißer Hai in einer Gruppe zu leben. Wenn die Jagdsaison vor Seal Island im September endet, zerstreuen sich die Räuber im Ozean. Manche Haie können ausdauernd schwimmen: Denn anders als bei fast allen Knochenfischen durchströmt ihre Muskeln warmes Blut, dessen Temperatur um bis zu 14 Grad Celsius höher als die des Wassers sein kann. Mit Satellitenpeilsendern, angebracht an der Rückenflosse, haben Forscher weltweit die Routen von Weißen Haien verfolgt: „Neale" - von der Südostspitze Australiens nach Norden, 2946 Kilometer in 113 Tagen. „Tipfin" - von Kalifornien nach Hawaii, 3800 Kilometer in 50 Tagen. Schließlich „Nicole": Ihr Trip führte von Südafrika nach Westaustralien - 11.100 Kilometer in 91 Tagen. Nicole ist womöglich eine Ausnahme. Aber relativ häufig schwimmen Weiße Haie von Südafrika die Küste entlang Richtung Norden, um nach etwa 2000 Kilometern haltzumachen - und einige Monate später zurückzuschwimmen. Folgen sie den Schwärmen von Fischen? Wandern sie zu Paarungsplätzen? Oder suchen sie eine Bucht, um ihre Jungen zur Welt zu bringen?

9

Diese Fragen werden die Wissenschaftler erst beantworten können, wenn sie viele weitere Sender an die Flossen der Weißen Haie geheftet haben werden. So wie Alison Kock im August 2005. Eigentlich wollte die Haiforscherin an jenem Tag ihre Untersuchung über das Verhalten der Männchen fortsetzen und zwei von ihnen mit Sendern versehen. Aber dann tauchte, wieder einmal, Rasta auf, und Kock entschloss sich spontan, die Wege ihres Lieblingshais zu verfolgen und sie mit einem „Pinger" zu markieren, einem akustischen Sender, dessen Signale von Stationen an der Küste aufgefangen werden. So erfuhr die Biologin, dass Rasta wenige Tage danach die Gegend verließ. Dass sie im Monat darauf vor der Küste Südafrikas patrouillierte. Und schließlich ins offene Meer hinausschwamm. Was danach geschah, weiß die Südafrikanerin nicht. Im Frühjahr 2006 wartete sie auf Rastas Rückkehr zur Robbeninsel - vergebens. Das Raubtier tauchte nicht auf, zum ersten Mal seit neun Jahren. Rasta müsste jetzt 4,50 Meter lang sein: ein etwa 16-jähriges, geschlechtsreifes Weibchen. Womöglich, vermutet Alison Kock, ist sie trächtig und nimmt deswegen eine Auszeit vom Jagen. Oder vielleicht ist sie unterwegs zu einem anderen, unbekannten Ort, um sich dort zu paaren. Das Rätsel Rasta - es ist das Rätsel Weißer Hai.

Text von Malte Henk

Aus: GEOkompakt Nr. 10-03/07 (gekürzt)

2. Dieser Zeitungstext ist in verschiedene Abschnitte gegliedert. Unten findest du zu den Textabschnitten 2 – 9 jeweils drei Überschriften. Nur eine davon passt genau zum Inhalt des entsprechenden Abschnitts. Kreuze jeweils diese eine passende Überschrift an.

2. Abschnitt (Z. 6-13)	5. Abschnitt (Z. 37-50)	8. Abschnitt (Z. 69-81)
O Rasta hat eine verkrüppelte Rückenflosse.	O Die evolutionäre Perfektionierung von Haien brauchte viel Zeit.	O Weiße Haie bewegen sich nach einem bislang unbekannten Plan in den Weltmeeren.
O Die Forscher beobachten Rasta.	O Weiße Haie sind von der Evolution gut zum Jagen ausgestattet.	O Weiße Haie schwimmen bis zu 11.100 Kilometer weit.
O Rasta schaut die Forscher auf dem Beobachtungsboot an.	O Weiße Haie sind geschickte Jäger.	O Weiße Haie zerstreuen sich nach der Jagdsaison in Seal Island in den Weltmeeren.

3. Abschnitt (Z. 14-26)	6. Abschnitt (Z. 51-56)	9. Abschnitt (Z. 82-94)
O Rasta ist eine geschickte Jägerin.	O Haie haben eine ölhaltige Leber als Energiespeicher.	O Die Haiforscherin Alison Kock beobachtet Rasta mit Hilfe eines Peilsenders.
O Rasta verfolgt eine Robbe.	O Haie unterscheiden sich erheblich von anderen Knochenfischen.	O Die Haiforscherin Alison Kock hält weiße Haie für ein Rätsel.
O Rasta ist eine geduldige Verfolgerin.	O Haie sind durch die Evolution begünstigt.	O Die Erforschung des Lebens der Weißen Haie steht erst am Anfang.

4. Abschnitt (Z. 27-36)	7. Abschnitt (Z. 57-68)
O Rasta verschlang schon im Mutterleib unbefruchtete Eier.	O Weiße Haie haben ein besonders Jagdverhalten entwickelt.
O Rasta wurde um das Jahr 1990 geboren.	O Weiße Haie jagen vor allem in Seal Island.
O Die Geburt von Haien.	O Forscher wissen noch wenig über das Zusammenleben von Haien.

8 P

3. Lies dir den Inhalt des ersten Abschnitts (Z. 1-5) noch einmal genau durch.
Fasse dann den Inhalt des Abschnitts in ein bis zwei Sätzen zusammen.

____

____

________________________________ 4 P

4. Der Text macht deutlich, welche Einstellung der Verfasser gegenüber den Weißen Haien hat.
Kreuze an, welche Aussage richtig ist:

O Der Verfasser mag Weiße Haie.	O Der Verfasser bedauert es, dass man nicht mehr über Weiße Haie weiß.
O Der Verfasser hält Weiße Haie für gefährliche Räuber.	O Der Verfasser ist von Rasta begeistert.
O Der Verfasser hält Weiße Haie für faszinierende Tiere.	O Der Verfasser möchte vor der Ausrottung der Weißen Haie warnen.

2 P

5. Überlege, welche Absicht der Text hat und für wen er geschrieben ist.
   Formuliere deine Antwort in eigenen Worten.

____

____

____

____ 4 P

Teil 2: Sprachkompetenz

✓ 18 / ⧗ 10 / 🕮 19/20

6. Der folgende Text enthält vier Ausdrucksfehler. Unterstreiche und verbessere sie!

> Der Weiße Hai erreicht eine Höchstlänge von etwa acht Metern und gehört damit zu den größten Haiarten. Die Weibchen werden deutlich größer wie die Männchen, die eine Länge von maximal fünf Metern erlangen. Weiße Haie sind in fast allen Weltmeeren und im Mittelmeer verbreitet. Sie besiedeln nahezu alle Klimazonen. Sie halten sich häufig in Küstennähe und in Robbenrevieren auf. Weiße Haie treten in der Regel einzeln oder paarweise an. Sie finden ihre Nahrung durch Jagd, fressen aber auch Aas. Tintenfische, Thunfische und Schwertfische gehören zu ihrer bevorzugten Beute, sie fressen aber auch Robben und Krebstiere. Ihre Fortpflanzungsgeeignetheit erreichen Haie mit etwa 13 Jahren. In der Regel werden zwei bis zwölf Jungtiere geboren.

____

____

____

____

____

____

____

____________________ 4 P

7. Ersetze in jedem Satz das fettgedruckte Wort durch einen Begriff aus dem Deutschen. Dabei darfst du aber den Sinn des Satzes nicht verändern.

   a) Einzelne Zähne oder ganze Gebisse von Haien sind geschätzte und teuer verkaufte **Souvenirs**. ____________________

   b) Manche Haiarten sind bereits ausgestorben. Andere Populationen sind schon so **dezimiert**, dass sie sich kaum noch erholen können. ____________________

   c) Wenn es nicht gelingt, Haie **effektiv** zu schützen, werden bald alle Arten ausgestorben sein. ____________________ 6 P

8. Kreuze an, ob die Kommas in den folgenden Sätzen richtig gesetzt sind oder nicht.

	richtig	falsch
1. Der Weiße Hai ist ein geschickter Jäger, der sich bei der Jagd mit seinen Artgenossen zusammenschließt.	○	○
2. Haie jagen zwar nicht in Gruppen stets sind aber Artgenossen in der Nähe.	○	○
3. Zu ihren bevorzugten Beutetieren gehören Schwertfische Thunfische und Tintenfische.	○	○
4. Sie fressen aber auch Robben, und kleinere und größere Krebstiere.	○	○

8 P

Teil 3: Formale Sprachbeherrschung

✓ 24 / ⧗ 10 / 📖 20

9. Bestimme bei den fettgedruckten Wörtern im folgenden Satz die jeweilige Wortart. Verwende dazu Fachbegriffe.

Wenn die **Forscher** auf **ihrem** Beobachtungsboot **standen**, konnte es vorkommen, **dass** Rasta den Kopf aus dem Wasser reckte **und die** Menschen anschaute.

wenn	
Forscher	
ihrem	
standen	
dass	
und	
die	

14 P

10. Lies den Auszug aus dem Artikel von Malte Henk noch einmal und vervollständige die unten stehenden Sätze so, dass sie in indirekter Rede stehen.

Sogar beim Verfolgungsrennen gegen kleine, wendige Gegner hat die Evolution dem Superjäger der Meere Chancen eingeräumt. Dank ihres Knorpelskeletts kann Rasta fliehenden Robben auf der Spur bleiben, kann ihren massigen Körper krümmen und verdrehen; undenkbar bei Knochenfischen dieser Größe.

Malte Henk schreibt, die Evolution ________________ sogar beim Verfolgungsrennen gegen kleine, wendige Gegner der Superjäger der Meere Chancen eingeräumt. Dank ihres Knorpelskeletts ____________________ Rasta fliehenden Robben auf der Spur bleiben, ____________________ ihren massigen Körper krümmen und verdrehen, was bei Knochenfischen dieser Größe ______________________________________ .

10 P

Die Mutprobe

Es hatte sich in diesem Sommer in den Ferien, im Juli, ergeben, dass eine Mutter mit ihrem Sohn Kolja für eine Woche siebzig Werst[1] weit in einen anderen Kreis auf Besuch zu einer entfernten Verwandten gefahren war, deren Mann auf einer Eisenbahnstation angestellt war. Dort besah sich Kolja gleich von vornherein die Eisenbahn aufs Genaueste und studierte alle ihre Einrichtungen; denn er sagte sich, dass er zu Hause vor seinen Kameraden auf dem Gymnasium mit seinen neuen Kenntnissen würde glänzen können. 1

Es traf sich, dass er dort einige andere Jungen kennenlernte, manche von ihnen wohnten auf der Station, andere in der Nachbarschaft: lauter junges Volk von zwölf bis fünfzehn Jahren, sechs oder sieben an der Zahl, darunter zufällig auch zwei aus unserem Städtchen. Die Jungen spielten zusammen und trieben allerhand Unfug, bis es dann nach vier oder fünf Tagen unter ihnen zu einer unerhörten Wette um zwei Rubel kam. 2

Kolja, der beinahe der jüngste von allen war und darum von den älteren Jungen ein bisschen verachtet wurde, vermaß sich aus Ehrgeiz oder unverzeihlicher Tollkühnheit, er wolle sich nachts, wenn der Elfuhrzug komme, mit dem Gesicht nach unten zwischen die Schienen legen und regungslos liegenbleiben, bis der Zug mit Volldampf über ihn hinweggefahren war. Allerdings waren vorher Versuche angestellt worden, aus denen sich ergeben hatte, dass es tatsächlich möglich war, sich zwischen den Schienen so platt hinzulegen, dass der Zug über den Liegenden hinwegfuhr, ohne ihn zu streifen – trotzdem, welche Leistung, so dazuliegen! Kolja behauptete mit aller Bestimmtheit, er werde liegenbleiben. 3

Zuerst lachten die anderen über ihn und nannten ihn einen Aufschneider und Prahlhans, doch dadurch wurde er nur noch mehr angereizt; diese Fünfzehnjährigen waren ihm gegenüber gar zu hochmütig und wollten ihn, den „Kleinen", zuerst nicht einmal als ihren Kameraden gelten lassen, was denn doch in unerträglichem Grad beleidigend war. Zu guter Letzt wurde also beschlossen, sich am Abend eine Werst weit von der Station wegzubegeben, damit der Zug nach dem Verlassen der Station schon seine volle Geschwindigkeit erreicht hatte. 4

Die Jungen versammelten sich. Es war eine mondlose, dunkle, fast schwarze Nacht. Zur richtigen Zeit legte sich Kolja zwischen die Schienen. Die fünf übrigen Jungen, die mit ihm gewettet hatten, warteten mit Herzklopfen und zuletzt mit Angst und Reue unten am Bahndamm im Gebüsch. Endlich war von fern der Zug zu hören, der die Station verlassen hatte. In der Dunkelheit blitzten zwei rote Laternen auf; das Ungeheuer nahte lärmend. „Schnell weg von den Schienen!", schrien die Jungen aus dem Gebüsch, halbtot vor Furcht, aber es war schon zu spät. Der Zug jagte heran und sauste vorüber. Die Knaben stürzten zu Kolja: Er lag da und rührte sich nicht. Sie schüttelten ihn und bemühten sich, ihn aufzuheben. Da stand er plötzlich auf und ging schweigend den Bahndamm hinunter. Unten erklärte er, er habe absichtlich wie besinnungslos dagelegen, um ihnen einen Schrecken einzujagen. 5

Die Wahrheit war jedoch, dass er wirklich das Bewusstsein verloren hatte, wie er später, erst lange danach, seiner Mutter auch gestand. Auf diese Weise hatte er den Ruhm der Tollkühnheit als festen Besitz für immer erworben. Leichenblass kehrte er zur Station zurück. Am anderen Tag erkrankte er an einem leichten Nervenfieber, war aber seelisch sehr heiter, froh und zufrieden. 6

Fjodor Dostojewski

[1] Werst: ca. ein Kilometer

1. Jeweils einer der folgenden Vorschläge erfasst den Kerngedanken eines Abschnitts am genauesten. Setze jeweils ein Kreuz!

Abschnitt 3 (Z. 12-19):
- O Kolja riskiert eine Wette mit sieben Jungen aus dem Ferienort.
- O Kolja ist zu einer Mutprobe bereit.
- O Die Wette ist viel ungefährlicher, als es zunächst scheint.
- O Die Jungen wetten um etwas Verbotenes. 1 P

Abschnitt 4 (Z. 20-26):
- O Die Wette soll nachts und auf freier Strecke durchgeführt werden.
- O Nur mit der Durchführung der Wette können die Jungen ihren Streit beenden.
- O Kolja, der „Kleine", setzt sich durch.
- O Kolja behauptet sich und die Wettbedingungen werden festgelegt. 1 P

Abschnitt 5 (Z. 27-37):
- O Kolja gewinnt die Wette, weil er das Bewusstsein verliert.
- O Die Jungen halten ihn zurück, doch Kolja gewinnt die Wette.
- O Kolja gewinnt die Wette und zeigt seine Überlegenheit.
- O Die Jungen fürchten Strafe, doch Kolja bleibt bei der Wette. 1 P

Abschnitt 6 (Z. 38-42):
- O Kolja hat nun, während der Ferien, den Ruf, ein verwegener Bursche zu sein.
- O Kolja genießt den Erfolg, auch wenn die Wette nicht spurlos an ihm vorbeigegangen ist.
- O Nachdem Kolja nach der Wette zur Station zurückgekehrt ist, erkrankt er an einem Nervenfieber.
- O Kolja muss später seiner Mutter die Täuschung eingestehen. 1 P

2. Überprüfe die folgenden Aussagen anhand des Textes und kreuze das Zutreffende an!

a) Koljas Mutter wählt diesen Ferienort, weil der Mann ihrer Verwandten dort eine Eisenbahnstation besitzt.
O richtig O falsch O nicht enthalten 1 P

b) Weil Kolja die Eisenbahn und alle ihre Einrichtungen zu Hause genau studiert hat, weiß er, dass sein Unternehmen gefahrlos ist.
O richtig O falsch O nicht enthalten 1 P

c) Weil Kolja den anderen unbedingt imponieren will, geht er ein gefährliches Risiko ein.
O richtig O falsch O nicht enthalten 1 P

d) Versuche am späteren Wettort haben ergeben, dass man bei dieser Wette mit dem Gesicht nach unten auf den Schienen liegen muss.
O richtig O falsch O nicht enthalten 1 P

e) Für die Durchführung der Wette denken die Jungen an einen bestimmten Zug.
O richtig O falsch O nicht enthalten 1 P

f) Kolja reagiert nicht mehr auf die warnenden Rufe der Jungen, weil er bereits bewusstlos ist.
O richtig O falsch O nicht enthalten 1 P

3. Die Abschnitte eines Textes spiegeln dessen gedanklichen Aufbau. Kreuze an, welche Formulierung für den jeweiligen Einzelabschnitt zutreffend ist! Setze jeweils ein Kreuz!

Abschnitt 1 (Z. 1-6):
- O Vorstellung der Hauptfiguren
- O Darlegung der Vorgeschichte
- O unvermittelter Einstieg
- O Formulierung des Konflikts — 1 P

Abschnitt 2 (Z. 7-11):
- O Vorbereitung der Haupthandlung
- O Einsetzen der Nebenhandlung
- O Veranschaulichung der Einleitung
- O Vorwegnahme des Höhepunkts — 1 P

Abschnitt 3 (Z. 12-19):
- O Schilderung der Atmosphäre
- O Wende in der Haupthandlung
- O Charakterisierung der Nebenfiguren
- O Entfaltung des bisher Angedeuteten — 1 P

Abschnitt 4 (Z. 20-26):
- O Rückblick auf die Einleitung
- O spannungssteigernder Einschub
- O Zuspitzung des Konflikts
- O Abschluss der Nebenhandlung — 1 P

Abschnitt 5 (Z. 27-37):
- O Kommentierung des Höhepunkts durch den Erzähler
- O Ausgestaltung des Höhepunkts
- O Vorbereitung des Höhepunkts
- O Hinauszögern des Höhepunkts — 1 P

Abschnitt 6 (Z. 38-42):
- O Zusammenführen von Haupthandlung und Nebenhandlung
- O vertiefte Einschätzung der Hauptfigur
- O Formulieren einer Lehre
- O Bewertung des Handlungsverlaufs durch den Erzähler — 1 P

4. Kreuze jeweils den Satz an, der die unter a) bis f) aufgeführten Aussagen aus der Geschichte treffend wiedergibt!

a) Kolja sagt sich, dass er in seiner Schule werde **„glänzen"** (Z. 6) können.
- O Kolja will bewundernde Aufmerksamkeit erhalten.
- O Kolja will immer auf andere herabschauen.
- O Kolja muss von eigenen Schwächen ablenken.
- O Kolja will andere mit seinen Einfällen blenden. — 1 P

b) In den Ferien lernte Kolja **„junges Volk"** (Z. 8) kennen.
- O ... junge Teufelskerle ...
- O ... junge Herumtreiber ...
- O ... junges Gesindel ...
- O ... junge Leute ... — 1 P

c) Zwischen Kolja und den Jungen kommt es zu einer **„unerhörten"** (Z. 11) Wette.
- O ... zu einer gefährlichen Wette
- O ... zu einer ungesetzlichen Wette
- O ... zu einer spektakulären Wette
- O ... zu einer geheimzuhaltenden Wette — 1 P

d) Im Text heißt es, Kolja **„vermaß sich"** (Z. 13), diese Wette einzugehen.
- O Kolja macht einen Fehler, den er später bereut, als er diese Wette eingeht.
- O Kolja muss sich lange überwinden, als er diese Wette anbietet.
- O Kolja hat bei dieser Wette für sich schon einen genauen Plan.
- O Kolja lässt sich unvorsichtigerweise zu dieser Wette hinreißen. 1 P

e) Die Jungen waren Kolja gegenüber **„gar zu hochmütig".** (Z. 22)
- O Die Jungen waren eitler als Kolja.
- O Kolja hatte Angst vor den Jungen.
- O Sie waren ihm gegenüber allzu überheblich.
- O Die Jungen zeigten mehr Mut als Kolja. 1 P

f) **„Zu guter Letzt"** (Z. 23/24) einigt man sich auf die Durchführung der Wette.
- O Man hofft, dass die Wette gut ausgehen wird.
- O Nach einigem Hin und Her wird eine Wette beschlossen.
- O Mit dieser Wette erwirbt sich Kolja einen guten Stand bei den Jungen.
- O Man beschließt endlich faire Wettbedingungen. 1 P

5. Eine Klassleiterin plant eine Exkursion zum Eisenbahnmuseum in Nürnberg. Dabei stößt sie auf folgende Internetseite:

Unsere Öffnungszeiten & Preise

Das DB Museum hat Dienstag bis Freitag von 9 bis 17 Uhr und am Wochenende von 10 bis 18 Uhr für Sie geöffnet. Montags ist das Museum geschlossen. Weitere Informationen zu den Öffnungszeiten und Eintrittspreisen des DB Museums in Nürnberg finden Sie hier.

Öffnungszeiten

- Montags geschlossen.
- Dienstag bis Freitag von 9.00 bis 17.00 Uhr geöffnet.
- Samstag, Sonntag und an Feiertagen von 10.00 bis 18.00 Uhr geöffnet.
- Während der Spielwarenmesse und im Advent auch montags geöffnet.
- Geöffnet am Ostermontag, Pfingstmontag, Tag der deutschen Einheit und am zweiten Weihnachtsfeiertag.
- Geschlossen am Karfreitag, 1. Mai, 24., 25. und 31. Dezember, 1. Januar.
- Die Bibliothek hat Samstag und Sonntag geschlossen.
- Das Freigelände ist von April bis Oktober geöffnet (Öffnungszeiten wie Museum).

Hinweis: Im Juli hat das Museum jeweils mittwochs länger geöffnet, und zwar von 9 bis 21 Uhr.

Eintrittspreise

Erwachsene	4,00 Euro
Familienkarte (2 Erwachsene, 4 Kinder)	8,00 Euro
Ermäßigter Eintritt*	3,00 Euro
Kinder, Jugendliche (6 – 17 Jahre)	2,00 Euro
Schulklassen (Gruppen aus Kindergärten, -heimen, -horten)	1,50 Euro
Kinder unter 6 Jahren frei	

* *Schüler, Studierende, Auszubildende, am Besuchstag abgestempelter DB-Fahrschein, Gruppen ab 10 Personen (je Person), Rentner, Pensionäre, Schwerbehinderte.*

Überprüfe die folgenden Aussagen anhand der Internetseite und kreuze das Zutreffende an! Setze bei jeder Aussage ein Kreuz!

	richtig	falsch	nicht auf der Internetseite enthalten
Das Museum ist an den Weihnachtsfeiertagen (25. und 26.12.), an Silvester und an Neujahr geschlossen.			
Außer am Ostermontag und am Pfingstmontag ist das Museum montags immer geschlossen.			
Das Eisenbahnmuseum bietet Führungen für Schulklassen an.			
Eine Ermäßigung mit einem DB-Fahrschein gibt es nur, wenn dieser am Besuchstag abgestempelt wurde.			
Auch wenn jemand nur montags nach 19 Uhr das Museum besuchen kann, hat er dennoch die Möglichkeit, das Freigelände zu besichtigen.			

5 P

6. Ersetze die sechs fett gedruckten Ausdrücke durch im Zusammenhang bedeutungsgleiche und füge diese in die Klammern ein! Verwende keine Umgangssprache!

Wirklich große Probleme **existieren** (____________________) bei Eisenbahnstrecken im Gebirge. **Schon** (____________________) beim Bau muss an Lawinenabgänge und Schneeverwehungen gedacht werden. Mit **aufsehenerregenden** (____________________) Bauwerken, sogenannten Lawinengalerien, erhält die Strecke an besonders exponierten Stellen gleichsam ein schützendes Dach. **Dennoch** (____________________) muss der Lokführer **auf der Hut** (____________________) sein, denn Lawinen oder Verwehungen drohen auch auf freier Strecke. Insgesamt aber **beweist** (____________________) die doch geringe Zahl an Unglücksfällen im Winter die Zweckmäßigkeit derartiger Konstruktionen.

6 P

7. Der folgende Text enthält fünf Ausdrucksfehler. Verbessere sie in der Zeile daneben! Der Sinn des Textes darf dabei nicht verändert werden!

Bis zum Jahre 1991 galt der Rubel als die bloße Währung in allen Staaten der Sowjetunion. Nach dem Zusammenkrachen der Sowjetunion wurde der Rubel in den Nachfolgestaaten vertauscht, und zwar durch eigene Landeswährungen; nur in Russland gab es die hergekommene Währung weiterhin. Erst 1992 erschienen neue Banknoten mit dem Namen der Russischen Zentralbank anstelle einer Landesbezeichnung. Nach einigen Jahren rascher Geldentwertung wurde festgemacht, dass 1000 alte Rubel einem neuen Rubel (RUB) entsprechen.

____

____

____

____

____

5 P

8. Ersetze in jedem Satz das fett gedruckte Wort durch ein passendes Fremdwort! Der Sinn des Satzes darf dabei nicht verändert werden!

a) Damit bei der Bahn ein **bestmöglicher** Betrieb möglich ist, ist viel Arbeit nötig.

______________________________ 1 P

b) Auch eine **sehr genaue** Buchführung trägt zur Sicherheit bei.

______________________________ 1 P

c) Alle Abläufe müssen regelmäßig **überprüft** werden.

______________________________ 1 P

d) Dafür werden leistungsfähige **Rechner** eingesetzt.

______________________________ 1 P

e) Über dies gibt es europaweite Vereinbarungen zur Zugsicherung und **Verständigung** zwischen den Eisenbahngesellschaften.

______________________________ 1 P

9. Ersetze die fett gedruckten bildlichen Ausdrücke durch passende sachliche! Dabei notwendige Änderungen im Satzbau sind zulässig. Der Sinn des Satzes darf aber nicht verändert werden!

a) Viele Jugendliche **setzen es sich in den Kopf,** ihr Ansehen in der Gruppe durch Mutproben zu steigern.

______________________________ 1 P

b) Sie **verschließen die Augen** vor der damit verbundenen, manchmal sogar tödlichen Gefahr.

______________________________ 1 P

c) Wenn man wegen der Ablehnung einer Mutprobe von anderen kritisiert wird, ist das sicher zunächst **eine bittere Pille**.

______________________________ 1 P

d) Dennoch ist es vernünftiger, den anderen **die Stirn zu bieten** und sich nicht auf fragwürdige Mutproben einzulassen.

______________________________ 1 P

10. Setze im folgenden Text die in Klammern angegebenen Infinitive in die passende Form! Vermeide die Umschreibung mit „würde"!

______________ (geben) es die weltweiten Warnungen vor einer Klimakatastrophe nicht, so ______________ (gehen) wir Menschen wohl weiterhin sorglos mit fossilen Brennstoffen um. In einem Gastvortrag an der Universität Passau behauptete ein renommierter Klimatologe, durch eine verstärkte Nutzung des Schienenverkehrs ____________ (sein) die Erwärmung der Erdatmosphäre zumindest zu verlangsamen. Dem ist, wenn man ehrlich zu sich selbst ist, nichts ______________________ (entgegensetzen). Wenn schon früher mehr alternative Energien wie Sonnenenergie ________________________ (nutzen), dann ________________ (befinden) wir uns jetzt gar nicht in dieser Situation. Umweltfreundliche Technik ist zu fördern – ______________ (kommen), was da wolle. 7 P

11. Im Deutschen kann man Satzglieder an den Anfang stellen, um sie dadurch zu betonen. Ein Beispiel wird dir vorgegeben:

Beispiel: Der Vater beschreibt dem Freund seines Sohnes ausführlich die Modelleisenbahn.

Betone durch Voranstellen des entsprechenden Satzglieds, wer etwas erfährt!

⟶ Dem Freund seines Sohnes beschreibt …

In einem Moskauer U-Bahnhof erklärt eine Studentin der Kunstgeschichte zur Aufbesserung ihrer Finanzen einer Touristengruppe aus den USA kenntnisreich Zusammenhänge zwischen Baustil und Entstehungszeit des Bahnhofs.

a) Betone durch Voranstellen des entsprechenden Satzglieds, wer den Erklärungen der Studentin gerade zuhört! (Der Rest des Satzes muss nicht abgeschrieben werden.)

________________________________ 1 P

b) Benenne das Satzglied genau, das du in Teilaufgabe a) an den Satzanfang gestellt hast! (lateinischer Fachbegriff)

________________________________ 1 P

c) Betone durch Voranstellen des entsprechenden Satzglieds, wie die Studentin erklärt! (Der Rest des Satzes muss nicht abgeschrieben werden.)

________________________________ 1 P

d) Benenne das Satzglied genau, das du in Teilaufgabe c) an den Satzanfang gestellt hast! (lateinischer Fachbegriff)

________________________________ 1 P

e) Betone durch Voranstellen des entsprechenden Satzglieds, was die Studentin erklärt! (Der Rest des Satzes muss nicht abgeschrieben werden.)

________________________________ 1 P

f) Benenne das Satzglied genau, das du in Teilaufgabe e) an den Satzanfang gestellt hast! (lateinischer Fachbegriff)**!**

________________________________ 1 P

12. Wandle die vorgegebenen Sätze vom Aktiv ins Passiv bzw. vom Passiv ins Aktiv um! Achte darauf, nichts wegzulassen und im vorgegebenen Tempus zu bleiben!

a) Verspätungen werden den Fahrgästen von der Bahn in der Regel rechtzeitig mitgeteilt.

____

________________________________ 2 P

b) Vor einiger Zeit jedoch wurden die Fahrgäste eines Zuges buchstäblich im Regen stehen gelassen,

____

________________________________ 2 P

c) nachdem ein vorausfahrender Zug ein auf den Schienen liegendes Hindernis überfahren hatte.

____

________________________________ 2 P

13. Im folgenden Text finden sich sieben Fehler. Verbessere sie in der Zeile daneben!
(Von Legasthenikern nicht zu bearbeiten)

Einer der ersten architecktonisch beindruckenden Neubauten war der Frankfurter Bahnhof. Er endstand im späten 19. Jahrhundert und war damals flächenmäßig der größte Bahnhof weit und breit. Mit den Bogen förmigen Stahlträgern und den verglasten Stirnwändengalt die 200 Meter lange Bahnhofshalle als Meillenstein der damaligen Ingeniörskunst. Dennoch zitiert sein Stiel auch die älteren Bahnhofsbauten.

7 P

14. Bei den folgenden Sätzen ist jeweils ein Wort bzw. Wortabschnitt fett gedruckt. Zeige, wie am Zeilenrand zu trennen wäre, indem du dieses Wort bzw. diesen Wortabschnitt in der Zeile darunter getrennt schreibst! Ein Beispiel wird dir vorgegeben.
(Von Legasthenikern nicht zu bearbeiten)

Beispiel: In Westeuropa haben die **Schienen**stränge einen einheitlichen Abstand.

Schie - nenstränge

a) Einige betrachteten Dampfmaschinen und Lokomotiven zunächst als **Hexen**werk. 1 P

b) Doch physikalisch betrachtet, ist Krafterzeugung durch Dampf keine Hex**erei**. 1 P

c) Im England der Industriellen Revolution versorgten Dampfloks bald die **Stofffa**briken mit der benötigten Baumwolle. 1 P

d) Meist gleiten ICEs ohne jedes **Ruckeln** mit 200 km/h durch Europa. 1 P

e) Heute steuern nur noch Eisenbahnfreunde, oft in **histo**rischer Kleidung, alte Lokomotiven. 1 P

f) Sie verstehen, das leiseste **Klopfen** in ihren Dieselmotoren zu deuten. 1 P

15. Setze im folgenden Text die sechs fehlenden Satzzeichen (Anführungszeichen für die wörtliche Rede sowie Kommas) ein! (Von Legasthenikern nicht zu bearbeiten)

In diesem Streik erklärt der Gewerkschaftsvertreter vor Reportern der wichtigsten Nachrichtenagenturen aus Deutschland wird es vor allem darum gehen die Schließung regional bedeutsamer Nebenstrecken und Bahnhöfe zu verhindern. 6 P

Gutes Deutsch ist auf dem Gymnasium schon die „halbe Miete", weil fast der gesamte Lernstoff in Deutsch vermittelt und geprüft wird.

Lies regelmäßig Zeitungen und Bücher. Das ist der beste Weg zu einem guten Ausdruck, einem gepflegten Sprachstil und einem breiten Allgemeinwissen.

Das Bayerische Staatsministerium für Unterricht und Kultus hat auf der Homepage www.leseforum-bayern.de interessante Bücher aufgeführt.

Geh doch mal wieder in die Schulbücherei!

Das Wort Esel, wenn es zurückgelesen wird, so heißt es: Lese!
Wahr ist es, wann jemand kein unverständiger Esel bleiben will,
so muss er Bücher lesen!

Abraham a Santa Clara

Claudia Mayr ist sehr gläubig und ihr Glaube zu Gott bestärkt sie in allen Lebenslagen. Ein lebendiges, Mut machendes Buch, das zeigt, dass das Leben immer weiter geht.

Claudia Mayr erzählt über ihren Kampf mit den Folgen einer seltenen Stoffwechselkrankheit und will durch ihr Buch vor allem jungen Menschen, die ebenfalls an einer Krankheit oder Behinderung leiden, Mut machen.

Besprechung aus dem Leseforum Bayern des Staatsinstituts für Schulqualität und Bildungsforschung München

In ihrem 14. Lebensjahr entdeckt Claudia, dass sie, wie bereits zwei ihrer Geschwister, an Morbus Pompe Typ II, einer gefährlichen Störung des Stoffwechsels, erkrankt ist. Die Krankheit wird durch einen Gendefekt verursacht und äußert sich vor allem in den Symptomen Muskelschwäche und Atembeschwerden. Es fällt Claudia immer schwerer, die Dinge des alltäglichen Lebens zu bewältigen, längere Strecken zu gehen, eine Treppe hinaufzusteigen. Dennoch kämpft sie um einen Schulabschluss, eine Ausbildung, eine sinnvolle Tätigkeit. Bald muss sie ständig ein Beatmungsgerät in ihrer Nähe haben, erleidet einen Atemstillstand, benötigt immer öfter und länger den Rollstuhl zur Fortbewegung. Trotz dieser Einschränkungen und vieler Krankenhausaufenthalte zieht sie sich nicht resigniert zurück, sondern nimmt im Freundeskreis, soweit es ihr möglich ist, am normalen Leben der Heranwachsenden teil.

Eines Tages beginnt sie, ihre Gedanken, Gefühle und Erlebnisse aus dieser Zeit in einem Buch zu beschreiben, um anderen kranken oder behinderten Menschen Mut zu machen, nicht aufzugeben, sondern dem Leben einen neuen Sinn abzugewinnen. Dieser lebensnahe, tagebuchähnliche Bericht in der Sprache Jugendlicher kann aber ebenso für gesunde junge Menschen eine Gewinn bringende Lektüre sein.

Er eignet sich auch gut als Diskussionsgrundlage und kann zu unterschiedlichen Themen in denFächern Deutsch, Religion, Ethik, Sozialkunde herangezogen werden. Ausschlaggebend für die positive Bewertung des Buches sind weniger stilistische Aspekte, sondern die glaubwürdige Intention der Autorin und die beeindruckende Haltung, mit der sie ihre Krankheit bewältigt. Zumal für jugendliche Leser eine in vielerlei Hinsicht lohnende Lektüre!

Erschienen im Bauer-Verlag, www.verlag-bauer.de, 144 Seiten, 11 Euro

I. Dictation (Elternheft Seite 27)

Diesen Text findest Du als Audiofile auf unserer Homepage www.verlag-bauer.de unter "Gym 8" 20 P

II. Grammar

1. Reported speech

Last August John Smith's plane crashed into the Australian outback. John was injured but he survived the next six weeks until he was rescued. A reporter interviewed him in hospital.

Interviewer:	John, how do you feel and what do the doctors say?
John:	My leg still hurts. I think I lost about 20 pounds.
Interviewer:	Did you have any food on board?
John:	As I could hardly move, I had trouble getting the emergency rations. There were days when I didn't eat at all.
Interviewer:	How long will you have to stay in hospital?
John:	I'll stay here for about two months. I might see my family at Christmas. I hope to return to the site of my crash in spring.
Interviewer:	Give me more details about the accident, please!

Later the reporter talked to a colleague about his interview with John. Write down what he and John said. Use five different introductory verbs („sagen", „antworten" etc.).

I asked John ____

____

____

____

____

____

____

____

____

____ 21 P

2. if-clauses. Uncle Henry the Great. Complete what the big show-off tells his nephew.

a) If you listen carefully, I ____________ (tell) you amazing things about my life. 1 P

b) If I ____________ (find) the right partner, I would have climbed Mount Everest. 1 P

c) I would sail to Australia if I ____________ (not suffer) from sea-sickness. 1 P

d) If I ____________ (not be) busy doing other things I would learn Chinese. 1 P

e) I could have married a billionaire's daughter if I ____________ (not prefer) my freedom as a young man. 1 P

f) I would be rich now if my boss and my wife ____________ (be) more helpful in the past. 1 P

III. Mediation

18 P

You are an author of a history book.
Write an article about the Renaissance.
Write complete sentences.

Schreibe,
- auf welches Zeitalter die Renaissance folgte,
- dass Architektur und Literatur eine wichtige Rolle spielten und nenne den wichtigsten Dichter Englands,
- wer der Entdecker Amerikas war und berichte zwei Dinge über ihn,
- zwei Informationen über Heinrich VIII,
- welche drei „Tätigkeiten" Sir Francis Drake ausübte

I. Reading comprehension: Read the text, then answer the questions in complete sentences.

The Torrey Canyon - a catastrophe for Cornwall

One morning in March 1967 a big oil-tanker, the Torrey Canyon, ran onto a rock near Land's End. The tanker was on its way from the Persian Gulf to Wales with a cargo of 118,000 tons of oil for British Petroleum. Now an oil-slick was slowly travelling west towards the beaches of Cornwall. Why could such a terrible accident happen? The answer is easy: As the weather was fine the captain had changed the usual course and tried to take a short cut. He had not heard of the dangerous "Seven Stones" between Land's End and the Scilly Isles where the tanker was stuck now. The Torrey Canyon couldn't be towed off the rock: Experts feared that she might explode. For many days fishermen and other locals tried to destroy the oil-slick and to save birds and fish with detergents (Reinigungsmittel). They were not very successful. And to make matters worse, the Torrey Canyon started to break in half about ten days after the accident. Now even more oil poured into the water. The government had to react quickly! They decided to sink the tanker with bombs and burn the rest of the oil. There was an enormous explosion and a cloud of absolutely dark smoke. The tanker was burning but it took three more days to sink her and to burn most of the oil. As the beaches were damaged now, a lot of tourists cancelled their holidays in Cornwall and went to other places. So in the end it was the people of Cornwall - landlords, owners of inns and bed and breakfast places - who had to pay for a captain's mistake.

1. Complete these sentences.

a) The accident happened because ______________________________

______________________________ 2 P

b) Locals reacted in the following way to the catastrophe: ______________________________

______________________________ 2 P

2. True, false or not in the text? Cross T or F or ?. Correct the false statements. 14 P

a) The weather in March 1967 was always terrible. T F ?

____

b) The Seven Stones are dangerous because you can't see them. T F ?

____

c) The situation was the same ten days after the accident. T F ?

____

d) The government's plan was to pull the tanker off the rock. T F ?

____

e) A lot of fish and birds died. T F ?

____

f) In summer 1967 the usual number of tourists came to Cornwall. T F ?

____

II. The passive. Change these sentences into the passive.

1. At the moment the teacher **is asking** Mark about tourism in Devon. The teacher **is watching** the other pupils carefully. Yesterday at the same time the English teacher **was asking** Tom. The other pupils were **laughing at** Tom because his answers were so funny. The teacher's last sentence was: "People are **looking for** new ways to protect Devon's beaches. We must **deal with** these problems".

   At the moment Mark is being asked about tourism in Devon by the teacher. The other pupils are being watched carefully. Yesterday at the same time Tom was being asked. At Tom was being laughed because his answers were so funny. For new ways is being looked to protect Devon's beaches. These problems must be dealt with. 12 P

2. Use the **personal passive** at least once!

   a) The guide described the excursion to the tourists.

   The excursion was described to the tourists by the guide. 2 P

   b) A man in the group explained his health problems to the others.

   His health problems were explained in the group to the others. 2 P

   c) After some miles the guide offered the tourists hot tea.

   After some miles hot tea was offered to the tourists 2 P

   d) The guide said: "Now I will show you the town of St Ives."

   The town of St. Ives will be showed to you now 2 P

   e) At Land's End the guide gave a brochure with information to the tourists.

   A brochure with informationen was given to the tourists at Land's End. 2 P

III. Textproduction

Schreibe, dass

- Cornwall mit seinen Klippen und kleinen Buchten eine ausgezeichnete Gegend für Schmuggler ist,
- die „englische Riviera" ein Paradies für Touristen ist, weil das Klima so mild und feucht ist, dass sogar Palmen dort wachsen können,
- "cream tea" eine Kanne Tee mit „süßen Brötchen", Sahne und „süßer Marmelade" ist,
- man nicht seekrank sein darf, wenn man den Ärmelkanal mit der Fähre überqueren will,
- Tintagel ein erstaunlicher Ort ist, weil es der Geburtsort des legendären König Arthur ist,
- es am „Land's End" oft so viel Dunst gibt, dass man nichts sehen kann.

30 P

I. Listening comprehension (Elternheft Seite 29)

Listen to the text, then answer the questions.

1. Thanksgiving Day is celebrated every year. When exactly is it?

______________________________ 2 P

2. What do many Americans do in the morning of that national holiday?

______________________________ 2 P

3. What do most people eat?

______________________________ 2 P

4. What, according to the text, did North America not have in 1620?

______________________________ 2 P

5. Who settled already on the eastern coast in the 17th century?

______________________________ 2 P

6. What problems did the Pilgrims have in their first winter?

______________________________ 2 P

7. Why had they left England?

______________________________ 2 P

8. What is the Mayflower?

______________________________ 2 P

II. Vocabulary

Explain the words. Write complete sentences.

1. A ransom ______________________________ 2 P

2. An inquiry ______________________________

______________________________ 2 P

3. A phone booth ______________________________ 2 P

4. A border ______________________________ 2 P

5. A servant ______________________________

______________________________ 2 P

6. A Puritan ______________________________

______________________________ 2 P

III. Grammar

Complete the sentences.

Sam and Tim ______________________ (would like/go) to the zoo today. They ______ ______________ (enjoy/watch) animals and ____________________ (love/feed) them. So they _______________ (decide/ask) their parents. Mum and Dad ____________________ (suggest/go) now because the weather is beautiful. Sam: "I am ____________________ (keen/see) the tigers and Tim ______________________________ (look forward/watch) the polar bears." Their dad ______________ (want/go) by train, but Mum answers: "______ ______________ (How about/take) our bikes? ____________________ (By/cycle) we can enjoy nature and save money!" Sam and Tim: "Good idea! We have always ________________ (dream/go) to the zoo by bike!" 11 P

IV. In English please.

1. Letztes Jahr bekamen die Smiths ein Baby.

   ____ 3 P

2. Für viele Eltern ist es ziemlich schwer, sich an (das) Leben mit einem Baby zu gewöhnen, aber die Smiths finden es faszinierend.

   ____

   ____ 6 P

3. Die Smiths sind die einzigen Eltern, die jeden Tag mit ihrem Baby spazieren gehen.

   ____ 4 P

4. Sie wollen, dass ihr Baby hübsch und gesund aussieht.

   ____ 3 P

5. Die Smiths denken, dass Spaziergänge (gerund!) mit ihrem Baby unvergesslich sind, und oft haben sie keine Lust, nach Hause zu gehen.

   ____

   ____ 6 P

6. „Unsere Träume wurden wahr! (Das) Leben mit Trixi ist unglaublich!"

   ____ 4 P

I. Reading comprehension
Read the text, then answer the questions in complete sentences.

Isaac Asimov, The fun they had (shortened)

On May 17, 2157 Margie wrote in her diary: "Today Tommy found a book!" It was a very old book. Margie's grandfather once said that his grandfather told him about a time when all stories were printed on paper.
They looked at it together, Tommy and Margie. It was funny to read words that didn't move on the page. "What a waste!", said Tommy. "When you finish the book, you just throw it away!"
"What's it about?", asked Margie.
"School!", he said.
Margie laughed. "School? What's there to write about school? I hate it."
Margie always hated school. The "teacher" was giving her test after test in geography and she was doing worse and worse. That was when the inspector came with a box of tools to look at the "teacher". "I think the geography sector was a little too quick. I have slowed it down."
Margie had hoped the inspector would take the "teacher" away altogether. So she said to Tommy: "Why write about school?"
Tommy said: "Because it's not our kind of school, stupid. This is the old kind of school that they had hundreds of years ago."
"What kind of school did they have all that time ago? Anyway they had a teacher."
"Sure they had a teacher. But it was a man."
"A man? How could a man be a teacher? A man can't know as much as a teacher. And I wouldn't want a strange man in my house to teach me."
"The teachers didn't live in the house. They had a special building and all the kids went there."
Suddenly Margie's mother called: "Margie! School!"
Margie went into the schoolroom. It was next to her bedroom, and the teacher was "on".
The screen was lit up and it said: "Today's arithmetic lesson is on the addition of fractions. Put your homework in the slot."
Margie did so. She was thinking about the old schools they had when her grandfather's grandfather was a little boy. The kids came, laughing and shouting, sitting together, going home together. And the teachers were people. She was thinking about the fun they had.

1. Name three aspects of school life in 2157. Write about things which are different from today's school life. Write three sentences.

   * ______________________________ 2 P

   * ______________________________ 2 P

   * ______________________________ 2 P

2. Name three aspects of school life today. Write about things they don't have in the year 2157. Write three sentences.

   * ______________________________ 2 P

   * ______________________________ 2 P

   * ______________________________ 2 P

II. Word order

Put the sentences in the correct order.

(Bob:) the go tonight Let's concert to. ____ 2 P

Moonkids well The always very sing. ____ 2 P

(Tom:) sure Moonkids I not Frankly are am the good if

____ 2 P

of But try course can we ____ 2 P

(After the concert. Tom:) was enough not good performance Bobby's

____ 2 P

got He enough hasn't experience ____ 2 P

were the The Millers at too concert, ____ 2 P

it They very obviously much liked ____ 2 P

(Bob:) for much coming you very thank I'd to Actually like

____ 2 P

III. Letter writing (Verwende hierfür ein separates DIN A4-Blatt!) 20 P

Schreibe einen Brief mit folgendem Inhalt:

- Anrede (du weißt nicht, wer zuständig ist)
- Du nimmst Bezug auf eine Anzeige vom 23. Juni
- Du erkundigst dich nach den Konzertkarten, die noch nicht eingetroffen sind
- Du schreibst, dass du dankbar wärst, wenn sie bald kämen
- Leider wirst du die Karten nicht nehmen können, wenn sie nicht sehr bald kommen
- Du fügst deinem Brief deine Telefonnummer hinzu
- Du bedankst dich für die Hilfe
- Du freust dich, bald von ihnen zu hören
- Schlussformel

IV. Vocabulary

Fill in.

1. If you use an ____________________, you make a bad situation worse. 1 P

2. A shy person does not have enough ____________________. 1 P

3. The ____________________ of a story is the place of the story. It also shows the time of the story. 1 P

4. Another word for "to say sorry" is to ____________________. 1 P

5. People who live in a different country live ____________________. 1 P

6. For German students English and French are ____________________ languages. 1 P

**I. Nigel Tough spent two months in Australia's outback in a tent.
Back at school, students asked him how he felt:**

"How did you feel alone in the outback?"
"Were you frightened of snakes?"
"Why did you travel to Australia?"
"Are you glad to be back in Nottingham?"
"Will you show us your photos?"
"Would you do it again?"

Turn these six questions into reported speech! Start with "They asked Nigel" or "They wanted to know".

1. They asked Nigel ______________________________ 1 P
2. They ______________________________ 1 P
3. They ______________________________ 1 P
4. They ______________________________ 1 P
5. They ______________________________ 1 P
6. They ______________________________ 1 P

II. For the school magazine Nigel wrote the following article:

"In Australia I bought several postcards with animals because I love Australia's wildlife. There are koalas and kangaroos, but you can also find poisonous snakes! I went surfing and I saw some Aborigines. I couldn't go diving because the sea was too rough. Have you ever been to Australia? Go there - it's worth it!"

Nigel's friend Tina sent an e-mail to her grandparents reporting about Nigel's article.
What did she write?

In his article Nigel reported that ______________________________

____

____

______________________________ 11 P

III. if-clauses. Fill in.

1. If Nigel goes to Australia next year, he ______________ (stay) for six months. 1 P
2. Nigel would buy a new camera if he ______________ (have) enough money. 1 P
3. If Nigel hadn't spent two months in Australia, he ______________ (cannot take) the lovely photographs. 1 P
4. If he hadn't travelled there, he ______________ (not/speak) English so well now. 1 P

I. Rewrite these six sentences in the passive. Write the by-agent, too.

1. Yesterday at 11 o'clock in Market Street in St. Austell.
   a) A man was making a phone call.
   b) Two children were eating ice cream.
   c) A woman was cleaning a shop window.

2. At the moment in a school in St. Austell.
   a) Tom is telling a joke to his neighbour.
   b) Lisa and Tina are writing little letters.
   c) Outside some men are repairing a street lamp.

1. a) A phone call was being made by a man. 2 P
   b) Ice cream was ~~ea~~ being eaten by two children. 2 P
   c) A shop window was being cleaned by a woman. 2 P
2. a) A Joke is being told to his neighbour by Tom. 2 P
   b) Little letters are being written by Lisa and Tina. 2 P
   c) A street lamp is being repaired by some men outside 2 P

II. In English please. Use the simple past! Wherever it is possible write two different translations!

1. Das Schloss wurde ihnen gezeigt.
   a) The Castle was shown to them. b) They were shown the castle 2 P
2. Das Problem wurde mir erklärt.
   a) I was ~~told about~~ explained the problem. b) The problem was told to me. 2 P
3. Die Broschüren wurden den Leuten gegeben.
   a) The people were given ~~some~~ the brochures. b) ~~Bro~~ The brochures were given to the people 2 P
4. Der Weg wurde den Touristen erklärt.
   a) The way was explained to the tourists. b) The tourists ~~was~~ were explained the way. 2 P
5. Ausflüge wurden den Leuten vorgeschlagen.
   a) Trips were suggested to the people. b) People were suggested trips 2 P
6. Man bot den Leuten Getränke an.
   a) Some drinks were offered to the people. b) The people were offered some drinks. 2 P

III. Vocabulary. Fill in. 15 P

Mr Green knows all about the importance (Bedeutung) of his ~~biomes~~ greenhouse (Gewächshaus). When he talks about his garden, he immediately refers to (sich beziehen auf) his amazing (erstaunlich) little paradise (Paradies). Its climate is humid (feucht), nearly ~~tt~~ tropical (tropisch), and he can even grow (züchten) the pineapple (Ananas). Each plant - and some of them are really rare (selten) - has got a nice print (Beschriftung), and Mr Green ~~changed~~ replaces (ersetzen durch) every old or dying plant by a new one. His rules are very ~~strikt~~ strict (streng). He waters (gießen) his plants three times a day. Furthermore (Außerdem) he sometimes talks to them.

I. Textproduction

Schreibe, dass
- Millers und Whalleys in England leben,
- Herr Miller Amerikaner ist,
- Frau Miller Lehrerin ist und dass sie zehn Stunden am Tag arbeitet,
- der kleine Bob Miller amerikanisches Essen liebt und dass Mathe sein bestes Fach ist,
- die Schule in England um 9 Uhr beginnt,
- Herr Whalley eine neue Brille und zwei neue Hosen hat,
- die neuen Möbel in seiner Küche gut aussehen,
- Frau Whalley den Obdachlosen Ratschläge, Informationen und neue Kleidung gibt.

____

____

____

____

____

____

____

____ 24 P

II. Mixed vocabulary. Fill in

1. The traditional Scottish skirt is the ______________________. 1 P
2. Tim's job is to repair cars: he is a ______________________. 1 P
3. Tim is in ______________________: His bus leaves in two minutes. 1 P
4. A very wide road where you can drive really fast is a ______________________. 1 P
5. In order to drive you need a special document: it is called a ______________________. 1 P
6. A line of people who are waiting for something is a ______________________. 1 P
7. A test in which you have to speak is an ______________________ test. 1 P
8. In the ______________________ from 1776 you can read that the American settlers broke away from Britain. 1 P

I. In English, please. 20 P

1. Einen Tag vor seinem Geburtstag beschloss Arthur, das Rauchen aufzugeben.

   ____

2. Arthurs Frau: Ich möchte eine Party organisieren. ______________________

3. Arthur: Es hat keinen Zweck, eine Party zu organisieren. Ich will es vermeiden, Leute zu treffen. Wie wäre es, wenn wir meinen Geburtstag auf (in) dem Land verbringen?

   ____

   ____

4. Arthurs Frau: Ich weiß nicht, was ich dort tun soll. Ich bin nicht interessiert am Wandern.

   ____

5. Arthur: Ich freue mich darauf, mit dir in einem Restaurant zu essen, ohne Leute zu sehen. Du weißt, auf einer Party ist es schwer, mit dem Rauchen aufzuhören.

   ____

   ____

II. Vocabulary: Fill in.

1. A thing which is ______________ lasts for a long time. 1 P
2. With the "Declaration of ______________" the American settlers broke away from Britain. 1 P
3. The opposite of "clean" is "______________". 1 P
4. The round hard pieces of money are called ______________. 1 P
5. There isn't much time left means: Time is ______________. 1 P
6. This is very easy to understand: This is quite ______________. 1 P
7. The officer caught the thief: He ______________ him. 1 P

III. Fill in the gaps. 10 P

glauben	
	unbelievable
vergessen	
	unforgettable
zerbrechen	
	unbreakable
mögen	
	likeable
sich vorstellen	
	unimaginable

Stegreifaufgabe 5

⌛ 15 / 📖 34

Dictation (Elternheft Seite 34)

Diesen Text findest du als Audiofile auf unserer Homepage www.verlag-bauer.de unter "Gym 8" 20 P

Stegreifaufgabe 6

✓ 20 / ⌛ 20 / 📖 35

Mediation

Lies folgendes deutsche Interview und verfasse einen **englischen Lexikoneintrag** anhand der Informationen!

- Wie hieß Daniel Defoe wirklich und wann lebte er?
  = Er hieß eigentlich Foe und lebte von 1660 bis 1731. Geburts- und Sterbeort war London.

- In welchem Alter schrieb er seinen ersten Roman und wie hieß dieser?
  = Mit fast 60 Jahren schrieb er "The life and strange adventures of Robinson Crusoe".

- Was schrieb er sonst noch?
  = Er schrieb einige andere Romane und viele politische Artikel. Einmal schrieb er über die Pest in London (plague).

- Warum schrieb er?
  = Es war ihm wichtig, dass seine Leser etwas über seine politischen und religiösen Ideen erfuhren.

Übung 1

1. A crossword puzzle

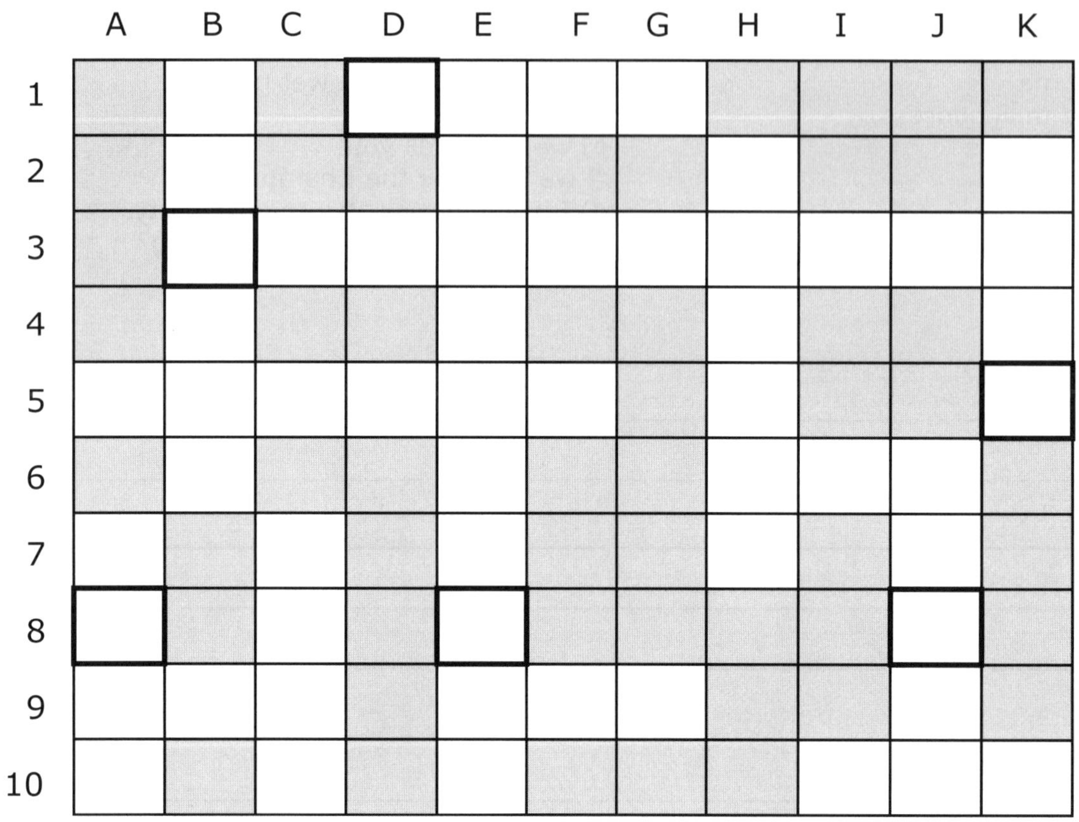

Across:
1D: A .... - Aboriginal can have a white mother and an Aboriginal father
3B: Something which can't be done
5A: I think my hopes will............
6H: If you break the ...., you will have problems
9A: A mouselike animal
9E: An Australian bird
10I: A spider catches insects in its ....

Down:
1B: There is nothing like it: It is ....
1E: The native people of Australia
7A: If you scratch yourself, you'll have a ....
7C: I really must do it: It is my ....
2H: He will probably come means that he is .... to come
6J: What a ....: You have thrown out all the empty papers
2K: I am so ugly in this photograph: I will .... it.

Put the letters in the bold boxes in the right position. The word tells you where you go when you break the law!

Solution: ________________________

Übung 2

1. Join the sentences and translate them afterwards.

a) If we knew the answer,
b) Will they come to dinner
c) If you had invited me,
d) If I give you my e-mail address,
e) He would be a millionaire
f) You'll catch a cold
g) I'll cut the grass
h) If we had played well,

a) will you write me a mail?
b) if he had worked harder.
c) if you go out with wet hair.
d) if you want.
e) we could tell you.
f) we could be the Champions.
g) I would have come to your party.
h) if they know we have a big dog?

a) ______________________________
b) ______________________________
c) ______________________________
d) ______________________________
e) ______________________________
f) ______________________________
g) ______________________________
h) ______________________________

Übung 3

1. Fill in and find the solution.

1. When you travel into a region to find out what it is like, you .... the region.
2. A .... is a man who works on a ship.
3. Charles Dickens was a famous English ....
4. When you leave your country and start a new life in another country, you ....
5. The adjective "free" has a corresponding noun: ....
6. One nasty student can .... the whole class negatively.
7. "To ...." means to kill a person in order to punish him or her.
8. This book will be of great .... to you: It can give you useful information.

__ __ [__] __ __ __ __ **1.**
__ __ __ __ [__] __ **2.**
[__] __ __ __ __ __ **3.**
[__] __ __ __ __ __ __ __ **4.**
__ [__] __ __ __ __ __ **5.**
__ __ [__] __ __ __ __ __ __ **6.**
__ __ __ __ [__] __ __ **7.**
__ __ [__] __ __ **8.**

Now read the letters in the box dowwards. The solution is a characteristic of Elizabeth I.

Solution: ______________________

2. The Renaissance. Write one sentence about

1. Elizabeth I
2. Sir Francis Drake
3. Christopher Columbus
4. Henry VIII
5. William Shakespeare

1. ______________________________
2. ______________________________
3. ______________________________
4. ______________________________
5. ______________________________

Übung 4

Vocabulary alphabeth

A: Look, Mike is walking ____________ the street.

B: The opposite of top: ____________ .

C: You need it to make chocolate: ____________ .

D: If you are frightened, you don't ____________ to do it.

E: The door or gate which you use to go in: ____________

F: A boat that transports people or cars: ____________

G: Salad is easier to grow there than outside: ____________

H: A castle where there are ghosts is ____________ .

I: An old word for pub: ____________

J: Dating from the age called Jura: ____________ .

K: Another word for nice is ____________ .

L: A man who runs a B&B place is a ____________ .

M: 12 o'clock at night is ____________ .

N: The opposite of a wide road is a ____________ road.

O: A tree that grows in southern Europe: ____________

P: The people who went to America on the Mayflower were called ____________ .

Q: Another word for fast: ____________

R: You need this material for wheels: ______________

S: In order to plant tomatoes you must plant ______________ .

T: You find it inside cigarettes: ____________

U: Your father's or your mother's brother is your ____________ .

V: Tomatoes, cucumbers and beans are ____________ .

W: The comparative of bad: ____________

X: The third letter from the end: ________

Y: A bright colour: ____________

Z: You can look at animals there: ________

Übung 5

1. Scotland: A mind map

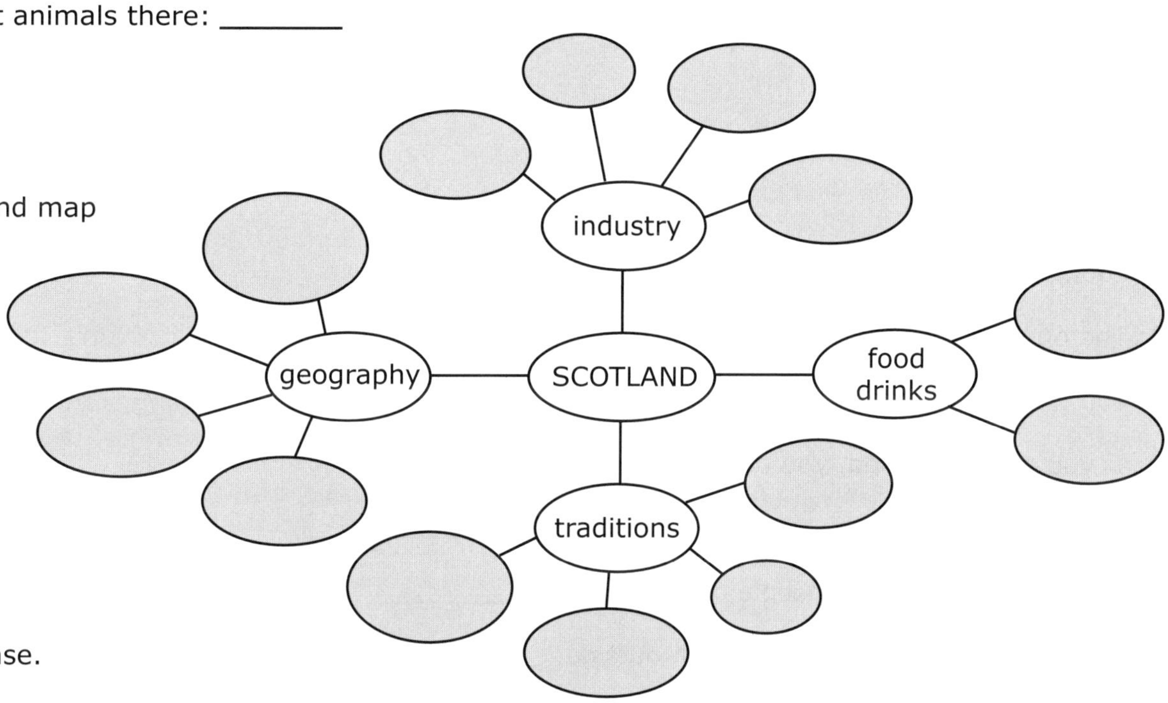

2. In English, please.

   a) Wir können mit dem Zug nach Glasgow fahren.
   b) Der Zug nach Glasgow ist nicht sehr teuer.
   c) Januar und Februar sind sehr schneereiche (snowy) Monate.
   d) Der Februar 2009 war besonders schneereich.
   e) In Schottland ist die Polizei sehr nett.
   f) Ist das Hochlandvieh auch nett?

a) ______________________________

b) ______________________________

c) ______________________________

d) ______________________________

e) ______________________________

f) ______________________________

3. Possessive pronouns. Fill in.

MUM: Is that your pen?

SON: Yes, it's ____________ .

MUM: Where are Dad's shoes?

SON: Look, these shoes must be ____________ .

MUM: And where is Susan's shampoo?

SON: Oh, I think this one must be ____________ .

MUM: Now I'm looking for the cats' balls. I can't find them.

SON: They aren't here. These balls aren't ____________ , they are ____________ !

____________ are in the garage.

Übung 6: Mediation (Verwende ein separates DIN A4-Blatt)

Schreibe einen englischen Artikel über Boston! Verwende folgende Informationen!

Einwohnerzahl:	ca. 600.000
Lage:	Ostküste der USA, Hauptstadt des Staates Massachusetts
Sehenswürdigkeiten:	Harvard University (gegründet 1636, kann besichtigt werden) Prudential Tower (230 Meter hoch, guter Blick auf die Staaten Vermont und New Hampshire)
Museen:	New England Aquarium, Boston Museum of Science
Atmosphäre:	in der Altstadt bei dem berühmten Faneuil Hall: Läden, Cafés, Straßenmusik

Übung 7

Britisch English	American English	German
		Mitte
neighbour		
	college	
		ich denke
garden		
	movie	
		Farbe
banknote		
	favorite	
		Laden

motorway		
	real good	
		Innenstadt

Übung 8 A: Find the word for a person who prepares and sells medical goods.

This letter is in Christmas, but not in far, ☐ that letter is in hour, but not in car. ☐

This letter is in friendly, but not in strong, ☐ that letter is in mobile, but not in long. ☐

This letter is in silly, but not in late, ☐ that letter is in sister, but not in great. ☐

This letter is in Betty, but not in Mark. ☐ Solution: ________________

Übung 8 B: What is the right order of these words?

A specialty in Maine is OBLTRSE. ________________

In many classrooms RANTSARPECINES are used. ________________

NODSWBAORNIG is like surfing in the snow. ________________

When you type you use a EBKAYDOR. ________________

For the use of many machines you need LECTERCIITY. ________________

Übung 9: The magic "i". Find the words.

1. to understand and enjoy something:
2. person who receives guests and amuses them:
3. another word for "to get":
4. way of feeling, thinking and behaving:
5. the opposite of "advantage":
6. to get somebody to believe something:
7. A person who wants to be very rich, famous and successful is
8. great, much, important:
9. People who are not happy with a situation often make a
10. small, not serious, not important:
11. a feeling which is caused by something sudden and unexpected:
12. An ..... girl goes abroad to learn a foreign language and to help a family.
13. If you want to sell your piano, you can put an ..... in the newspaper.

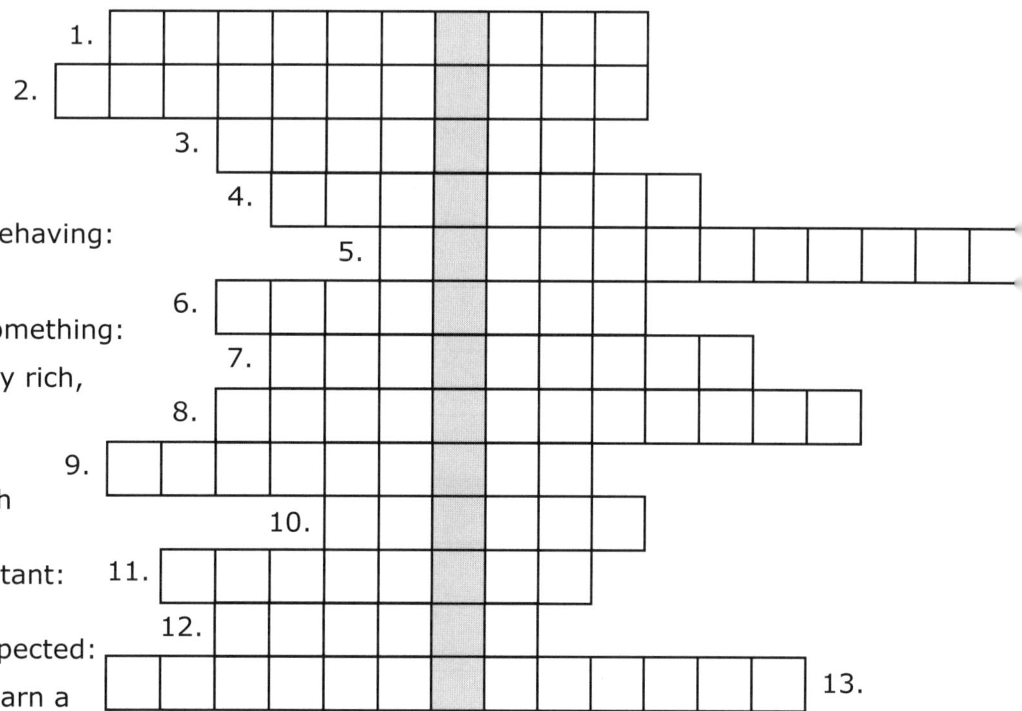

I. Übersetzung: Am Badesee

1. Marius in quadam nave sedens Caesarem imitatur et Fredericum hortatur:

2. „Aggrediamur magistrum, qui in aqua versatur! Dominice, noli remanere!

3. Ne veritus sis magistrum, sed persequere istum!"

4. Haec verba locutus desiluit.

5. Omnes incredibili audacia et celeritate profecti sunt;

   magistrum aggressi sunt et arena aquaque sparserunt.

6. Quamobrem magister quam celerrime e lacu egressus est. Sed postridie magister questus est:

7. „Quis vestrum multum temporis et operae in discendo consumpsit?

8. Certe obliti estis verborum vestrorum. Sed me ut latrones repente premere malebatis."

II. Aufgabenteil

1. Ersetze die Verben durch die angegebenen Deponentien und übersetze sie!

   a) intravistis (ingredi) ________ ________ 2 P

   b) tolerabunt (pati) ________ ________ 2 P

   c) fuisses (versari) ________ ________ 2 P

2. Setze die eingeklammerten Wörter im richtigen Kasus ein und übersetze!

   a) Sequebar (amicus) ________ ________ 2 P

   b) Utamini bene (libri) ________ ________ 2 P

   c) Magister irascetur (pueri) ________ ________ 2 P

3. Erkläre folgende Fremdwörter durch Angabe des zugrunde liegenden lateinischen Verbs (Inf. Präs.) und seiner Bedeutung!

   a) Experte ________ ________ ________ 1,5 P

   b) Prospekt ________ ________ ________ 1,5 P

4. Nenne außer Archimedes noch zwei weitere griechische Mathematiker!
   Wofür sind diese heute noch bekannt?

   * ________ 1 P

   * ________ 1 P

5. Mit welchen Helden des Mythos verglich sich Alexander? ________ 1 P

I. Übersetzung: Pädagogische Regeln aus der Vergangenheit für die Gegenwart

1. Quintilianus, vir docendi peritus, nobis summa eloquentia multa praecepta dedit, quemadmodum liberi optime instituendi essent.

2. Nonnulli Romani filios servis Graecis educandos tradiderunt.

3. Sed Quintilianus praecepit: Optandum est, ut pueri a parentibus in scholam mittantur, non solum humanitatis augendae causa, sed etiam ad firmas amicitias coniungendas.

4. Praeceptor autem cogitet, quomodo discipuli ad discendum excitentur.

5. Alii magistro reprehendendi, alii saepe laudandi sunt.

6. Quare parentibus magna est adhibenda cura, ut liberi magistro idoneo docendi mandentur.

II. Aufgabenteil

1. Welcher der folgenden Sätze enthält einen: Irrealis – Jussiv – Imperativ – Prohibitiv – Realis – Potentialis - Deliberativ – erfüllbarer Wunsch – unerfüllbarer Wunsch?

   a) Desiste clamare! b) Paene cecidi. c) Ne clamaveris! 3 P

   d) Tibi idem eveniat! e) Utinam istud vidissem! f) Hoc nemo credat. 3 P

2. Gib an, ob es sich um Gerund oder Gerundiv handelt, tausche die Konstruktionen und übersetze!

   a) occasio amici videndi 2 P

   b) cupidus carmen audiendi 2 P

   c) libris legendis multa discere 2 P

3. Nenne neben Quintilian einen weiteren berühmten Autor, der in lateinischer Sprache pädagogische Themen behandelt hat. Wann lebte er und wie nennt man die Geistesrichtung dieses Autors? 3 P

4. Benenne und belege drei Stilmittel in folgendem Text: Philosophia nos hortatur, ut deo libenter pareamus, ut deum sequamur, ut casus fortunae fortiter feramus. 3 P

Schulaufgabe 3 LmF bis Kap. 98

I. Übersetzung

Wie sollen die römischen Machthaber mit den Christen umgehen? C. Plinius, der Statthalter von Bithynien, einer Provinz in Kleinasien, fragt bei Kaiser Trajan an.

1. Meministis epistularum Plinii, cuius avunculum eruptione[1] Vesuvii perisse legistis.

2. Plinius diu in Bithynia versatus est, ubi magnus numerus Romanorum victum Christianorum contemnebat atque oderat.

3. Cum multum Plinii interesset iustitiam fieri, ausus est ad imperatorem epistulam scribere, ut cognosceret, quemadmodum in Christianos consulendum esset.

4. Plinius: „Isti numinibus nostris et imagini tuae immolare nolunt.

5. Qui fit, ut quidam supplicio affici gaudeant neque ad bonam mentem revertantur?

6. Quid faciam? Responde mihi, qui consilio tuo confidere soleo!"

[1] eruptio, -onis = Ausbruch

II. Aufgabenteil

1. Übersetze folgenden verschränkten Relativsatz auf vier verschiedene Arten!
   Hercules, quem fortem fuisse constat, multos labores subiit.

   ______________________ 1 P

   ______________________ 1 P

   ______________________ 1 P

   ______________________ 1 P

2. Ersetze scire durch cognovisse (bzw. umgekehrt) und übersetze die Formen!

   a) sciebam ____________ ____________ 1 P

   b) cognoverunt ____________ ____________ 1 P

c) cognovissemus ____________ ____________ 1 P

d) scies ____________ ____________ 1 P

3. Finde den Irrläufer (mit Begründung)!

a) passus, cantus, rursus, victus

____________ ____________ ____________ 1 P

b) eicienti, eiecto, eiciendo, eiecturo

____________ ____________ ____________ 1 P

c) tametsi, ob, quamvis, quoniam

____________ ____________ ____________ 1 P

d) absolutus sum, solitus sum, ausus sum, confisus sum

____________ ____________ ____________ 1 P

4. Bilde die Tempusreihe (Präsens, Imperfekt, Futur I, Perfekt, Plusquamperfekt, Futur II) von gaudere in der 2. Person Singular Indikativ!

____________________________________ 3 P

5. Unter welchem römischen Kaiser fand die letzte große Christenverfolgung statt? Wann war dies etwa? Wie verhielt sich der römische Staat sonst gegenüber fremden Religionen?

____________________________________ 3 P

✓ 18 / ⌛ 45 / 📖 44 **Schulaufgabe 4** LmF bis Kap. 103

I. Übersetzung

Der Philosoph Seneca (1. Jahrhundert n. Chr.) klagt in einem Brief über die Zuschauer und deren Verhalten bei den Gladiatoren„spielen".

1. Nihil magis contemnendum est quam spectaculum[1].

____

2. Nam libido sanguinis hominem crudeliorem reddere videtur.

____

3. Crebri autem spectatores[2] dicant:

____

4. „Multi in arena contendunt, in quos optimo iure vindicatur; alii furta fecisse, alii homines occidisse dicuntur.

____

____

5. Cum scelera turpia commiserint, puniantur! Gladiatores nihil habeant, quo tegantur! Libenter et celeriter moriantur!"

____

____

6. Pugnantes non leonibus, sed spectatoribus obiciuntur. Exitus omnium pugnantium mors est.

7. Spectatores[2] non habent, quod tam crudelia spectacula[1] aspiciant.

8. Qua de causa facile intellegi potest turbam esse vitandam.

9. Sunt enim, qui mala exempla dent.

[1] spectaculum, -i = Gladiatorenspiel [2] spectator, -oris = Zuschauer

II. Aufgabenteil

1. Übersetze folgende NcI-Konstruktion auf vier verschiedene Möglichkeiten!
Cicero Athenis multos philosophos audivisse traditur.

1 P

1 P

1 P

1 P

2. Kasuslehre: Übersetze!

a) periculo liberare

b) Nobis laborandum est.

2 P

c) oculis videre

d) magno usui esse

2 P

e) amor patriae

f) magna audacia esse

2 P

g) multos annos bellum gerere

h) Tu maior amico es.

2 P

3. Was bedeuten folgende italienische Wörter? Gib auch das zugrunde liegende lateinische Wort an!

a) la consolazione

b) la dottrina

c) il ferro

3 P

4. Sokrates versuchte seine Mitbürger zu einem sittlich guten Leben zu führen.

a) Welche Einsicht war die Voraussetzung für ethisch richtiges Handeln?

1 P

b) Welche Vorwürfe führten zu seiner Verurteilung zum Tod? 2 P

1. Übersetze! Achte genau auf die Formen!

Pueri hortabantur
hortaberis
hortati essetis
hortemur
hortamur
hortabuntur
hortatus es
hortata erat
minor
miror
mirer
mirarer
mirare
mirari
mirus
caedere
cadere
cedere
credere 19 P

2. Gib die Bedeutung der Verben an! Finde ein Fremdwort und erkläre es!

tueri
imitari
confiteri
pati
aggredi
loqui 12 P

3. Setze zu folgenden Wörtern die passende Form des Indefinitpronomens quidam!

pueri 1
pueri 2
puellae 1
puellae 2
puellae 3 6 P

✓ 18 / ⌛ 20 / 📖 46 Stegreifaufgabe 2 LmF Kap. 90/91

1. Übersetze den Satz und benenne die Modusverwendung im Hauptsatz!

   a) Si adfuissem, eum reprehendissem. 2 P

   b) Utinam tacuisses! 2 P

   c) Quid tibi respondeam? 2 P

   d) Qui dedit beneficium, taceat; narret, qui accepit! 2 P

   e) Vix quisquam putet vos verum dixisse. 2 P

   f) Longum est omnes poetas Graecos nominare. 2 P

2. Erkläre die folgenden Fremdwörter! Du musst auch das zugrunde liegende lateinische Wort und dessen Bedeutung anführen! (Beispiel: total: vollständig, von totus, ganz)

   a) Visite 1 P

   b) Emission 1 P

   c) exakt 1 P

   d) oral 1 P

   e) Präferenz 1 P

   f) requirieren 1 P

Stegreifaufgabe 3 LmF Kap. 96/97 ✓ 18 / ⌛ 20 / 📖 46

1. Beuge!

   cantus suavis

   9 P

2. Übersetze die Subjunktion und gib die Sinnrichtung an!

   a) Si bene laboraveritis, hae sententiae difficiles non erunt. 1,5 P

   b) Discipuli in scholam eunt, ut discant. 1,5 P

   c) Tantus erat timor, ut omnes fugerent. 1,5 P

   d) Donec eris felix, multos numerabis amicos. 1,5 P

3. Bilde die Tempusreihe (Präsens, Imperfekt, Futur I, Perfekt, Plusquamperfekt, Futur II) von excedere in der 3. Person Plural Indikativ. 3 P

1. a) Bestimme zu den abgebildeten Graphen jeweils einen passenden Definitions- und Wertebereich! Gib auch an, ob es sich bei der zu Grunde liegenden Zuordnung um eine Funktion handelt oder nicht!

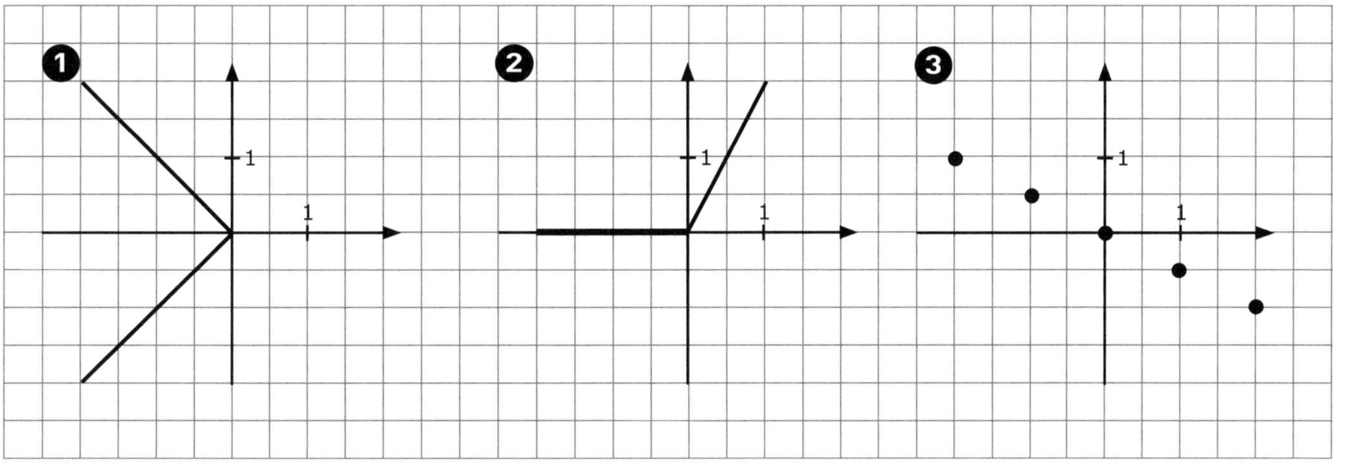

	1	2	3
Definitionsbereich			
Wertebereich			
Funktion			

9 P

b) Betrachte nun nur den Graphen der Zuordnung von Bild (3)! Gib die zu Grunde liegende Zuordnungsvorschrift an!

$x \mapsto$

2 P

c) Gib die Zuordnungsvorschrift einer Zuordnung an, die zu jedem **n**-ten Bruchteil eines Kreises (Halbkreis, Drittelkreis, Viertelkreis,…) den zugehörigen Mittelpunktswinkel zuordnet!

$n \mapsto$

3 P

d) Gib die Zuordnungsvorschrift einer Zuordnung an, die zu jedem Radius **r** eines Kreises den zugehörigen Flächeninhalt zuordnet!

$r \mapsto$

3 P

2. a) Gib für nebenstehende Graphen die Funktionsgleichungen der Geraden f und g an und berechne die Koordinaten ihres Schnittpunktes S!

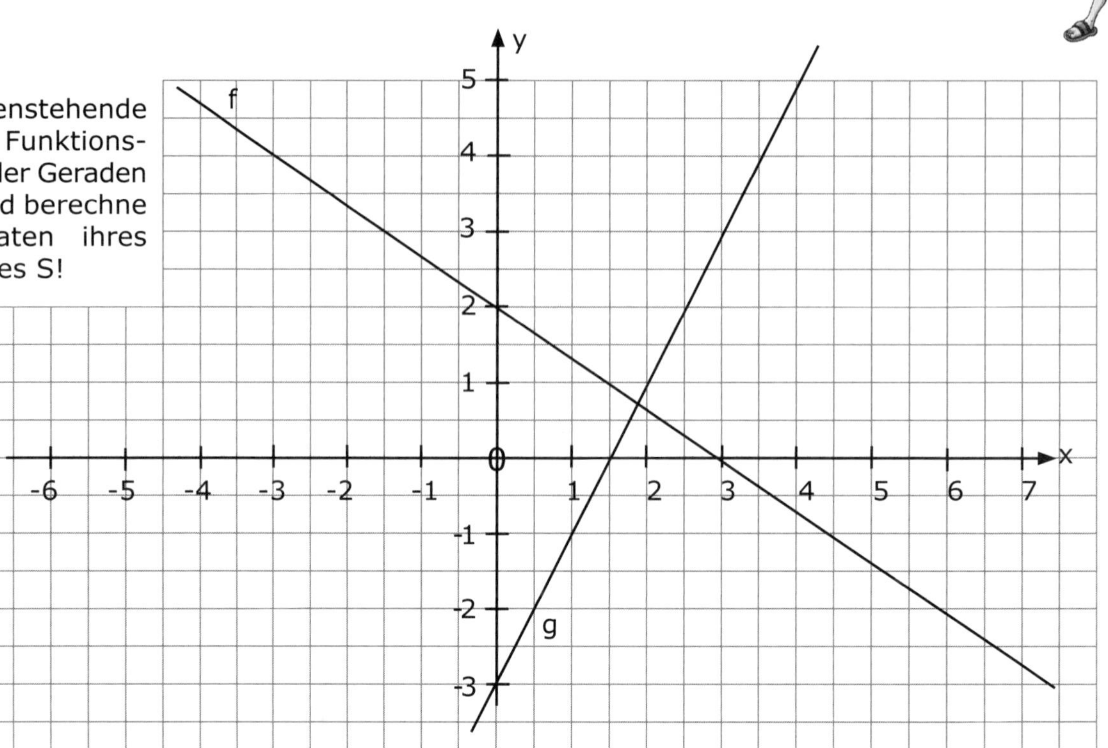

10 P

b) Zeichne in das Koordinatensystem die Punkte A(6|0) und B(5|3) sowie die Gerade h, gegeben durch die Gleichung $y = \frac{3}{4}x + 3$, ein! 4 P

c) Bestimme durch Rechnung die Gleichung der Geraden durch A und B!

5 P

d) Bestimme durch Rechnung, ob der Punkt P mit den Koordinaten (2|4,6) auf der Geraden h liegt!

4 P

1. a) Bei einem Zahnrad ist die Zahl der Zähne proportional zum Radius. Was bedeutet dieser Satz? 4 P

b) Zwei Zahnräder greifen ineinander. Wenn man das eine Zahnrad (Zahnrad 1) 5 mal dreht, so dreht sich das andere Zahnrad (Zahnrad 2) 13 mal. In welchem Verhältnis stehen die Radien der Zahnräder und welches ist größer? 3 P

2. a) Gib für nebenstehende Graphen die Funktionsgleichungen der Geraden f und g an und berechne die Koordinaten ihres Schnittpunktes S! 7 P

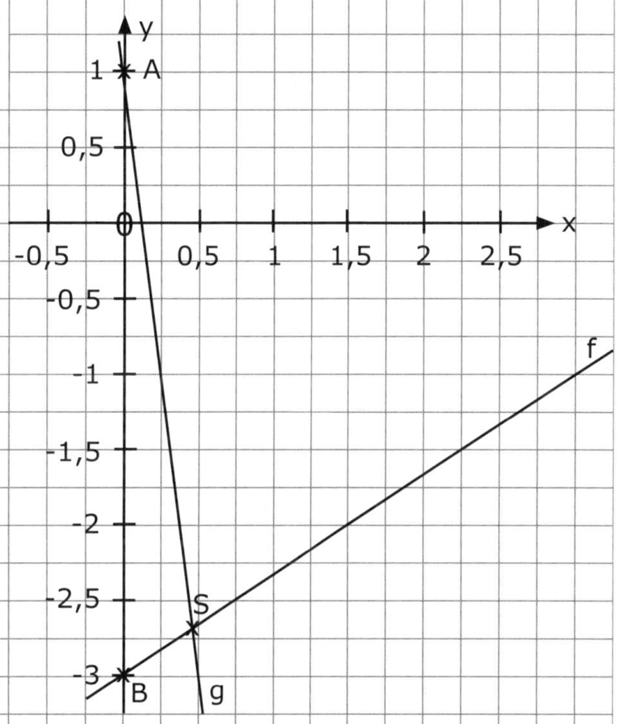

b) Berechne den Flächeninhalt des Dreiecks ABS! 5 P

c) Zeichne in das Koodinatensystem den Graphen der Funktion h: $y = -\frac{1}{4}x - 2$ ein! 5 P

d) Berechne den Flächeninhalt eines Kreises um den Punkt S, der die y - Achse berührt. 5 P

e) Bestimme durch Rechnung, ob der Punkt P (1|-2,24) auf der Geraden h liegt, darüber oder darunter!

5 P

f) Markiere im Koordinatensystem die Punktmenge, die alle drei Ungleichungen erfüllt!

$y \leq -\frac{1}{4}x - 2 \qquad y \geq \frac{2}{3}x - 3 \qquad y \geq -8x + 1$

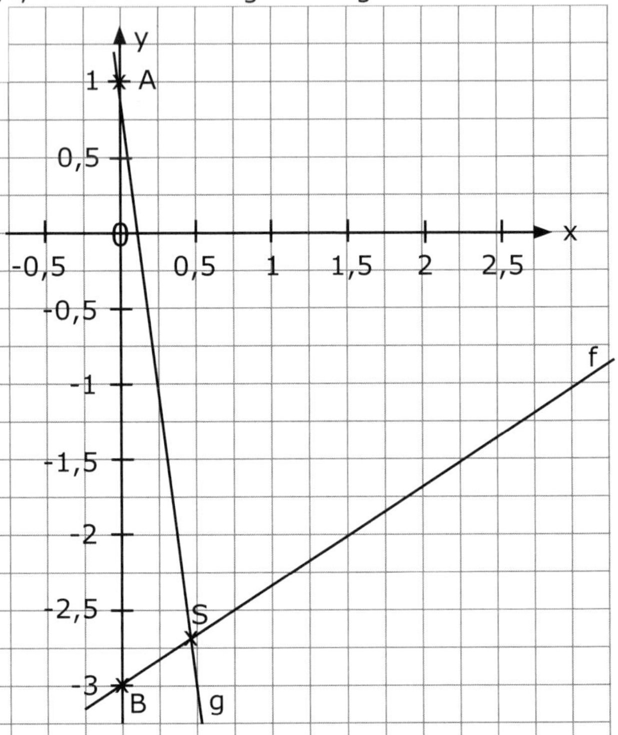

6 P

1. Gegeben ist das lineare Gleichungssystem:

   I. $5x + 2y = 3$
   II. $x + 4y = 16$

   Bestimme die Lösung rechnerisch mit dem Einsetzungsverfahren!

8 P

2. Bauer Maier hat zwei Arten Nutzvieh im Stall: Kühe und Gänse. Wenn am Morgen die Stalltür öffnet blicken ihn 200 Augen an. Die Tiere haben zusammen 322 Beine. Wie viele Kühe und wie viele Gänse hat der Bauer im Stall, wenn alle Tiere normalsichtig sind?

8 P

3. Bei einem Fußballspiel nimmt der Veranstalter 772.100 Euro ein. Das Spiel ist mit 56.255 zahlenden Zuschauern ausverkauft. Für einen Sitzplatz in Kategorie A bezahlt jeder Zuschauer mit Sitzplatz 20 Euro, für jeden Stehplatz der Kategorie B 12 Euro. Stelle ein Gleichungssystem auf, mit dessen Hilfe die Aufgabe gelöst werden kann. Die Lösung selbst ist nicht verlangt!

4 P

4. Löse graphisch: I. $x - y = 2$
II. $2x + 3y = 6$

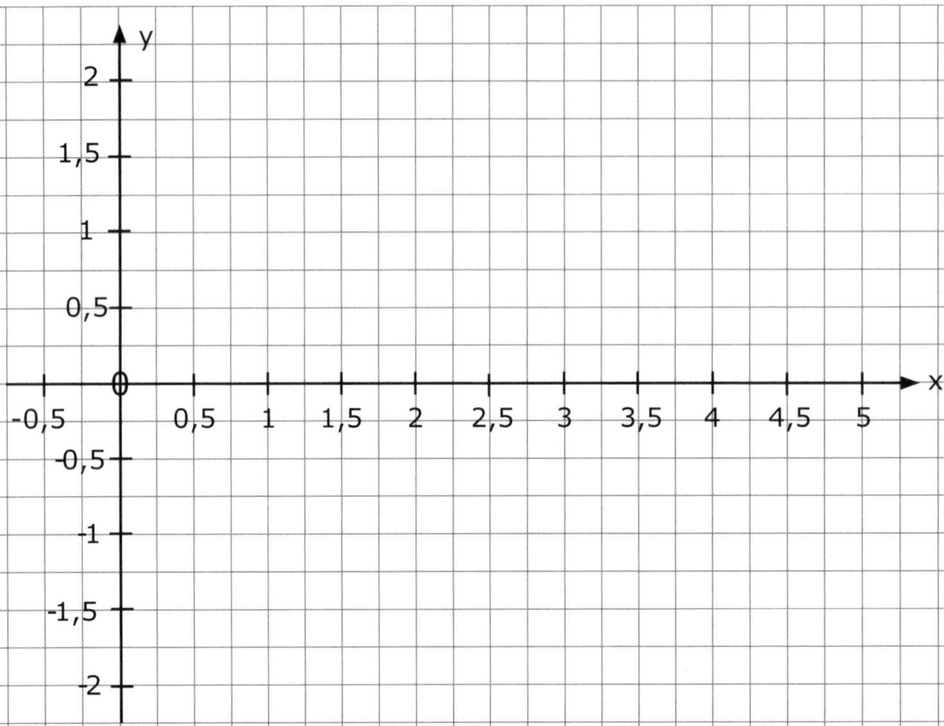

x =
y =

6 P

5. Gib für die folgenden Zufallsexperimente einen möglichst feinen Ergebnisraum Ω und seine Mächtigkeit $|\Omega|$ an!

a) Zwei Münzen und ein Würfel werden nacheinander geworfen. 5 P

b) Ein Zahlenschloss mit drei Rädern wird verstellt. 5 P

6. Gib bei folgenden Zufallsexperimenten an, ob LAPLACE-Annahmen gerechtfertigt sind oder nicht!

a) Es gibt 12 Monate. Also ist die Wahrscheinlichkeit, dass jemand im März Geburtstag hat 1/12.
☐ LAPLACE ☐ kein LAPLACE ☐ weiß nicht 1 P

b) Es gibt 7 Wochentage. Also ist die Wahrscheinlichkeit, dass eine zufällig ausgewählte Person an einem Sonntag Geburtstag hat 1/7.
☐ LAPLACE ☐ kein LAPLACE ☐ weiß nicht 1 P

c) Es gibt 7 Wochentage. Also ist die Wahrscheinlichkeit, dass der 1. Advent dieses Jahr auf einen Sonntag fällt 1/7.
☐ LAPLACE ☐ kein LAPLACE ☐ weiß nicht 1 P

d) Jeder Knopf hat zwei Seiten. Also ist die Wahrscheinlichkeit, dass er auf eine Seite fällt 50 %. 1 P
☐ LAPLACE ☐ kein LAPLACE ☐ weiß nicht

1. Löse mit Hilfe von Gleichungssystemen!

a) Eine zweistellige Zahl wird um 9 größer, wenn man ihre Ziffern vertauscht. Ihre Zehnerziffer ist halb so groß wie ihre Einerziffer. Wie lautet die Zahl?

8 P

b) Als Ergebnis einer Divisionsaufgabe erhält eine Grundschülerin 12 Rest 9. Ihre ältere Schwester aus der 6. Jahrgangsstufe erhält bei der gleichen Rechnung 12,75. Wie lautet die Aufgabe?

8 P

2. Frau Meier kauft Orangen und Äpfel. Sie bezahlt insgesamt 7,20 €. Ihre Nachbarin kauft 1 kg Orangen mehr, dafür 1 kg Äpfel weniger als Frau Meier und bezahlt 6,60 €.
Wie groß ist der Preisunterschied zwischen Orangen und Äpfeln?

8 P

3. Löse graphisch:

I. $x + y - 3 = 0$
II. $2y = -9 - x$

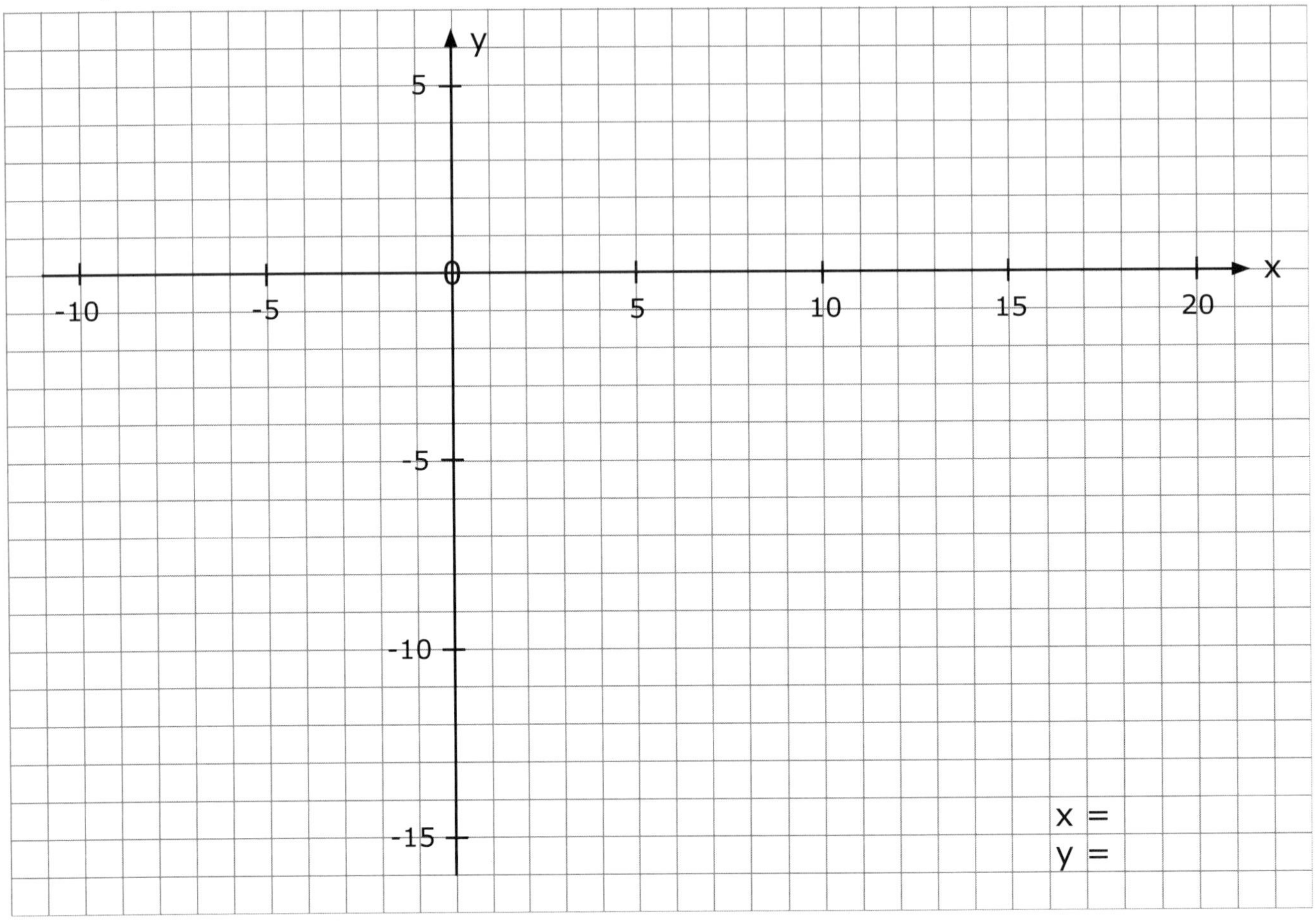

8 P

4. Mit welcher Wahrscheinlichkeit ist eine 5-stellige Zahl

a) gerade:

4 P

b) durch 5 teilbar:

4 P

1. Löse folgende Sachaufgabe: Ein Löwe, eine Hyäne und ein Geier fressen ein Zebra. Würde der Löwe allein am Zebra fressen, so würde er 2 Stunden benötigen, um es ganz aufzufressen, die Hyäne 4 Stunden und der Geier 6 Stunden. Wie lange benötigen die drei Tiere, wenn sie gemeinsam das Zebra verspeisen? (Ansatz und Rechnung, Ergebnis in Minuten)

8 P

2. Löse folgende Gleichungen mit mehreren Variablen jeweils nach der in den eckigen Klammern angegebenen Variablen auf!

a) $W = U \bullet I \bullet t$ [I]   b) $\frac{b + g}{b \bullet g} = \frac{1}{f}$ [g]   c) $(r + h) \bullet r = M$ [h]   11 P

3. Bestimme Definitions- und Lösungsmenge der folgenden Gleichung!

$$x - 2 - \frac{4}{x - 2} = x \bullet \frac{x - 4}{x - 2}$$

7 P

4. In untenstehender Abbildung (nicht maßstabsgetreu) gilt: AB||CD.

a) Berechne x, y und z!

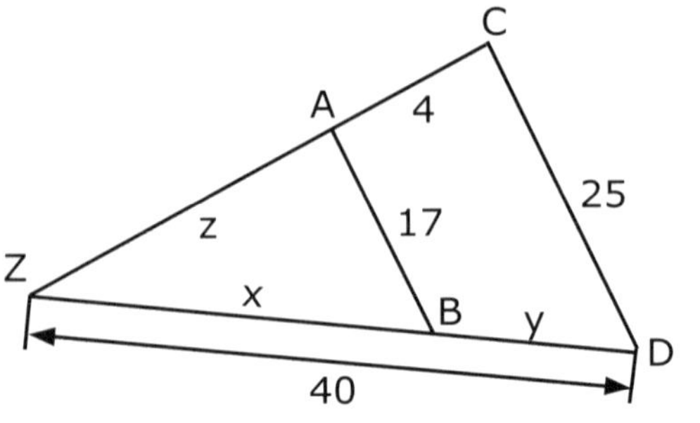

8 P

b) Angenommen das Dreieck AZB hat den Flächeninhalt 25.
Welchen Flächeninhalt hat dann das Dreieck CZD?

6 P

1. Herr Müller muss geschäftlich nach Hamburg. 600 km kann er über Autobahn zurücklegen, die restlichen 180 km benutzt er Landstraßen. Hier kommt er nur halb so schnell voran, wie auf der Autobahn. Mit welcher Durchschnittsgeschwindigkeit muss Herr Müller die Autobahnen befahren, wenn er in 8,5 h in Hamburg sein will?

8 P

2. Löse folgende Gleichungen mit mehreren Variablen jeweils nach der in den eckigen Klammern angegebenen Variablen auf!

a) $s = \frac{a}{1 - q}$ [q] b) $z = \frac{1}{x} - \frac{1}{y}$ [y] c) $\frac{u - v}{uv} = w$ [v]

a) 3 P

b) 5 P

c) 3 P

3. Bestimme Definitions- und Lösungsmenge der folgenden Gleichung!

$$\frac{2}{x} = \frac{1}{x - 1} + \frac{1}{x + 2}$$

7 P

4. In untenstehender Abbildung gilt: AB||DE. Die Strecke [BD] ist 7,69 LE lang.

a) Berechne $\overline{AZ}$, $\overline{ZB}$ und $\overline{ZD}$
(Zwischenergebnisse auf 2 Dezimalen runden)!

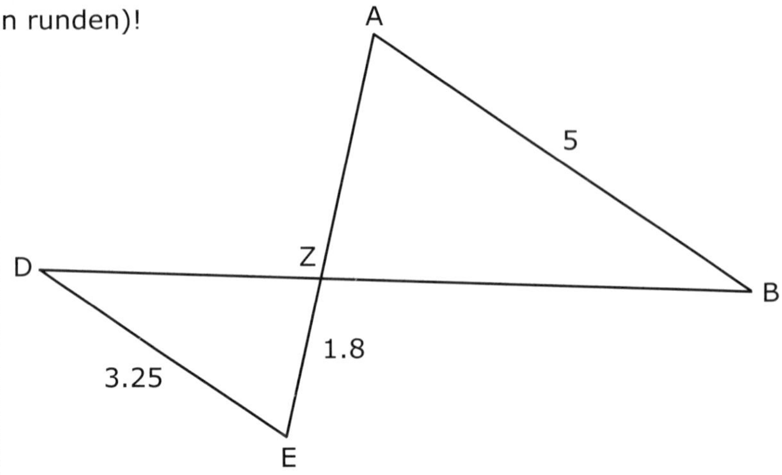

8 P

b) Angenommen das Dreieck AZB hat den Flächeninhalt 6,53 FE.
Welchen Flächeninhalt (auf 2 Dezimalen gerundet) hat dann das Dreieck EZD?

6 P

MATHEMATIK

Stegreifaufgabe 1

✓ 20 / ⌛ 20 / 📖 54

1. An einer Tankstelle tanken nacheinander 6 Fahrzeuge an der gleichen Zapfsäule Diesel.

   a) Vervollständige die nachfolgende Wertetabelle! Runde auf ganze Liter bzw. ganze Euro!

Menge in l	55		47		80
Kosten in €	60	77		80	

6 P

   b) Berechne aus dem ersten Wertepaar den Dieselpreis in Euro auf zwei Nachkommastellen genau!

3 P

2. Die Zapfsäulen aller Tankstellen eines Mineralölkonzerns in Bayern sollen gewartet werden. Dafür stehen 45 Techniker zur Verfügung, die jeweils 8 Stunden am Tag arbeiten.

   a) Wie lange dauert die Wartung insgesamt, wenn ein Techniker im Mittel am Tag 8 Zapfsäulen schafft und es in Bayern 15.000 Zapfsäulen gibt? (Ergebnis auf ganze Tage genau!)

5 P

   b) Wie lange dauert die Wartung insgesamt, wenn nach zwei Arbeitstagen 5 der Techniker krank werden? (Ergebnis auf ganze Tage genau!)

6 P

1. Zeichne die Graphen der folgenden linearen Funktionen in das Koordinatensystem ein!

a) $y = 2x - 1$

b) $3y + 2x = -3$

c) $y = -\frac{2}{3}x + \frac{7}{2}$

d) $y = \frac{7}{8}x - 2$

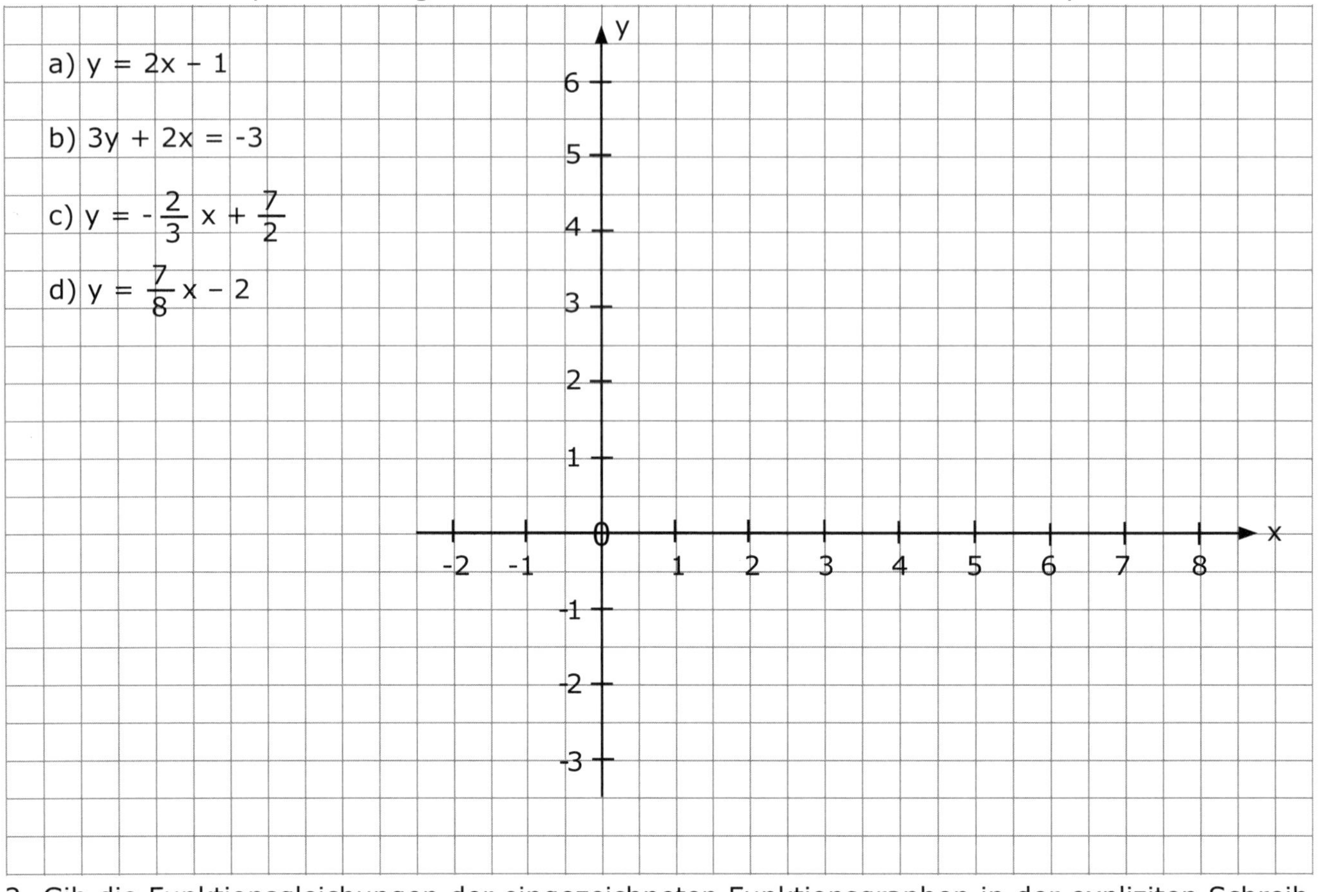

10 P

2. Gib die Funktionsgleichungen der eingezeichneten Funktionsgraphen in der expliziten Schreibweise an!

a) f (x) =

b) g (x) =

c) h (x) =

d) i (x) =

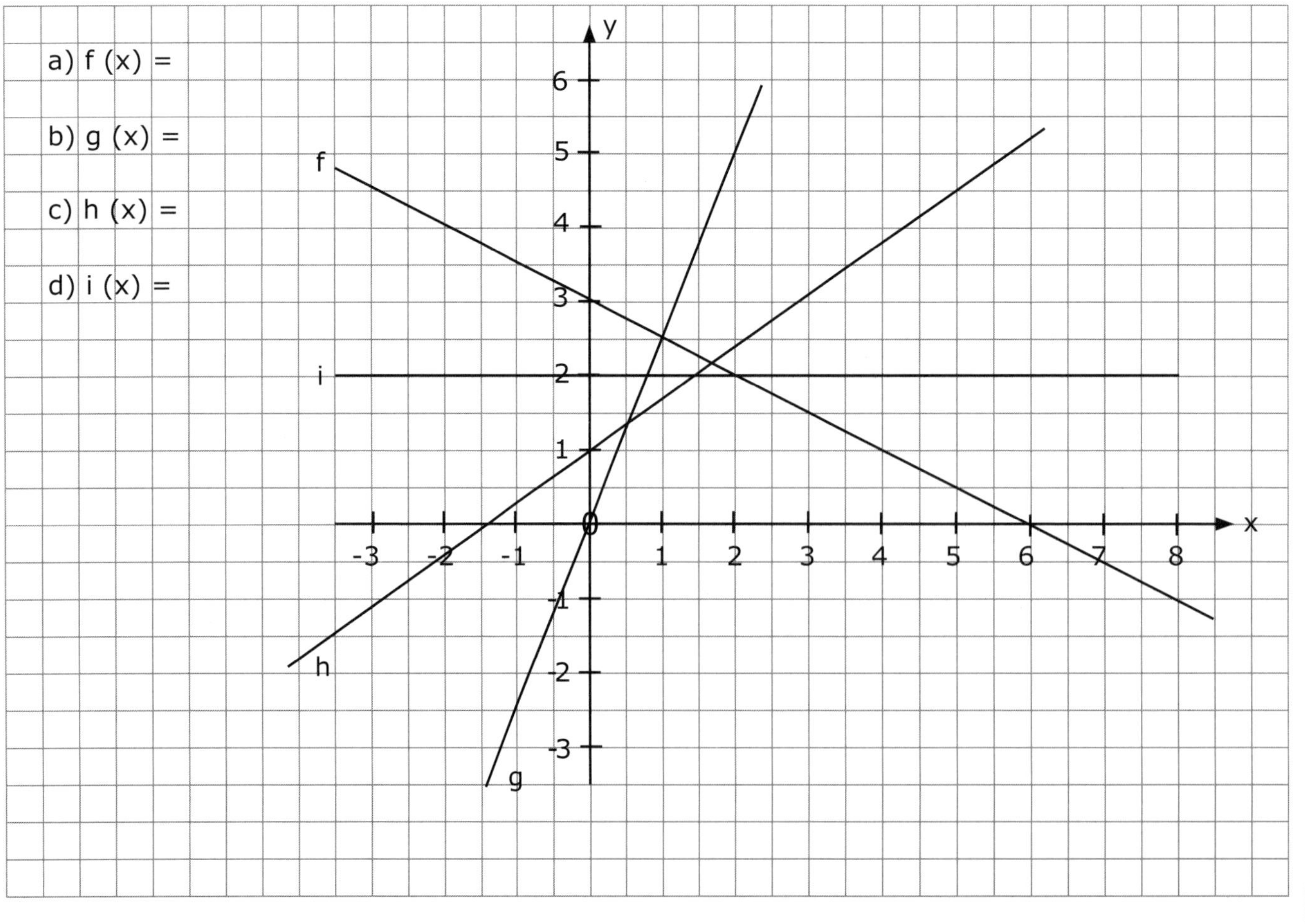

10 P

Stegreifaufgabe 3

✓ 20 / ⧗ 20 / 📖 55/56

1. In einem mitteleuropäischen Land wird eine Studie zur Leistungsfähigkeit 11-jähriger Schüler (im Folgenden kurz „Schüler" genannt) an 1.000 Schülern durchgeführt. Dabei stellt sich heraus:

   (1) Nur 30 % der (getesteten) Schüler erfassen beim Lesen eines Textes dessen Sinn **(S).**
   (2) Von den Schülern unter (1) haben immerhin 70 % Problemlösekompetenz **(P).**
   (3) Unter den (getesteten) Schülern mit Verständnisschwierigkeiten beim Lesen findet man nur 20 % mit Problemlösekompetenz.

   a) Fülle die folgende Vierfeldertafel vollständig und korrekt aus!

	P	$\overline{P}$	
S		0,09	
$\overline{S}$		0,50	0,70
	0,41	0,59	1,00

9 P

   b) Wie viele Schüler haben insgesamt Problemlösekompetenz!

4 P

   c) Welcher Anteil der Schüler hat keine Problemlösekompetenz und kann trotzdem sinnerfassend lesen?

3 P

   d) Einer der getesteten Schüler wird durch einen Zufallsmechanismus „rein zufällig" ausgewählt. Wie groß ist die Wahrscheinlichkeit, dass er sinnerfassend lesen oder Probleme lösen kann? (mathematische Formulierung und Lösung!)

4 P

Stegreifaufgabe 4

✓ 20 / ⧗ 20 / 📖 56

1. Gib den Definitionsbereich folgender Bruchterme an!

   a) $\frac{1}{x + 3}$ b) $\frac{7x}{5x + 4}$ c) $\frac{a}{a^2 + 4}$ d) $\frac{x}{8x^3 - 24x^2}$

7 P

2. Vereinfache folgende Bruchterme!

   a) $\frac{27x + 18}{12 + 18x} =$ 4 P

   b) $\frac{(2x - 6)(x-2)}{x^2 - 9} =$ 4 P

   c) $\frac{15\,x^2 + 60x + 60}{5x + 10} =$ 5 P

1. Welcher der folgenden Brüche hat den kleinsten Wert?

a) $\frac{7}{8}$ b) $\frac{66}{77}$ c) $\frac{555}{666}$ d) $\frac{4444}{5555}$ e) $\frac{3333}{4444}$

2. Zwei Zahnräder greifen ineinander. Der Radius des großen Zahnrades ist 3 mal so groß wie der des kleinen. Wie oft und in welche Richtung hat sich das kleine Zahnrad gedreht, wenn sich das große einmal linksherum gedreht hat?

3. Eine Tüte Äpfel kostet 2 Euro, eine Tüte Pfirsiche 3 Euro und eine Packung Pflaumen 4 Euro. Für einen Wandertag werden 8 Packungen für insgesamt 23 Euro gekauft. Welches ist die größtmögliche Zahl an Pflaumenpackungen dieses Einkaufs?

4. In einer Zoohandlung kann man Mäuse kaufen: Ein Viertel der angebotenen Mäuse ist weiß, der Rest schwarz. Von den weißen Mäusen hat die Hälfte blaue Augen, von den schwarzen Mäusen ein Fünftel. Alle Mäuse haben entweder blaue oder braune Augen. Steffi zählt alle Mäuse mit blauen Augen: 99. Steffi weiß nun, wie viele Mäuse es insgesamt in der Zoohandlung gibt. Und Du?

5. In Kanada spricht ein Teil der Bevölkerung nur Englisch, ein Teil der Bevölkerung nur Französisch. Es ist bekannt, dass 83% englisch und 71% französisch sprechen. Welcher Mindestanteil der Bevölkerung spricht beide Sprachen?

6. Bei einem Wandertag kommt eine Klasse an einem Eisstand mit 8 unterschiedlichen Eissorten vorbei. Der Klassensprecher sagt zur Verkäuferin: „Wir hätten gerne pro Person zwei unterschiedliche Sorten Eis und jeder Schüler soll eine andere Tüte bekommen, als die anderen.“ Darauf entgegnet die Verkäuferin: „Das würde ich gerne machen, aber dafür seid ihr einer zu viel in der Klasse.“ Wie groß ist die Klassenstärke? a) 22 b) 28 c) 35 d) 29 e) 31

1. Aus einem Quader wurde an einer Ecke ein Würfel herausgeschnitten (vergleiche nebenstehende Abbildung). Berechne das Volumen des Restkörpers!

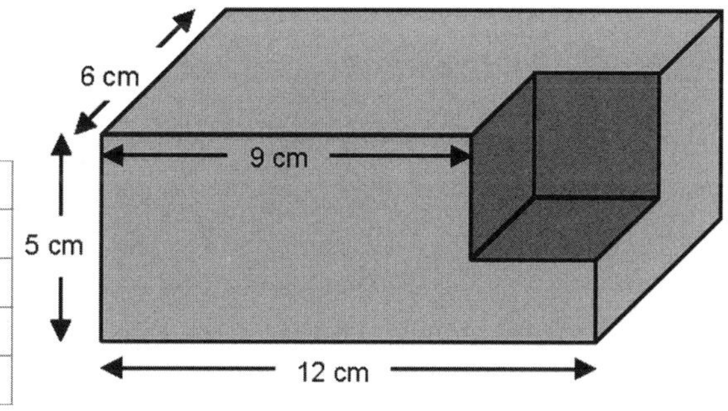

2 P

2. Nebenstehende Tabelle zeigt, wie viele Euro-Geldscheine am 31. Mai 2007 in Umlauf waren. Beispielsweise befanden sich von den 200 €-Scheinen 153 Millionen Stück in Umlauf.

Wert	Anzahl der Scheine in Millionen
500 €	429
200 €	153
100 €	1116
50 €	3983
20 €	2244
10 €	1804
5 €	1325

a) Wie hoch war der Gesamtwert aller 50 €-Scheine?

- ☐ ca. 200 000 Euro
- ☐ ca. 2 Milliarden Euro
- ☐ ca. 20 Milliarden Euro
- ☐ ca. 200 Milliarden Euro
- ☐ ca. 2 Billionen Euro

1 P

b) Ungefähr wie viel Prozent aller in Umlauf befindlichen Scheine waren 20 €-Scheine? Die notwendigen Rechnungen brauchen nicht exakt ausgeführt zu werden, es genügt jeweils ein Überschlag. Der Lösungsweg muss nachvollziehbar sein!

2 P

3. a) Bestimme die Lösung der Gleichung $12 - 6 \cdot \left(\frac{1}{3}x + 3\right) = 4x$!

2 P

b) Durch welche Zahl muss in obiger Gleichung die Zahl 12 ersetzt werden, damit $x = 0$ Lösung der neuen Gleichung ist?

1 P

4. Im Rahmen des Verkehrsunterrichts wurden die Fahrräder der Unterstufenschüler überprüft. Die einzelnen Mängel wurden in folgender Liste zusammengefasst:

- mangelhafte Beleuchtung an jedem 6. Fahrrad
- mangelhafte Bremsen an 15 % der Fahrräder
- mangelhafte Reifen an $\frac{1}{5}$ der Fahrräder

a) Welcher Mangel wurde am häufigsten festgestellt? Begründe deine Antwort durch einen Größenvergleich der in der Liste genannten Anteile!

1 P

b) Peter schaut sich die obige Liste mit den Ergebnissen der Überprüfung an, rechnet kurz und sagt dann: „Nach dieser Liste sind mehr als 50 % aller untersuchten Fahrräder mangelhaft." Begründe, dass Peter nicht unbedingt Recht hat!

1 P

5. Die Summe der Innenwinkel in einem n-Eck beträgt $(n - 2) \cdot 180°$.

a) Wie viele Ecken hat ein n-Eck mit der Innenwinkelsumme 720°?

1 P

b) Ein n-Eck mit lauter gleich langen Seiten und gleich großen Innenwinkeln heißt reguläres n-Eck. Berechne die Größe eines Innenwinkels im regulären Zehneck!

1 P

6. a) Von einer Raute sind die Diagonalenlängen e und f bekannt. Überlege, wie man daraus den Flächeninhalt der Raute ermitteln kann und gib eine entsprechende Formel an!

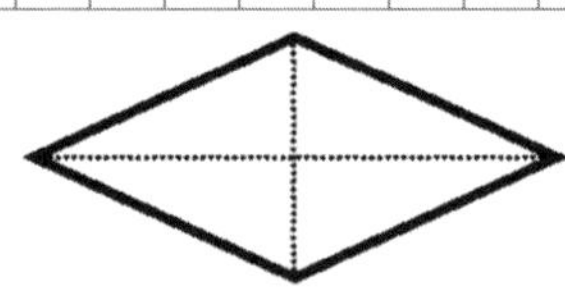

Raute

1 P

b) Konstruiere nur mit Zirkel und Lineal eine Raute, bei der ein Innenwinkel 60° beträgt!

2 P

7. Berechne den Wert des Terms 0,1 • (2,4 : 0,6)!

1 P

8. a) Gib zwei Zahlen mit verschiedenen Vorzeichen an, so dass auf der Zahlengeraden die Zahl 20 in der Mitte zwischen diesen beiden Zahlen liegt!

1 P

b) Bestimme den Mittelwert der Zahlen $\frac{1}{3}$ und $\frac{1}{2}$!

1 P

9. Die Nationalfahne der Schweiz zeigt ein weißes Kreuz auf rotem Grund. Für die vier kongruenten Arme des Kreuzes ist durch Beschluss der Schweizer Bundesversammlung aus dem Jahr 1889 festgelegt: Die Länge ℓ eines Arms ist um $\frac{1}{6}$ der Breite b größer als b (vergleiche nebenstehende Abbildung!).

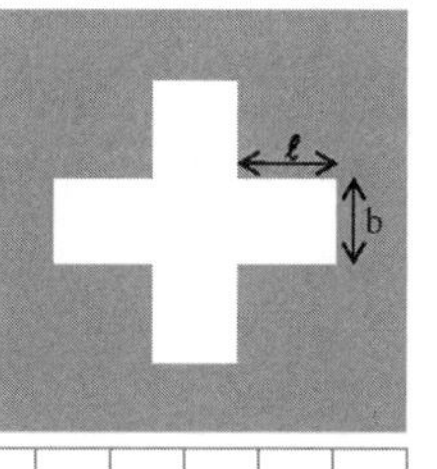

a) Wie lang ist ein Arm, wenn seine Breite 18 cm beträgt?

1 P

b) Stelle einen Term auf, der den Flächeninhalt des weißen Kreuzes in Abhängigkeit von der Breite b eines Arms beschreibt. Fasse den Term, in dem nur noch b als Variable vorkommen soll, so weit wie möglich zusammen!

2 P

1. Ein Gummiball prallt zur Zeit t=0 vom Boden ab. Das dargestellte Diagramm zeigt den Bewegungsablauf eines Gummiballs im folgenden. Die Rechtswertachse ist die Zeit in Sekunden, die Hochwertachse die Energie in Joule. Dargestellt ist der Graph der potentiellen Energie.

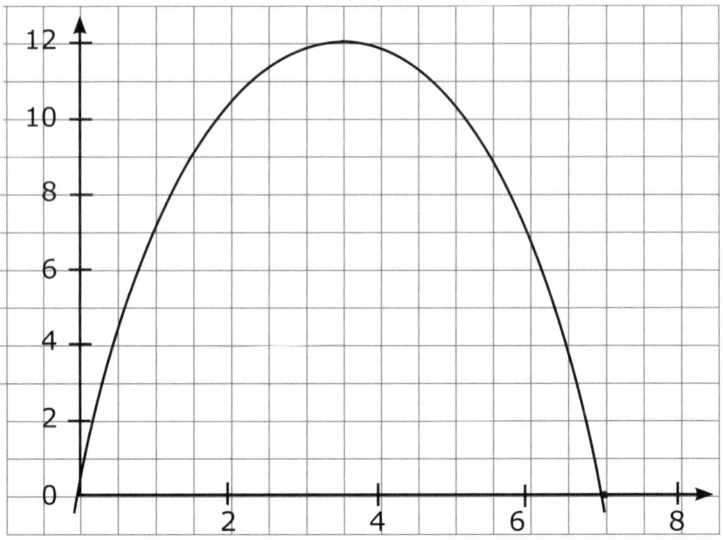

a) Beschreibe allgemein die auftretenden Energieumwandlungen und gib an, wenn Maximalwerte erreicht sind. 5 P

b) Zeichne den Graphen für die kinetische Energie in das Diagramm ein, wenn keine andere Energieform beteiligt ist. 5 P

c) Welche Höhe über dem Boden erreicht der Ball, wenn seine Masse 400 Gramm beträgt? 4 P

d) Welche Geschwindigkeit hat der Ball beim Aufprall? 5 P

e) Peter ergänzt das Diagramm, indem er den gleichen Graphen nach rechts verschoben nochmals zeichnet. Warum kann man es sich in der Realität nicht so einfach machen? 7 P

2. Beim Verladen von Kraftfahrzeugen zieht ein Hafenkran einen PKW der Masse m = 1,45 t hoch. Dabei bewegt sich der PKW mit einer Geschwindigkeit von 7,50 km/h aufwärts um eine Gesamtstrecke von 8,0 m.

a) Berechne die Gewichtskraft des PKW! 3 P

b) Berechne die Hubleistung des Elektromotors des Krans! 3 P

Schulaufgabe 1 A ✓ 40 / ⧗ 45 / 📖 60

c) Berechne wie groß die Energie ist, die man dem Kran zuführen muss, um den PKW anzuheben, wenn der Elektromotor einen Wirkungsgrad von 80 % besitzt!

4 P

d) Der Kran verwendet nun einen Kraftwandler zum Anheben des PKW. Wie wirkt ein Kraftwandler? Um wie viel verlängert sich der Zugweg, wenn zum Anheben nun eine Kraft von 500 N erforderlich ist?

5 P

Schulaufgabe 1 B ✓ 40 / ⧗ 45 / 📖 61

1. Ein Springfrosch (m=25,0 g) wird mit einem Saugnapf unter Spannen einer Feder an einer Tischkante befestigt. Nach kurzer Zeit springt er in die Höhe, weil der Saugnapf nicht mehr hält. Seine Flugbahn ist etwas seitlich, so dass er beim Herabfallen die Tischkante verfehlt und bis zum Boden fällt.

a) Beschreibe allgemein die auftretenden Energieumwandlungen und gib an, wenn Maximalwerte erreicht sind!

8 P

b) Die Feder (D=450 N/m) wird vor dem Start um 3,50 cm eingedrückt.
Berechne die Spannenergie!

3 P

c) Welche Höhe über dem Tisch erreicht der Frosch?

4 P

d) Welche Geschwindigkeit hat der Frosch zu Beginn des Abhebens?

5 P

e) Die Tischkante ist 0,865 m über dem Fußboden.
Welche Gesamtenergie hat der Frosch im Moment des Aufpralls?

3 P

Vergleiche die Ergebnisse von b) und e)! Woher kommt die zusätzliche Energie?
Warum ist der Energieerhaltungssatz nicht verletzt?

3 P

2. Der Bergsteiger Sepp Kraxelmaxl, der einschließlich seiner Ausrüstung eine Masse von 90,0 kg hat, besteigt von der Höllentalanger-Hütte (1379 m) aus in 4,00 Stunden die Zugspitze (2963 m).

a) Welche Hubarbeit verrichtet er (in MJ) und wie groß ist seine Leistung?

5 P

b) Durchschnittliche Bergwanderer erbringen bei „normaler Anstrengung" eine Hubleistung von 75,0 W. Welche Hubarbeit verrichten sie dann in einer Stunde?

3 P

c) Welcher Höhenunterschied ergibt sich aus b) für einen durchschnittlichen Bergwanderer (Masse 90,0 kg inklusive Gepäck), den er in einer Stunde bewältigt?

3 P

d) Fred Gemütlich wandert von der Höllentalanger-Hütte ebenfalls zur Zugspitze. Allerdings benützt er einen wesentlich flacheren (und doppelt so weiten) Weg als Kraxelmaxl. Auf Grund welchen Prinzips verrichtet Fred die gleiche Hubarbeit wie Sepp?
Nenne das Prinzip und formuliere es!

3 P

1. a) Was bedeutet es für die Teilchen eines Körpers, wenn seine Temperatur erniedrigt wird. Wie weit kann man einen Körper abkühlen?

4 P

b) Welche Nachteile hätte Wasser als Thermometerflüssigkeit? Erkläre in diesem Zusammenhang auch, was man unter der Anomalie des Wassers versteht.

4 P

c) Warum benutzt man zum Braten Öl und nicht Wasser? Kreuze das Richtige an:

☒ Öl hat eine kleinere Wärmekapazität und wird deshalb schneller heiß.
☐ Öl hat eine höhere Siedetemperatur und wird deshalb heißer.
☒ Die Wärmeleitfähigkeit von Öl ist besser.
☐ Öl hat ein besseres Kriechvermögen und dringt besser in das Fleisch ein.
☐ Öl ist gesünder als Wasser.

2 P

d) Eine Stahlniete, die zwei Bleche verbindet, besitzt bei einer Temperatur von 20° C eine Länge von 8,46 mm. Sie wird bei einer Temperatur von 600° C eingelegt. Um wie viel zieht sie sich beim Abkühlen dann zusammen? ($\alpha_{Stahl} = 1{,}1 \cdot 10^{-5}\,\frac{1}{K}$)

4 P

e) Welche Anfangstemperatur hatte eine glühende Kupferkugel von der Masse 63,0 g, die, in 300 g Wasser von 18,0° C geworfen, dieses auf 37,0° C erwärmt? ($c_{Kupfer} = 0{,}39\,\frac{kJ}{kg \cdot K}$)

6 P

2. In der dargestellten Schaltung ist $R_1 = 25\ \Omega$, $R_2 = 17\ \Omega$ und $R_3 = 32\ \Omega$. Es liegt eine Gesamtspannung von 12 V an.

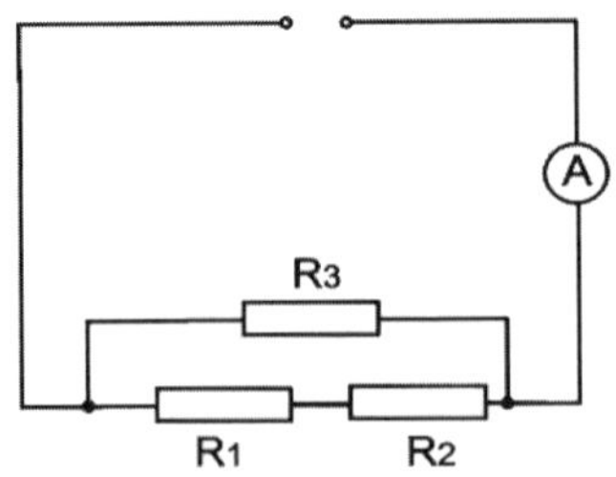

a) Berechne den Ersatzwiderstand der gesamten Schaltung!

4 P

b) Welche Stärke hat der elektrische Strom, der durch das Messgerät fließt? Welche Stärke hat der Strom durch den Widerstand R_3?

6 P

c) In einer Küche soll ein Mikrowellengerät mit 800 W und eine Kochplatte mit 2 kW gleichzeitig betrieben werden. Die Sicherung in diesem Stromkreis trägt die Aufschrift: „10 A".
Wird die Sicherung den Stromkreis unterbrechen?

5 P

d) Ein Vertreter bietet deiner Familie einen elektrischen Durchlauferhitzer an, der 8,0 l heißes Wasser (das um 45° C erwärmt wurde) pro Minute liefern soll. Der Hauptvorteil sei, dass „... Sie nicht einmal Ihre 10-A-Sicherung auswechseln brauchen!"
Empfiehlst du deinen Eltern den Kauf oder werft ihr den Kerl gemeinsam hinaus?
(Beides mit physikalischer Begründung und Rechnung!)

5 P

1. a) Skizziere den Aufbau eines Flüssigkeitsthermometers!

6 P

b) Was kann man bei einem Flüssigkeitsthermometer alles verändern, damit die Steighöhe der Flüssigkeitssäule bei einer bestimmten Temperaturänderung möglichst groß wird?

3 P

c) Was versteht man unter Normpunkten und wo liegen sie bei der Celsius-Skala und bei der Kelvin-Skala?

6 P

2. In eine Bleiplatte ist ein elektrisches Thermometer eingelassen. Nun schlägt man mit einem Hammer auf die Bleiplatte. Was wird zu beobachten sein? Beziehe Dich in deiner Erklärung auf die Begriffe „Innere Energie" und „Arbeit"!

5 P

3. a) Welche Arten des Energietransports sind beteiligt, wenn man eine Flüssigkeit in einem Kochtopf auf einem Elektroherd erwärmt? Unterscheide zwischen Transport von Herd zu Topf und innerhalb der Flüssigkeit.

4 P

b) Warum deckt man den Kochtopf mit einem Deckel zu? Präzise physikalische Erklärung unter Verwendung von Fachbegriffen!

3 P

4. a) Die folgenden vier Bilder sind in der falschen Reihenfolge abgedruckt. Schreibe unter jedes Bild den Namen des entsprechenden Taktes und bringe in die richtige Reihenfolge:

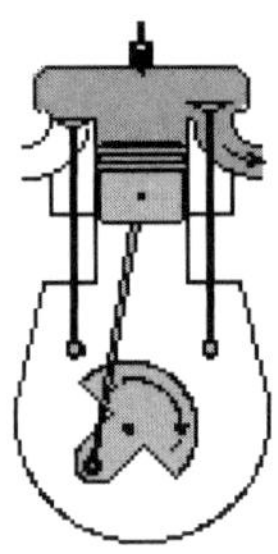	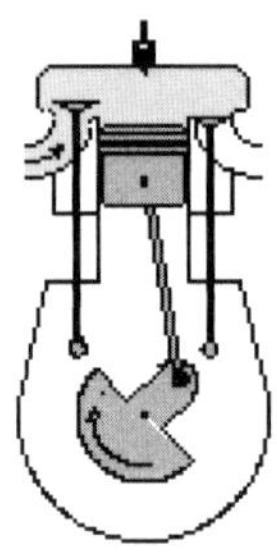	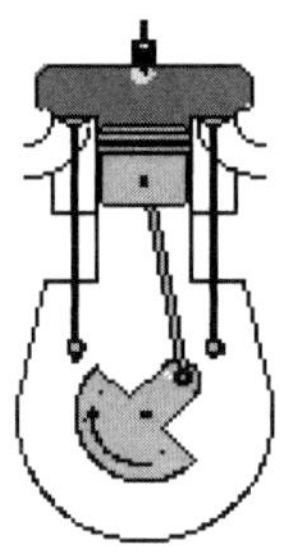	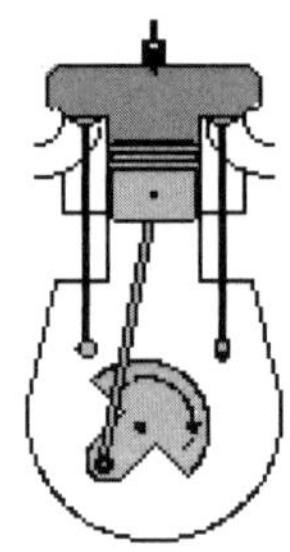

8 P

b) Was ist der prinzipielle Unterschied zwischen einem Otto- und einem Dieselmotor?

2 P

c) „Der Wirkungsgrad eines Ottomotors beträgt in etwa 40 %". Was bedeutet diese Aussage?

3 P

Stegreifaufgabe 1

✓ 20 / ⧗ 20 / 📖 65

1. Die Pferdestärke (engl. horsepower) ist eine veraltete, besonders in der Technik bis Ende 1977 üblich gewesene Einheit. Gegenwärtig darf in der Automobilwerbung PS nur als Zusatzangabe zur Leistungsangabe in der SI-Einheit aufgeführt werden.

   a) Von welcher **physikalischen Größe** war die Pferdestärke eine Einheit? Wie lautet die **heutzutage** übliche Einheit dieser Größe? Mit welcher Größe wurde das PS aufgrund des Namens häufig **falsch** in Verbindung gebracht?

   3 P

   b) 1 PS ist definiert als die Leistung, die erbracht werden muss, um eine Masse m = 75,0 kg entgegen des Schwerkraftfeldes auf der Erde (bei Erdbeschleunigung 9,81 m/s²) mit einer Geschwindigkeit von 1,00 m/s zu bewegen. Berechne den Wert von 1 PS in der heutzutage gebräuchlichen Einheit!

   5 P

2. a) Welche Leistung in kW muss der Motor einer Hebebühne zum Anheben von Kraftfahrzeugen haben, wenn eine Last mit der Gewichtskraft 12 kN in der Zeit t = 15 s um 1,75 m angehoben werden soll?

   6 P

   b) Der Motor einer Seilwinde leistet 8,0 kW. Welche Masse kann mit dieser Seilwinde in 1,5 Minuten um 30 m gehoben werden?

   6 P

1. Verzweigter-, unverzweigter Stromkreis

	Parallelschaltung	Reihenschaltung
Skizze		
Spannung		
Stromstärke		
Widerstand		
technische Anwendung		

10 P

2. a) Berechne den Gesamtwiderstand der Schaltung!

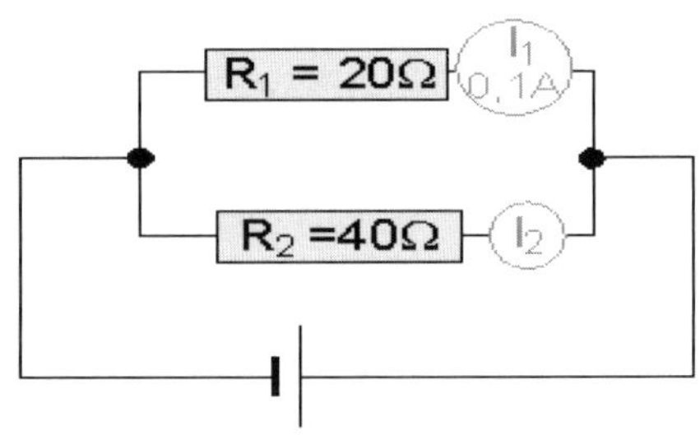

3 P

b) Berechne die Spannung am Widerstand R_1!

2 P

c) Berechne die Stromstärke durch den Widerstand R_2!

3 P

d) Berechne die Gesamtspannung U!

2 P

1. In den Pressluftflaschen von Tauchern herrscht ein hoher Druck

a) Der Inhalt der Flasche steht etwa unter einem Druck von 20 MPa.
Berechne die Kraft, die von Innen auf die 3,80 dm^2 große Bodenfläche wirkt.

3 P

b) Wie groß ist die Kraft, die der Schweredruck des Wassers in 30 m Tauchtiefe auf den Boden ausübt?

3 P

c) Erkläre, warum auch Cola-Flaschen aus Glas gefährlich sein können, wenn sie geschüttelt werden oder lange in der Sonne stehen?

2 P

2. a) Schiffe sind meistens aus Stahl (ρ = 7,8 g/cm^3). Ein Quader aus Stahl geht in Wasser sofort unter. Warum schwimmen jedoch die Schiffe trotzdem?
Wie lautet das Prinzip von Archimedes?

3 P

b) Ein Mann hat die Masse 70,0 kg und ein Köpervolumen von von 71,5 dm^3 wenn er voll eingeatmet hat. Warum kann dieser Mann im Süßwasser nicht auf dem Wasser liegen (wie im Toten Meer), sondern muss Schwimmbewegungen machen?

4 P

c) Wie viel Prozent des Körpervolumens ragen bei einem Eisberg aus dem Wasser, wenn die Dichte von Eis 920 kg/m^3 beträgt?

5 P

I. Übersetzung: Olympia (68 LW)

1. Temporibus antiquis iuvenes fortissimi undique Olympiam proficiscebantur, ut in illo loco sanctissimo de victoria certarent.

2. Homines aedificia clarissima Olympiae admirabantur, imprimis eam aedem, quam Graeci ad maiorem gloriam Iovis moliti erant.

3. Athletae inter se acerrime contendentes labores maximos subibant et summo studio vincere conabantur.

4. Qui magnam gloriam peperisse et praemia ampla meruisse traduntur.

5. Hodie quoque nobis certi athletae summae admirationi sunt, cum fortius ac melius aliis viris pugnent.

II. Aufgabenteil

1. Übersetze folgende Formen!

a) arbitrabuntur

b) secutus erat 2 P

c) irascitur

d) verebatur 2 P

2. Setze das Wort in die angegebene Form!

a) celerem > Superlativ

b) malus > Komparativ 2 P

c) acer > Komparativ

d) vehementer > Superlativ 2 P

3. Fragen zu Olympia

   a) Von wem stammt die berühmte Statue des Zeus-Tempels in Olympia? ____________________ 1 P

   b) Welcher Schriftsteller beschreibt authentisch die Olympischen Spiele der Antike? __________ 1 P

   c) Was versteht man unter dem Begriff „Ekecheiria"?

   ____ 1 P

   d) Wer hat Ende des 19. Jahrhunderts maßgeblich zur Wiedereinführung der Olympischen Spiele beigetragen?

   ____ 1 P

4. Fragen zu Archimedes:

   a) Was bedeutet der berühmte Ausspruch „Heureka"? ____________________ 1 P

   b) Nenne **eine** Entdeckung und **eine** Erfindung des Archimedes!

   ____ 2 P

✓ 15 / ⧗ 45 / 📖 69 **Schulaufgabe 2** cursus Kap. 40 - 42

I. Übersetzung: „Bruderzwist ..." (72 LW)

1. Cum scelera immania detecta[1] essent, Oedipus Thebis excedens filiis imperavit:

   ____

   ____

2. „Eteocles regnum prior teneat, anno post Polynices rex sit!

   ____

   ____

3. Ne ausi sitis regnum certando perdere!"

   ____

4. Sed postquam Eteocles fratri regnum tradere noluit, Polynices fratrem infestum contemnens consilium oppidum aggrediendi cepit.

   ____

   ____

5. Fratribus occisis Creon, qui rex factus erat, Polynicem sepeliri passus non est, quod illum nocentem esse arbitrabatur.

   ____

   ____

6. Antigona, quae Oedipode mortuo Thebas reverterat, se morti obtulit, quod sententiam regis non sequebatur.

____

____

[1] detegere, detego, detexi, detectum: aufdecken

II. Aufgabenteil

1. Bestimme die Funktion des Konjunktivs und übersetze die Ausdrücke!

   a) Quo fugiamus? ______________ ______________ 1 P

   b) Ne profectus sis! ______________ ______________ 1 P

   c) Si profecti essetis ... ______________ ______________ 1 P

   d) Omnes currant! ______________ ______________ 1 P

   e) Quis hoc nesciat? ______________ ______________ 1 P

2. Übersetze die Deponentien!

   a) indignatus sum ______________ b) consequebatur ______________ 1 P

   c) imitemur! ______________ d) tutabuntur ______________ 1 P

3. Erkläre folgende Fremdwörter und weise das jeweilige lateinische Ursprungswort (+ deutsche Übersetzung!) nach!

   a) der Konsument ______________ ______________ ______________ 1 P

   b) der Advent ______________ ______________ ______________ 1 P

   c) infantil ______________ ______________ ______________ 1 P

4. Finde für die fünf Stufen zur erfolgreichen Rede die deutschen Entsprechungen und bringe sie in die richtige Reihenfolge!

   memoria – dispositio – inventio – pronuntiatio – elocutio

   ____ 5 P

I. Übersetzung: Kaiser Konstantin und seine Mutter Helena (75W)

1. Scutis[1] militum signo crucis affectis Constantinus exercitum Maxentii vicit bellumque turpe confecit.

2. Imperator cum homines in Christum credentes iuturus esset, sibi hoc edendum esse rebatur:

3. „Christianis facultas religionem suam sequendi detur! Omnes ceteri eam religionem sequantur, quam velint!"

4. Etiam Helena, mater proba, se Constantino auctore ad religionem Christianam transgressuram esse dixit.

5. Amore Christi confirmata divitiis suis ad homines miseros adiuvandos utebatur.

6. Compluribus annis post Helena iter molestum in Palaestinam fecisse dicitur, ut crucem Christi reperiret.

[1] scutum,-i : der Schild

II. Aufgabenteil

1. Vervollständige den Text! 6 P

Flavius Valerius **CONSTANTINUS,** auch bekannt als Konstantin der Große oder Konstantin I., war von 306 bis 337 römischer Kaiser. Allein, das heißt ohne Mitherrscher oder Konkurrent, herrschte er jedoch erst ab 324.

Historisch bedeutend ist Konstantins Regierungszeit vor allem wegen der von ihm eingeleiteten konstantinischen ________________, mit der der Siegeszug des Christentums begann. Diese nahm ihren Ursprung in der Verwendung des Christusmonogramms in der Schlacht an ________________________________ im Jahr 312. Konstantin schrieb seinen Sieg eben diesem Monogramm zu. 313 folgte das ________________________ von Mailand, das im ganzen Reich Religionsfreiheit garantierte und damit auch das Christentum erlaubte. Konstantin unterstützte das Christentum in der Folgezeit weiterhin und berief 325 das erste ____________ von Nicäa ein, um innerchristliche Streitigkeiten beizulegen.

324/26 verlegte Konstantin den Kaisersitz in den ____________ des Reiches, nach Nova Roma („Neues Rom"), das nach seinem Tode ihm zu Ehren allgemein ____________ genannt wurde.

2. Nenne die entsprechende lateinische Rechtsregel!

   a) „Auch die andere Seite soll gehört werden!" ____________ 1 P

   b) „Es darf nicht zweimal wegen ein und desselben Vergehens geurteilt werden!"

   ____________ 1 P

   c) „Wem nützte die Tat?" ____________ 1 P

   d) „Verträge müssen eingehalten werden." ____________ 1 P

3. Übersetze folgende Ausdrücke!

   a) Caesare necando ____________ 1,5 P

   b) Caesare necato ____________ 1 P

   ____________ 1 P

   c) Caesare necante ____________ 1,5 P

Schulaufgabe 4 cursus bis Kap. 47

✓ 15 / ⧖ 45 / 📖 71

I. Übersetzung: Fluch über Nero (81 LW)

Unmittelbar nachdem Kaiser Konstantin im Jahr 313 n.Chr. die Ausübung des christlichen Kultes für das ganze römische Reich erlaubt hat, verfasst der Kirchenschriftsteller Laktanz eine harte Abrechnung mit den Kaisern, die die Christen verfolgt haben. Er beschreibt, wie diese Kaiser auf z. T. schreckliche Weise zu Tode kamen. Als erster Christenverfolger wird Nero (Nero, Neronis) erwähnt:

1. Nerone imperatore Petrus Romam venit. Hic miraculis[1] perficiendis multis hominibus persuasit, eos in Christum credere.

   ____

   ____

2. Nero autem, cum comperiret non modo Romae, sed multis in oppidis numerum Christianorum crescere, hanc fidem exstinguendam esse censuit.

   ____

   ____

3. Itaque Petrus crucifixus[2], Paulus gladio interfectus est.

   ____

[1] miraculum, -i : das Wunder

4. Postremo deus noster, cum inopiam[3] populi sui videret, Neronem poena gravi afficiendum esse arbitratus est:

5. Hostibus saevis eum dedidit ad necandum et effecit, ut iste homo nullo loco terrarum videri posset; nam omnis memoria huius bestiae crudelis tollenda erat.

nach Laktanz, „De mortibus persecutorum"

[2] crucifigere : kreuzigen [3] inopia,-ae : Not 2 P

II) Aufgabenteil

1. Wann und wie endete das Oströmische Reich? 2 P

2. Was versteht man unter den Carmina Burana? 1 P

1 P

3. Was wird im hippokratischen Eid dem Arzt verboten? Nenne 3 Aspekte! 1 P

*

*

1 P

*

1 P

4. Übersetze folgende Verbformen! 1 P

a) agendum est 1 P

b) laesus eram 1 P

c) confecturus est 1 P

d) peperceratis 1 P

e) merebis 1 P

f) laetati sunt

g) reperiebatur

h) iunget

Stegreifaufgabe 1 cursus Kap. 38

1. Bilde zu den Formen von putare die entsprechenden Formen von opinari und übersetze sie!

   a) putas ______ ______ 1 P

   b) putavistis ______ ______ 1 P

   c) putaverat ______ ______ 1 P

   d) putaremus ______ ______ 1 P

   e) putavissem ______ ______ 1 P

   f) putabunt ______ ______ 1 P

2. Übersetze!

   a) admiratus est ______ d) potiebaris ______ 2 P

   b) moraberis ______ e) fatemur ______ 2 P

   c) veriti essemus ______ f) conata erat ______ 2 P

3. Erkläre folgende Fremdwörter und weise das jeweilige lat. Ursprungswort (+ dt. Übersetzung!) nach!

   a) frustriert ______ ______ ______ 1,5 P

   b) Experiment ______ ______ ______ 1,5 P

Stegreifaufgabe 2 cursus bis Kap. 44

✓ 15 / ⌛ 20 / 📖 72

1. Wandle um! culpa quaedam -> Genitiv -> Plural -> Dativ -> Singular -> Akkusativ -> Plural

   Genitiv: ______ Plural: ______

   Dativ: ______ Singular: ______

   Akkusativ: ______ Plural ______ 6 P

2. Übersetze!

   a) Pecunia mihi solvenda est. ______ 1 P

   b) Officium pecuniae solvendae ______ 1 P

   c) Ceterum censeo Carthaginem esse delendam. ______ 1 P

   d) Mihi tempus libri legendi non est. ______ 1 P

   e) Liber quidam tibi legendus non est. ______ 1 P

   f) Libri legendi causa quietem quaero. ______ 1 P

3. Erkläre folgende Fremdwörter und weise das jeweilige lat. Ursprungswort (+ dt. Übersetzung!) nach!

   a) Orient ______ ______ ______ 1,5 P

   b) Konjunktion ______ 1,5 P

   ______ ______

I. Übersetzung: Römer und Germanen (79 LW)

Im Gegensatz zu Lucius, der sich in Germanien wohl fühlt (vgl. Kap. 43), kann der Soldat Quintus nichts Positives an Germanien und seinen Bewohnern finden. Bei einem Urlaub zuhause in Italien erzählt er:

1. „Certe audivistis consuetudinem vitae Germanorum multo a moribus nostris differre.
2. Memoravine Germanos ira incensos deis immortalibus etiam homines immolare[1]?
3. Isti barbari semper cupidi bellum inferendi et parati ad caedendum sunt.
4. Milites in pugnam ituros Veledam quandam de rebus futuris interrogare audivi; hanc feminam ut deam coli scio.
5. Recte fit, ut imperator Domitianus fines imperii munitionibus tegat.
6. Utinam ne a Germanis in servitutem ducamur! Utinam semper incolumes e Germania redeamus!
7. Speremus barbaros numquam victoriam atram de populo Romano parturos esse!"

[1] immolare = opfern

II. Aufgabenteil

1. Wandle in das andere Genus verbi um und übersetze die neu gebildete Form!
   a) fecerat 1 P
   b) fieri 1 P
   c) faceres 1 P
   d) fiamus 1 P
2. Wandle in die entsprechenden Formen der anderen Partizipien um! 4 P
   a) praecipientem
   b) comprehensos
   c) prolatura
   d) relinquentibus

3. Erkläre folgende Fremdwörter und gib das zugrunde liegende lateinische Wort und dessen deutsche Bedeutung an!

   a) Solarium ______ ______ ______ 1,5 P

   b) Nonsens ______ ______ ______ 1,5 P

4. Übersetze folgende Sätze, die jeweils eine –urus-Form enthalten!

   a) Germani oppidum capturi conveniunt. (2 Übersetzungsvarianten, kein Relativsatz!)

   ______ 2 P

   b) Germani urbem capturi erant.

   ______ 1 P

   c) Romani Germanos urbem capturos esse putabant.

   ______ 1 P

5. a) Wie hieß die römische Befestigungsanlage, die Domitian an der Grenze zum freien Germanien erbauen ließ? ______ 1 P

   b) Nenne zwei wichtige Bestandteile dieser Befestigungsanlage! ______ 2 P

Schulaufgabe 2 prima III bis Kap. 50 ✓ 18 / ⧖ 45 / 🕮 74

I. Übersetzung

Ein (heidnischer) Römer und ein Christ unterhalten sich über das Thema Religion (79 LW)

Romanus: „Nos Romani ad religionem alienarum gentium respiciendam parati sumus."

______

______

Christianus: „Deus noster universis hominibus colendus et diligendus est, quoniam etiam peccantibus veniam dat."

______

______

Romanus: „Cupidus sum Christianorum reperiendorum, qui odio incensi homines doloribus afficiunt et liberis edendis[1] se alunt, ut audivi."

______

______

Christianus: „Aio id, quod ultimum dixisti, omnino falsum esse. Inter Christianos, qui in unum deum credunt, constat homines ab iniuriis temperare debere. Ne iudicaveris Christianos nefarios esse. Quid addam? Quis dubitet Iesum miraculis[2] efficiendis multis hominibus providisse?"

______

______

II. Aufgabenteil

1. Übersetze folgende Gerundivkonstruktionen!

   a) Hae litterae nobis legendae sunt.

   ______________________________ 1 P

   b) Illae litterae tibi legendae non sunt.

   ______________________________ 1 P

   c) Vobis tempus litterarum legendarum deest.

   ______________________________ 1 P

2. Übersetze und gib die Bezeichnung für den jeweiligen Konjunktiv an!

   a) Utinam domi mansissem!

   ______________________________ 1 P

   b) Ne me spectaveritis!

   ______________________________ 1 P

   c) Utinam omnes bene discant!

   ______________________________ 1 P

   d) Speremus!

   ______________________________ 1 P

   e) Pueri taceant!

   ______________________________ 1 P

   f) Hoc nemo crediderit.

   ______________________________ 1 P

   g) Cur id permittam?

   ______________________________ 1 P

3. Welche Bedeutung haben folgende englischen Wörter?
   Gib jeweils auch das zugrunde liegende lateinische Wort an!

   a) to oppress ______________ ______________ 1 P

   b) brief ______________ ______________ 1 P

   c) conscious ______________ ______________ 1 P

   d) to omit ______________ ______________ 1 P

4. Wer passt zu wem? Verbinde! (Vorsicht: 2 Irrläufer!)

   1) Nero
   2) Minucius
   3) Helena
   4) Konstantin
   5) Augustus
   6) Titus

   a) erster Kaiser, der das Christentum erlaubt
   b) Eroberer Jerusalems
   c) einer der ersten Schriftsteller, die das Christentum darstellen
   d) findet das angebliche Kreuz Christi in Jerusalem

   4 P

I. Übersetzung

Baderegel: Gehe nie erhitzt ins Wasser – auch Alexander bekam ein eiskaltes Bad nicht: (73 LW)

1. Alexander in Asiam profectus est, ut Dareum, regem infelicem Persarum, aggrederetur.

____

2. Alexandrum copias Persarum vicisse et magnam gloriam consecutum esse scimus.

____

3. Tum in Ciliciam progressus in Cydnum flumen in-gressus est[1], ut lavaretur.

____

4. Sed subito vires eum deficere coeperunt.

____

5. Milites opinati regem moriturum esse veriti sunt, ne pernicies certa instaret. Itaque ingens metus in castris ortus est.

____

____

6. Milites his verbis questi sunt: „Quis nos tuebitur? Auxilio nobis opus est."

____

7. Tandem Alexander salvus fieri videbatur.

____

[1] in-gressus est – die Bedeutung lässt sich von e-gressus est ableiten.

II. Aufgabenteil

1. Ersetze die Formen von dicere durch die entsprechenden Formen von loqui und übersetze!

a) diceretis ______________ ______________ 1 P

b) dixisti ______________ ______________ 1 P

c) dicet ______________ ______________ 1 P

d) dixeramus ______________ ______________ 1 P

e) dicunt ______________ ______________ 1 P

f) dixissem ______________ ______________ 1 P

2. Gib beim fett gedruckten Wort an, um welche genaue Kasusfunktion es sich handelt und übersetze!

a) **Patri** domus magna est. ______________________________ 1 P

b) Spes **salutis** apud omnes magna erat. 1 P

c) **Nobis** discendum est. 1 P

d) Caesar **magna audacia** erat. 1 P

3. Der einheitliche Kulturraum des imperium Romanum zerfällt im Mittelalter in drei verschiedene Kulturen. Nenne sie und gib ihre geographische Lage an! 3 P

4. Ersetze in folgendem Text die fett gedruckten Wörter durch Fremdwörter!
Auch heute noch müssen **Rechtsgelehrte** die **Folgen** der **Verstaatlichung der Klöster** 1803 aufarbeiten. Denn der **Angriff** der einzelnen weltlichen Staaten auf die Klöster verursachte zahlreiche auch heute noch wirkende **Streitereien.** 5 P

✓ 18 / ⌛ 45 / 📖 76 **Schulaufgabe 4** prima III bis Kap. 56

I. Übersetzung: Dionysios, der Tyrann von Syrakus auf Sizilien, fürchtete Anschläge; da wird ein junger Mann namens Damon verhaftet … (80 LW)

1. Dionysius, quem multos annos in Sicilia regnavisse constat, tyrannus crudelissimus fuisse dicitur.

2. Plurimis vitia eius expertis nemo erat, qui quicquam agere auderet.

3. Damo autem, qui fortior ceteris esset, consilium tyranni interficiendi cepit.

4. Sed eo a custodibus capto Dionysius ira incensus hortatus est: „Confitere! Cum merces insidiarum mors esse soleat, morieris."

5. Damo: „Precor, ut mihi moram trium dierum des.

6. Nisi revertero, polliceor amicum meum pro me mortem subiturum esse."

7. Amicus verbis Damonis confisus est – et Damo profecto amicum non deseruisse traditur.

II. Aufgabenteil

1. Übersetze folgenden verschränkten Relativsatz auf vier verschiedene Arten!
Hercules, quem fortem fuisse constat, multos labores subiit.

____

____

____

____ 4 P

2. Bilde die Tempusreihe (Präsens, Imperfekt, Futur I, Perfekt, Plusquamperfekt, Futur II) von gaudere in der 2. Person Singular Indikativ!

____ 3 P

3. Ergänze die fehlenden Steigerungsformen (berücksichtige Kasus, Numerus und Genus)!

	minoribus		1 P
bonam			1 P
miserae			1 P
		maximi	1 P

4. Erkläre folgende Fremdwörter und gib das zugrunde liegende lateinische Wort und dessen deutsche Bedeutung an!

a) Vehikel ____________ ____________ ____________ 1,5 P

b) Assimilation ____________ ____________ ____________ 1,5 P

5. Wer passt zu wem? Verbinde! (Vorsicht: 2 Irrläufer!)

1) Diogenes
2) Aristoteles
3) Sokrates
4) Platon
5) Marc Aurel
6) Pythagoras

a) Stoiker

b) Lehrer Alexanders

c) Lehrer des Aristoteles

d) Kyniker

4 P

Stegreifaufgabe 1 prima III Kap. 43 ✓ 18 / ⌛ 20 / 📖 77

1. Beuge! hiems aspera ______

______ ______

______ ______

______ ______

______ ______ 6 P

2. Übersetze, bilde den Konjunktiv und übersetze ihn!

a) vocatur ______ ______ ______ 1,5 P

b) vocabatur ______ ______ ______ 1,5 P

c) vocatus erat ______ ______ ______ 1,5 P

d) deduco ______ ______ ______ 1,5 P

3. Übersetze!

a) Utinam ne amicas rideatis!

______ 1 P

b) Dei te servent!

______ 1 P

c) Puer paucis verbis respondeat!

______ 1 P

d) Amicos exscpectemus!

______ 1 P

e) Utinam tacuisses!

______ 1 P

f) Utinam hostes neminem ceciderint!

______ 1 P

1. Übersetze folgende Sätze! Benenne die Konjunktive!

a) Hoc faciat! ____________________ | ____________ 1 P

b) Utinam maneret! ____________________ | ____________ 1 P

c) Hoc faciamus! ____________________ | ____________ 1 P

d) Quid faciam? ____________________ | ____________ 1 P

e) Ne hoc feceris! ____________________ | ____________ 1 P

f) Utinam maneat! ____________________ | ____________ 1 P

2. Erkläre folgende Fremdwörter! Gib auch die lateinische Wurzel und deren Bedeutung an!

a) Edition ____________ ____________ ____________ 1 P

b) Präteritum ____________ ____________ ____________ 1 P

c) Nudist ____________ ____________ ____________ 1 P

d) Judikative ____________ ____________ ____________ 1 P

e) fiktiv ____________ ____________ ____________ 1 P

f) Solo ____________ ____________ ____________ 1 P

3. Übersetze folgende ablativi absoluti mit Unterordnung und Präpositionalausdruck in den angegebenen Sinnrichtungen!

	Unterordnung	Präpositionalausdruck	
a) His verbis dictis			
temporal	____________	____________	1,5 P
konzessiv	____________	____________	1,5 P
b) Liberis flentibus			
kausal	____________	____________	1,5 P
modal	____________	____________	1,5 P

Stegreifaufgabe 3 prima III Kap. 51 ✓ 18 / ⌛ 20 / 📖 78

1. Ersetze die Formen von monere durch die entsprechenden Formen von hortari und übersetze!

monet	______	______	1 P
monuisti	______	______	1 P
monebimus	______	______	1 P
monuissetis	______	______	1 P
monete	______	______	1 P
monueram	______	______	1 P
monebant	______	______	1 P
moneres	______	______	1 P

2. Übersetze!

veriti estis	______	1 P
egrediamur	______	1 P
moraretur	______	1 P
morietur	______	1 P
usi essemus	______	1 P
tributum erat	______	1 P

3. Finde zu folgenden lateinischen Worten je ein Fremdwort und erkläre es!

tueri	______	______	1 P
loqui	______	______	1 P
servire	______	______	1 P
videri	______	______	1 P

I. Übersetzung: Kaiser Nero (78 LW)

1. Nero imperio potitus munere principis primo prudentissime et diligentissime functus est.

2. Imperator quam iustissimus videri cupivit et pauperibus multa largitus est.

3. Nero enim a pueritia Senecam, magistrum suum, verebatur imitabaturque.

4. Magistro contigit, ut Nero moribus optimis uteretur.

5. Postea autem Nero ratus verba magistri vincula inutilia esse expertus est voluntatem suam sequi.

6. Non iam consiliis magistri nitebatur, sed vita frui orsus est.

7. Vitam artificis, non imperatoris degebat; in circo morans equos celerrimos admiratus est, in theatro versans carmina cantavit.

II. Aufgabenteil

1. Setze die fehlenden Steigerungsformen ein!

Positiv	Komparativ	Superlativ
magnus		
	plus	
		pessimam
similis		

4 P

2. Ersetze die Formen von monere durch solche von hortari und übersetze sie!

a) monuisset ______ ______ 1 P

b) monebamus ______ ______ 1 P

c) monebitis ______ ______ 1 P

d) monuisti ______ ______ 1 P

e) mone! ______ ______ 1 P

f) monerem ______ ______ 1 P

3. Erkläre folgende Fremdwörter! Gib auch die lateinische Wurzel und deren Bedeutung an!

a) komplex ______ ______ ______ 1,5 P

b) Kolloquium ______ ______ ______ 1,5 P

c) Konfession ______ ______ ______ 1,5 P

d) Orient ______ ______ ______ 1,5 P

4. Führe vier zentrale Informationen zu Delphi an!

* ______ 1 P
* ______ 1 P
* ______ 1 P
* ______ 1 P

✓ 20 / ⌛ 45 / 📖 80 Schulaufgabe 2 auspicia III bis Kap. 21

I. Übersetzung: Olympische Spiele (77 LW)

1. Eo tempore, cum certamina fiebant, omnes cives gavisi sunt.

______

2. Multi homines soliti sunt ludos Olympiacos, quos clarissimos totius Graeciae fuisse constat, spectare.

______

______

3. Qua de causa domo profecti sunt athletas aspecturi.

______

4. Quae cum ita sint, spectatores athletas incitabant:

______

5. „Honores adipiscimini! Nam digni et apti estis, qui gloriam insignem consequamini. Confidite viribus vestris!"

______

______

6. Certamen, quod „Pancration" nominabatur, periculosissimum erat.

______

7. Athletae, qui quantos dolores paterentur scitis, maxima fortitudine pugnabant.

______

8. Aliqui athletae, cum de victoria desperarent, tamen pugnaverunt, violati sunt, occisi sunt.

______

II. Aufgabenteil

1. Übersetze folgende feste Wendungen!

   a) nemo est, qui ________________________________ 1 P

   b) rerum scriptor ________________________________ 1 P

   c) dicturus sum ________________________________ 1 P

   d) ne quis ________________________________ 1 P

2. Bilde die Zeitenreihe im Indikativ (Präsens, Imperfekt, Futur, Perfekt, Plusquamperfekt, Futur II) von audere in der 2. Person Plural und übersetze alle Formen!

   ____

   ____

   ________________________________ 6 P

3. Erkläre folgende Fremdwörter! Gib auch die lateinische Wurzel und deren Bedeutung an!

   a) kontinuierlich ____________ ____________ ____________ 1,5 P

   b) Detektiv ____________ ____________ ____________ 1,5 P

   c) reversibel ____________ ____________ ____________ 1,5 P

   d) Tribunal ____________ ____________ ____________ 1,5 P

4. Nenne 4 Punkte, in denen sich die antiken von den modernen Olympischen Spielen unterscheiden!

   * ________________________________ 1 P
   * ________________________________ 1 P
   * ________________________________ 1 P
   * ________________________________ 1 P

Schulaufgabe 3 auspicia III bis Kap. 30 ✓ 20 / ⧖ 45 / 🕮 81

I. Übersetzung: Die frühen Christen und der römische Staat (82 LW)

1. Christiani, cum doctrinam assidue praedicarent, saepe proditionis accusabantur.

   ____

2. Qui aeque atque viri scelesti ab imperatoribus, qui iustitiae participes non erant, in vincula dabantur.

   ____

   ____

3. Imperator Nero ad carmen de incendio Troiae canendum urbem Romam incenderat.

   ____

4. Neroni Christiani rei faciendi erant, ut se crimine urbem evertendi liberaret.

   ____

5. Quare Nero eos sine quaestionibus aut iudicio capitis damnavit.

____

6. Nam vitam eorum minimi aestimabat.

____

7. Quo factum est, ut Christiani frequentes patientia laudanda in circo a bestiis omnis generis violarentur necarenturque.

____

____

8. Petro Pauloque quoque Romae vita erepta est.

____

II. Aufgabenteil

1. Erkläre folgende englische Wörter; führe auch die lateinische Wurzel und deren Bedeutung an!

community	______	______	______	1,5 P
autumn	______	______	______	1,5 P
administration	______	______	______	1,5 P
granny	______	______	______	1,5 P

2. Benenne und übersetze folgende Genitive!

a) satis praemii	______	______	1 P
b) iniuriae convincere	______	______	1 P
c) milites sociorum	______	______	1 P
d) puellae magnae sapientiae	______	______	1 P
e) magni esse	______	______	1 P
f) amici est	______	______	1 P

3. Übersetze folgende Gerund- bzw. Gerundivkonstruktionen!

a) facultas orationem habendi	______	1 P
b) occasio libertatis servandae	______	1 P
c) Haec epistula tibi legenda non est.	______	1 P
d) Do tibi illam epistulam legendam.	______	1 P

4. Cato der Ältere gilt als Beispiel eines echten Römers. Führe 4 charakteristische Wesenszüge bzw. Taten dieses Mannes an!

* ______________________________ 1 P
* ______________________________ 1 P
* ______________________________ 1 P
* ______________________________ 1 P

✓ 20 / ⌛ 45 / 🕮 82/83 **Schulaufgabe 4** auspicia III bis Kap. 41 — LATEIN 2

I. Übersetzung: Wie soll ein Lehrer erziehen? (81 LW)

1. Optimus quisque magister nullam occasionem praetermittat sapientiam discipulorum augendi.

____

____

2. Qui animos eorum, quos docendos accepit, intellegere conetur.

____

3. Diligenter igitur probet, quibus rebus uti possit, ut discipuli quam plurimum memoria teneant.

____

____

4. Quemadmodum discipuli educentur?

____

5. Alteri pueri severitate educandi sunt, quia putant se solum ad ludendum natos esse.

____

6. Sed ne hi pueri otiosi quidem crudelitate torquendi sunt.

____

7. Quidam pueri autem a magistro territi timent, ne poena afficiantur.

____

8. Quos pueros magister timore ac lacrimis liberet et laude incitet, ut sua sponte litteris operam dent.

____

____

II. Aufgabenteil

1. Übersetze folgende NcI-Konstruktion mit 4 Lösungsmöglichkeiten!

Catoni inimicitiae graves non defuisse dicuntur.

* ______________________________ 1 P
* ______________________________ 1 P
* ______________________________ 1 P
* ______________________________ 1 P

2. Nenne die entsprechende lateinische Rechtsregel!

a) „Auch die andere Seite soll gehört werden!" ______________ 1 P

b) „Es darf nicht zweimal wegen ein und desselben Vergehens geurteilt werden!"

______________________________ 1 P

c) „Eine Tat kann nur bestraft werden, wenn sie zum Zeitpunkt ihrer Ausführung verboten war."

______________________________ 1 P

d) „Verträge müssen eingehalten werden." ______________ 1 P

e) „Strengste Befolgung des Rechts kann schlimmstes Unrecht werden." 1 P

____

Schulaufgabe 4 auspicia III bis Kap. 41 ✓ 20 / ⌛ 45 / 📖 83

3. Thales und Sokrates waren beide Philosophen. Nenne 4 Unterschiede zwischen ihnen!

* ______________________________ 1 P
* ______________________________ 1 P
* ______________________________ 1 P
* ______________________________ 1 P

4. Benenne und übersetze folgende Ablative!

a) ordine ______________ ______________ 1 P
b) solis ortu ______________ ______________ 1 P
c) multo maior ______________ ______________ 1 P
d) iussu ______________ ______________ 1 P
e) manu tenere ______________ ______________ 1 P
f) spe carere ______________ ______________ 1 P
g) equestri loco ortus ______________ ______________ 1 P

✓ 20 / ⌛ 20 / 📖 84 Stegreifaufgabe 1 auspicia III Kap. 4

1. Übersetze!

a) polliciti estis ______________________________ 1 P
b) reor ______________________________ 1 P
c) visi erant ______________________________ 1 P
d) fatereris ______________________________ 1 P
e) tuebamini ______________________________ 1 P
f) hortati essemus ______________________________ 1 P
g) conare! ______________________________ 1 P

2. Übersetze folgende Wendungen!

a) Miror errorem tuum. ______________________________ 1 P
b) Miror forum. ______________________________ 1 P
c) Moror amicum. ______________________________ 1 P
d) Vereor precari. ______________________________ 1 P
e) Vereor deum. ______________________________ 1 P
f) Vereor, ne cadam. ______________________________ 1 P
g) In re publica versor. ______________________________ 1 P

✓ 20 / ⏳ 20 / 📖 84 Stegreifaufgabe 1 auspicia III Kap. 4

3. Ergänze die fehlenden Formen und gib die Bedeutung des Adjektivs an!

Positiv	Bedeutung	Komparativ	Superlativ
audax			
			acerrimos
		facilius	
recentium			

6 P

Stegreifaufgabe 2 auspicia III Kap. 15 ✓ 20 / ⏳ 20 / 📖 85

1. Erkläre folgende Fremdwörter! Gib auch die lateinische Wurzel und deren Bedeutung an!

a) Konzert ____________ ____________ ____________ 1,5 P

b) Initiative ____________ ____________ ____________ 1,5 P

c) Potenz ____________ ____________ ____________ 1,5 P

d) Judikative ____________ ____________ ____________ 1,5 P

2. Übersetze folgende Sätze mit „cum" und gib an, um welches „cum" es sich handelt!

a) Cum ludi Olympiaci erant, Graeci pacem servabant.

____________________________________ 2 P

b) Cum ludi Olympiaci sint, tota Graecia pax servatur.

____________________________________ 2 P

c) Cum leges non sinerent feminas Olympiae spectatores esse, aliquando mulier ausa est ad ludos venire.

____

____________________________________ 2 P

d) Solum viri ludis Olympiacis intererant, cum feminis non liceret Olympiae versari.

____________________________________ 2 P

e) Mulier aliqua cum ludos Olympiacos spectare vellet, detecta est.

____________________________________ 2 P

3. Beuge!

aliqui vir	____________
____________	____________
____________	____________
____________	____________
____________	____________

4 P

Hinweise zum Diktat: Das Diktat wird aus dem Lösungsheft ohne Satzzeichen folgendermaßen vorgelesen: Satz für Satz, jeder Satz jeweils zweimal. Danach immer eine kleine Pause machen. Die Schüler müssen den fehlenden Begriff in der Lücke richtig einsetzen. Zum Schluss soll das Diktat noch einmal im Ganzen vorgelesen werden.

Falls Sie, liebe Eltern, in Französisch nicht so fit sind: Das Lückendiktat steht für Sie auf unserer Homepage unter Gymnasium / Gym 8 als Audiofile zum Download bereit. Weitere Hinweise finden Sie im Elternheft auf Seite 9.

I. Dictée à trous (Lückendiktat) (Elternheft Seite 86)

Comme ________ les Carbonne ________ à Fécamp, au bord de la mer. Ils ________ déjà bien ________ et Marie ________ déjà ________ pas mal de copines, qui, elles aussi, ________ à Fécamp en été. Un jour, lorsque les filles ________ au volley sur la plage, un joli garçon ________ a commencé à s'intéresser au match. Mais Marie a tout de suite vu qu'il ________ ________. Pourquoi pas? Il ________ ... Salut! Je suis Marie. Tu ________ jouer avec nous? ________ jouer à côté de moi.» Cinq minutes après, l'équipe de Marie ________ le match. Et c'est comme cela que Marie ________ son copain Pierre, qui ________ à Fécamp. 20 P

II. Grammaire

A) La comparaison. Complétez le texte.

Anne est ________ (fille; canon ++) de notre quartier. Je pense qu'elle est presque ________ (beau =) que Shakira. Elle a ________ (notes; bon ++) de toute la classe et c'est ________ (fille; intéressant ++) que je connaisse. Il est vrai qu'elle est un peu ________ (sportif -) que moi, mais cela ne fait rien. 10 P

B) Reliez les phrases.
Employez les équivalents français des conjonctions allemandes «nachdem» (1x) et «bevor» (1x).

1. Situation: Hier Mme Brun s'est levée très tôt.
   6 h 00: Mme Brun prend son bain. 6 h 30: Mme Brun boit un café.

   ________ 3 P

2. Situation: Les journées sont toujours les mêmes.
   7 h 00: Elle fait les lits. 7 h 10: Elle quitte la maison.

   ________ 3 P

C) Passé composé – plus-que-parfait. Reliez les phrases.

Isabelle a pris des notes pour écrire un article dans le journal de son lycée.

1. 9h 00: Pierre – tomber malade.
2. 10h 00: Nous – visiter Strasbourg. Pierre - ne pas venir.

4 P

III. Ton journal de bord.

Mache einen Tagebucheintrag von einem Urlaubstag nach den folgenden Angaben.

- Ferien mit deinen Eltern im Südwesten Frankreichs
- während dein Vater immer badete, las deine Mutter ein Buch am Strand
- für dich war das nicht interessant: Angabe des Grundes
- Rauchverbot von deinen Eltern
- aber du wolltest so cool aussehen wie die anderen Jungs/Mädchen
- deshalb: Kauf von Zigaretten und einer Sonnenbrille, die „in" war
- dann: Gang zum Strand
- Ankunft eines Jungen/Mädchens, der/das sich neben dich gelegt hat
- er/sie fährt nicht auf Jungs/Mädchen ab, die rauchen
- du hast sofort aufgehört zu rauchen und hast ihr/ihm vorgeschlagen, einen Spaziergang zu machen
- er/sie hat sich über dich lustig gemacht und dir einen Ratschlag gegeben: 1-2 Sätze deiner Wahl

30 P

Diesen Text findest du als Audiofile auf unserer Homepage www.verlag-bauer.de unter "Gym 8"

I. Test de compréhension oral (lire le texte deux fois!)

A) Vrai ou faux? Cochez la bonne réponse et corrigez les phrases qui sont fausses. 15 P

	VRAI	FAUX
1. Babaka a quatre sœurs.		
2. Il a travaillé dans un laboratoire.		
3. Il a quitté le lycée et son village.		
4. C'est jour et nuit qu'il faisait du foot.		
5. On lui a offert un avion, une maison et une grande voiture.		
6. Babaka ne jouait pas très bien en France.		
7. En Europe c'est l'argent qui compte pour les footballeurs.		
8. Après son aventure en Europe Babaka était malheureux.		

____

____

____

____

____

B) Répondez aux questions suivantes:

1. Pourquoi est-ce que Babaka n'aimait pas les hivers en France?

   Il ne les aimait pas ____________________________________ . 2 P

2. Qui se moquait de Babaka?

   C'étaient ____________________________________ . 1 P

3. Qu'est-ce que Babaka a tout de suite fait après les moqueries?

   ____________________________________ . 2 P

II. Grammaire et vocabulaire

A) Complétez les définitions suivantes par des pronoms relatifs (pas «où») et trouvez les mots qu'on cherche (avec les articles!):

1. la langue ____________ les jeunes prononcent les mots et les syllabes (Silben) à l'envers: ____________ 2 P
2. quelqu'un ____________ les parents viennent d'Afrique du Nord, mais ____________ est né en France: ____________ 3 P
3. ____________ on peut dire pour 33,33%: ____________ 2 P
4. L'examen ____________ on pense à la fin du lycée: ____________ 2 P
5. Si un automobiliste fait ____________ est interdit, la police lui donne ça: ____________ 2 P

B) Complétez le texte par les formes correctes du comparatif (+; -) et du superlatif (++; - -).

Marie parle ____________________(bon; +) le français que son copain Jean. Mais tout le monde sait que Marie est ____________________(bon; ++) élève de toute la classe et qu'elle chante ____________________ (bon; ++). Les élèves qui chantent ____________________ (bon; - -), ce sont Luc et Pierre. Ils quittent toujours la salle de musique ____________________ (so schnell wie möglich). 5 P

C) Marie, Luc, Jean et Lisa parlent de leur avenir. Employez le futur simple.

1. Marie: vivre à la campagne / avoir trois enfants / être heureux

   Marie: Je vivrai à la campagne et j'aurai trois enfants. Je serai heureuse. 3 P

2. Luc: apprendre des langues / devenir professeur / devoir aider les enfants quand ils - avoir - des problèmes

   Luc, lui, apprendra des langues. Il deviendra professeur. Là, il devra aider les enfants quand ils auront des problèmes. 4 P

3. Jean et Lisa: acheter un appartement / faire le ménage ensemble / recevoir souvent des amis

   Jean et Lisa: Nous achèterons un appartement. Nous ferons le ménage ensemble et nous recevrons souvent des amis. 3 P

III. Production de texte: Ecrire une lettre (dix phrases à peu près)

Du beantwortest den Brief deines französischen Brieffreundes, in dem er dir über die Schule in Frankreich berichtet hat und in dem er dich gebeten hat, ihm darüber, wie die Schule bei uns abläuft, zu schreiben (Unterrichtszeiten, Klassenzimmer, Essen etc.).

____

____

____

____

____

____

____

____

____

____

____________________ 30 P

____

I. Le discours indirect - Dialogue

1. Votre prof: «Pourquoi est-ce que tu es en retard?»
2. Toi: «Parce que mon réveil n'a pas marché.»
3. Votre prof: «Qu'est-ce que tu vas faire vendredi après-midi?»
4. Toi: «Je ne sais pas encore.»
5. Votre prof: «Les élèves, qu'est-ce qui peut être plus amusant que de passer une heure supplémentaire à l'école?»

Le soir tu racontes cette petite conversation à ta mère. Mettez le dialogue au discours indirect. Employez les équivalents français des verbes allemands entre parenthèses au passé.

1. (jemanden fragen) ______________________________

____

2. (jemandem antworten) ______________________________

____

3. (wissen wollen) ______________________________

____

4. (jemandem erklären) ______________________________

____

5. (die Schüler fragen) ______________________________

______________________________ 15 P

II. La proposition conditionnelle I: Le professeur parle à ses élèves. Formez des phrases entières.

1. Il dit à toute la classe: «vous - avoir des bons résultats dans le test - vous - travailler bien»

Vous aurez des bons résultats dans le test, si vous travaillez bien. ✓

2. Il dit à Marie: «tu - ne pas parler à sa voisine tout le temps - tu - pouvoir mieux se concentrer»

Tu pourras mieux se concentrer, si tu ne parles pas à ta voisine tout le temps. ✓

3. Il parle des garçons de la classe: «les garçons - apprendre le vocabulaire - ils - faire moins de fautes»

Si les garçons apprennent le vocabulaire, ils feront moins de fautes. ✓ 9 P

III. Complétez le texte. Remplacez les expressions en caractères gras (fett gedruckt) par les pronoms corrects dans les réponses.

1. Luc: «Tu aimes passer tes vacances **en Provence?»**

Jean: «Oui, je/j' ______________________________ (aimer/aller) en août.»

2. Luc: «Quel temps fait-il **dans le Midi?»**

Jean: «Il ______________________________ (faire) souvent beau temps.»

3. Luc: «Tu achètes aussi **du parfum** quand tu es **à Grasse?»**

   Jean: «Oui, bien sûr, nous ______________ (acheter) toujours quand

   nous ______________ (être).»

4. Luc: «Tu penses aussi **aux gens qui n'ont pas encore passé leurs vacances sur la Côte d'Azur?»**

   Jean: «Non, je ______________ (ne jamais/penser).» 8 P

IV. En français, s'il vous plaît.
Wie sagst du auf französisch... (umgangssprachliche Ausdrücke beachten!)

1. ... dass Jean offensichtlich schlecht riecht?

____

2. ... dass er zwar gerne singt, aber oft falsch singt?

____

3. ... dass er boshaft über seine Kumpels spricht?

____

4. ... dass aber seine Klamotten deiner Meinung nach cool sind?

____

5. ... dass du hoffst, dass er bald beginnen wird, für die Schule zu schuften?

______________ 18 P

V. Thème. Traduisez les phrases suivantes en allemand.

1. In der Provence brennen oft die Wälder.

____

2. Die Brände zerstören die Wälder.

____

3. Es gibt immer mehrere Verletzte und sogar Leute, die in den Flammen sterben.

____

4. Für die Feuerwehr ist es nicht leicht, die Brände zu löschen.

____

5. Oft sind es die Touristen, die nicht aufpassen und Feuer im Wald machen.

______________ 20 P

VI. Production de texte (auf separatem Blatt)

Tu écris un petit texte d'à peu près 12 phrases dans lequel tu parles d'un rêve que tu as fait cette nuit.
Il faut employer les expressions françaises des expressions allemandes qui suivent: 30 P

- der/ein Kobold	- die Zigarette ausmachen
- die Zigarette wegwerfen	- trocken (z.B. Wald)
- zerstören	- sich beschweren/beklagen (über)
- ins Gefängnis werfen	- trösten
- Vertrauen haben zu jemandem	- einen si-Satz

I. Lire et écrire. Test de compréhension (Leseverstehenstext): Le code secret

Tous les élèves savent bien que quand on veut parler avec les copains en classe, c'est difficile parce que la maîtresse vous gêne tout le temps. Bien sûr, vous pouvez parler avec le copain qui est assis à côté de vous; mais même si vous essayez de parler tout bas, elle vous entend et vous dit: «Si vous avez envie de parler, venez au tableau, nous allons voir si vous êtes toujours aussi bavard[1]!» et elle vous demande les noms des départements, et ça fait des histoires. On peut aussi envoyer des bouts de papier où on écrit ce qu'on a envie de dire; mais là aussi, presque toujours, la maîtresse voit passer le papier et il faut le lui apporter sur son bureau, et comme il y a écrit dessus «Rufus est bête, faites passer», elle vous met en retenue[2].
C'est pour ça qu'à la première récréation, ce matin, on a trouvé terrible l'idée de Geoffroy.
- J'ai inventé un code secret que nous serons seuls à comprendre.
Et il nous a montré; pour chaque lettre on fait un geste. Par exemple: le doigt[3] sur le nez, c'est la lettre «a», le doigt sur l'œil gauche, c'est «b», le doigt sur l'œil droit, c'est «c». Il y a des gestes différents pour toutes les lettres.
Nous étions tous d'accord sauf Clotaire pour qui l'alphabet était déjà un code secret. Plutôt que d'apprendre l'orthographe pour parler avec les copains, il préférait attendre la récré pour nous dire ce qu'il avait à nous dire.
Mais tous les autres, on trouvait que ce code était très bien. Alors, on a demandé à Geoffroy de nous l'apprendre, son code. On s'est tous mis autour de lui et il nous a dit de faire comme lui: il a touché son nez avec son doigt et nous avons tous touché nos nez avec nos doigts... Tout le monde a vite compris le code.
En classe, la maîtresse nous a dit de sortir nos cahiers et de recopier les problèmes d'arithmétique qu'elle allait écrire au tableau. Et puis, pendant qu'elle écrivait sur le tableau, on s'est tous tournés vers Geoffroy, et on a attendu qu'il commence son message, ce qu'il a tout de suite fait. Je dois dire que ce n'était pas facile de le comprendre, parce qu'il allait vite, et puis il s'arrêtait pour écrire dans son cahier, et puis comme on le regardait, il commençait à faire des gestes, et il était rigolo, là, à se mettre les doigts dans les oreilles et à se donner des tapes sur la tête.
Et comme il était long, son message! Et c'était embêtant parce qu'on ne pouvait pas recopier les problèmes, nous. C'est vrai, on avait peur de rater des lettres du message et de ne plus rien comprendre; alors on devait regarder tout le temps.
- Oui, Geoffroy, a dit la maîtresse tout d'un coup. Je suis comme vos camarades: je vous regarde faire des bêtises. J'en ai assez. Pour demain, vous allez écrire cent fois: «Je ne dois pas faire le clown en classe et détourner mes camarades de leur devoir.»
Nous, on n'avait rien compris au message. Alors, à la sortie de l'école, on a attendu Geoffroy, et quand il est arrivé, on a vu qu'il était en colère.
- Qu'est-ce que tu nous disais, en classe? j'ai demandé.
- Laissez-moi! a crié Geoffroy. Et puis, le code secret, c'est fini!
C'est le lendemain que Geoffroy nous a expliqué son message. Il nous avait dit: «Ne me regardez pas tous comme ça; ____ »

Extrait de: Sempé-Goscinny, Le petit Nicolas (texte abrégé et adapté)

[1] être bavard: qn qui aime parler
[2] mettre qn en retenue: un élève doit rester ou venir à l'école en dehors des heures de cours parce qu'il a fait des bêtises
[3] des doigts (m): on en a cinq à la main

Répondez aux questions suivantes. Formez des phrases entières.

1. Ajoutez une deuxième phrase qui fait du sens (= sinnvoll sein) que Geoffroy dit quand il explique son message à la fin de l'histoire.

____

____ 4 P

2. Pourquoi est-ce que les élèves ont trouvé terrible l'idée de Geoffroy?

____

____

____ 6 P

3. Quel était le problème de Clotaire?

____

____ 4 P

4. Pourquoi est-ce qu'il était difficile de comprendre le message de Geoffroy?

____

____

____

____ 6 P

II. Subjonctif ou indicatif? Formez des phrases: À la maison

1. Mme Brun: «Rangez vos chambres.»

   Je veux que vous rangiez vos chambres. ✓

2. Luc: «Ma chambre est déjà propre.»

   Je suis d'avis que ma chambre est déjà propre. ✓

3. Marie: «Et ma chambre n'a jamais été sale.»

   Je trouve que ma chambre n'~~a~~ jamais sale. (été)

4. Mme Brun: «Vous êtes toujours contre.»

   Je trouve bête que vous soyez toujours contre. ✓

5. M. Brun: «Faites les devoirs maintenant.»

   Je propose que ~~tu~~ vous fass~~e~~ les devoirs maintenant.

6. Mme Brun: «Et tu écriras une lettre à ta tante après, Luc.»

   Il est important que tu écrives une lettre à ta tante après, Luc.

7. M. Brun: «Oui. Elle recevra la lettre avant son anniversaire.»

   J'aimerais qu' elle reçoive la lettre avant son anniversaire.

8. Luc: «Elle m'offrira un petit cadeau quand elle viendra nous voir la semaine prochaine.»

   J'espère qu' elle m'offrira un petit cadeau quand elle viendra nous voir la semaine prochaine.

9. Mme Brun: «Tu as une tante très gentille. C'est une chance.»

   C'est une chance que tu aies une tante très gentille.

10. Luc: «Oui. Mais pourquoi est-ce qu'elle vient toujours seule?»

    Ça ne me plaît pas qu' elle vienne toujours seule. 10 P

9,0 / 4,9 — recev / recevra / reç / reçoit

III. Le professeur pose des questions auxquelles les élèves répondent plus ou moins gentiment. Mettez les verbes entre parenthèses au passé composé et remplacez les expressions soulignées par les pronoms corrects. Attention à l'accord!

1. Le prof: «Jean, pourquoi est-ce que tu ______________________ (ne pas mettre) ta nouvelle cravate?»

   Jean: «Je ______________________ parce que je ne la trouve plus.»

2. Le prof: «Marie, tu nous montres les photos que tu ______________ (prendre) pendant notre voyage de classe?»
   Marie: «Non, monsieur, parce que ce sont des photos qu'on ne montre pas à un prof.»

3. Le prof: «Luc, pourquoi as-tu copié les exercices?»

   Luc: «Je ______________________ parce que je n'avais pas le temps de les faire moi-même.» 8 P

IV. Production de texte. Erstelle einen Dialog nach den folgenden Vorgaben.

1. Marie möchte gerne, dass ihr Pierre Informationen über Marseille gibt. Sie braucht sie für das Internetprojekt, das sie machen will.
2. Pierre sagt, dass er keine Zeit hat, dass sie sich auf eine Internetseite einloggen kann, auf der sie alles, was man wissen muss, finden kann.
3. Marie fragt nach, warum er keine Zeit hat, ob etwas passiert ist.
4. Pierre beruhigt seine Schwester.
5. (Marie will aber mehr wissen). Sie will wissen, wo Pierre hingeht und warum er ein schönes Hemd angezogen hat.
6. Zunächst will Pierre nichts herausrücken, aber dann gesteht er, dass er eine neue Freundin hat. Sie heißt Anne und er habe sie heute Abend ins Restaurant eingeladen.
7. Marie drückt ihre Überraschung aus!

20 P

I. Adjectif ou adverbe? Comparatif (+; -) ou superlatif (++; --)? Complétez le texte.

Beaucoup de gens pensent qu'à Paris on vit beaucoup __________ (bon; +) qu'à la campagne. Ils disent que la qualité de la vie y est bien __________ (bon; +) que dans une petite ville où on a __________ (peu; -) de possibilités que dans la capitale. Mais à Paris on vit __________ (sûr) __________ (dangereux; +) qu'en province parce qu'il y a __________(beaucoup; +) de voitures que dans les autres villes. Moi __________ (personnel), je crois que vivre dans une grande ville comme Bordeaux, Strasbourg ou Nice est la __________ (bon; ++) solution. Ce qui me plaît __________ (beaucoup; ++) à Nice par exemple, c'est la mer et son climat __________ (agréable).

II. Les noms des pays: prépositions et articles. Complétez le texte.

1. Nos enfants ont beaucoup de copains qui viennent __________ __________ __________ (aus: Marokko, Russland, Belgien, Niederlande, Türkei, Dänemark) par exemple.
2. Ils ont déjà passé leurs vacances __________ __________ __________ (in: Kanada, Türkei, Polen, Kroatien, Portugal, Niederlande)
3. Notre fille étudie __________ __________ (türkisch, portugiesisch, russisch)
4. Notre fils parle bien __________ (italienisch), parce qu'il a une copine (italienisch).

III. Imparfait ou passé composé? Complétez le texte. Annotation: «jouer aux dés»: würfeln

Pendant que Paule __________ (faire) ses devoirs, Paul __________ (être) dans sa chambre et __________ (jouer) aux dés. Comme Paul __________ (ne pas aimer) travailler, sa mère, qui __________(savoir) qu'il __________ (être) paresseux, __________(entrer) dans sa chambre et lui __________ (dire) d'arrêter de jouer aux dés. Puis elle __________ (quitter) la chambre et __________ (se remettre) au travail. Quand Paul __________ (être) seul dans sa chambre, il __________ (d'abord/essayer) de travailler. Mais il __________ (ne pas réussir) à se concentrer, et ainsi il __________ (arrêter) de travailler.

IV. Imparfait ou passé composé? Complétez le texte.

Ce/C' ___ (être) l'hiver. Il ___ (faire) froid et il y ___ (avoir) un vent très fort. Mme Brun ___ (être) au volant (Lenkrad) de sa voiture. Comme elle ___ (être) fatiguée, elle ___ (commencer) à rêver. Pendant qu'elle ___ (rêver) de ses enfants, la neige ___ (tomber) doucement. Quand elle ___ (être) à deux kilomètres de sa maison, elle ___ (voir) un camion qui ___ (avancer) vers elle. Mais comme Mme Brun ___ (rêver), elle ___ (ne pas laisser) passer le camion, qui ___ (être) trop large (=breit) pour cette petite route. Un moment après, elle ___ (sentir) une douleur (= Schmerz) terrible et elle ___ (se réveiller), mais trop tard.

V. Remplacez les expressions en caractères gras (fett gedruckt) par les pronoms «y» et «en».

Marie: «Viens avec moi, **au club d'escalade.**»

Jean: «Je ___ (ne pas pouvoir; aller) aujourd'hui, parce que je n'ai pas le temps.»

Marie: «Ah, tu n'as pas le temps! Tu rêves **d'un rendez-vous** avec ta copine, n'est-ce pas?»

Jean: «Je ___ (ne plus rêver) parce qu'on s'est séparés. Et toi, Marie, tu penses toujours **à l'amour.** Il y a encore autre chose dans la vie.»

Marie: «Non, Jean. Je ___ (ne pas penser) toujours, mais souvent. C'est important dans la vie. Réfléchis **à ce que je te dis.**»

Jean: «Oui, je ___ (aller; réfléchir), ma chérie.»

VI. Les verbes pronominaux (reflexive Verben).

Le professeur parle à ses élèves. Mettez les verbes entre parenthèses à la forme correcte.

1. Le prof: «Pierre et Nadine, à quelle heure est-ce que vous ___ (se lever; p.c.) ce matin?»

   Pierre: «Nous ___ (se lever; p.c.) à 7h30.»

   Le prof: «C'est trop tard. Vous ___ (devoir se lever; présent) à six heures et demie pour ne pas arriver en retard.»

2. Le prof: «Marie, pourquoi est-ce que tu ___ (se disputer; p.c.) avec ta voisine?»

   Marie: «Je ___ (ne pas se disputer; p.c.) avec Anne, mais avec Jean.»

   Le prof: «Marie, nous ___. (ne personne/se disputer avec; présent) dans notre classe. Nous sommes tous des amis.»

3. Le prof: «Emma et Julie, je vous ___ (connaître; présent) depuis très longtemps. Quand vous ___ (être; imparfait) petites, vous ___ (se promener; imparfait) toujours devant notre collège, n'est-ce pas?»

   Emma: «Oui, on ___ (s'amuser; imparfait) bien à faire des grimaces à nos amis qui ___ (travailler; imparfait) avec vous, monsieur.»

VII. Le futur simple. Mettez les verbes entre parenthèses au futur simple.

Michel: «Martine, qu'est-ce que tu feras (faire) après le bac?»

Martine: «J'espère que je pourrai (pouvoir) gagner un peu d'argent. Je travaillerai (travailler) d'abord dans un supermarché. Avec l'argent que je gagnerai (gagner), je m'achèterai (s'acheter) une petite voiture et je/j' irai (aller) à l'étranger pour un certain temps. Quand je serai (être) de retour, il faudra (falloir) que je continue mes études à l'université. C'est ce que j'ai promis à mes parents. Et toi?»

Michel: «Ma copine et moi, on verra (voir) ce qu'on fera (faire). Peut-être que nous aurons (avoir) un enfant. Si c'est une fille, on l' appellera (appeler) Martine comme toi. C'est un joli prénom...»

VIII. La proposition conditionnelle (la condition réelle).
Traduisez les phrases suivantes en français.

1. Wenn Marie nach dem Abitur eine gut bezahlte Arbeitsstelle findet, wird sie nicht mehr zu Hause wohnen (=leben).
   Si Marie trouve un bon job après le bac, elle ne vivra plus à la maison.
2. Marie: „Ich werde versuchen, eine hübsche Wohnung zu finden, falls ich genug Geld verdiene."
   J'essaierai trouver un apartement joli, si je ~~reçois~~ gagne assez d'argent.
3. Jeannette: „Wenn du eine kleine Wohnung in der Stadt suchst, werden dir meine Eltern sicher helfen können."
   Si tu cherches un petit apartement en ville, mes parents pourront sûre me t'aider.
4. Marie: „Dankeschön! Falls deine Eltern heute Abend zu Hause sind, besuche ich sie, einverstanden?"
   Merci! Si tes parents sont à la maison ce soir, je ~~vais~~ irai les voir, d'accord?

IX. Complétez le texte par «ce qui, ce que, dont, lequel + ses formes».
Quelquefois il faut ajouter une préposition.

La fille ______ Jean est tombé amoureuse s'appelle Céline. ______ lui plaît avant tout, c'est qu'elle est belle, ouverte et sympa en même temps. Ils discutent de tout: de ______ les intéresse, de ______ il faut faire et de ______ est important dans leur relation. Comme Jean est très fier (stolz) de sa copine, il a toujours des photos de Céline sur lui: des photos ______ on trouve sa bien-aimée dans toutes sortes de poses. La photo ______ il parle et ______ il pense le plus souvent montre Céline en bikini sur la plage. Mais c'est exactement la raison ______ ses camarades de classe évitent (meiden) Jean. ______ ils n'aiment pas, c'est son arrogance!

X. Subjonctif ou indicatif? Wie sagst du auf französisch, dass... (auf separatem Blatt)

1. ... du glaubst, dass ihr nächstes Jahr nach Québec fahren werdet,
2. ... eure Eltern wollen, dass ihr dort viel Sport treibt,
3. ... du hoffst, dass deine Schwester und du viele Tiere in den Parks sehen werdet,
4. ... es möglich ist, dass dein Vater in Kanada Klettern lernt,
5. ... ihr viele Fotos machen müsst, um sie, wenn ihr wieder zurück seid, euren Freunden zeigen zu können.

I. British history (Green Line Unit 1/2)

1. Complete the text and put in the correct form of the verbs within brackets.

Interested pupils know that the name Britain comes from the __________, a __________ tribe, and that England got its name from the __________ and __________, who originally came from __________. The __________ had already left from AD 400 onwards, so it was easy for the invaders to push the __________ north to __________ and west to __________.

2. The British think that 1066 is a very important date for them because it was in 1066 that Britain __________ (to invade) for the ______ time in its history – by __________ of __________, who brought an army from __________. King __________ of England __________ (to defeat) at the __________.

Tourists can see scenes of this battle when they come to the Norman town of __________, where they can visit the famous __________. 20 P

II. Grammar

1. Read the latest news about President Bambo. Put the sentences in the passive. Leave out the agent where possible.

a) They killed Ben Bambo, President of Bamboland.

__________ 2 P

b) They took him to hospital immediately after the attack, but it was too late.

__________ 2 P

c) The killer first got away, but the police arrested him when he was driving out of Bambo City, the capital.

__________ 2 P

d) They now report that the killer is dead, too.

__________ 2 P

e) Somebody found his body in the River Queng.

__________ 2 P

f) (The whole country is in chaos now.) The army has shut down the radio station.

__________ 2 P

2. Some rules for the pupils. In English, please. Use a passive in each sentence.

Wie sagst du auf Englisch, dass...

a) Hausaufgaben jeden Tag gemacht werden **müssen?**

____

b) Schüler **nicht** geschlagen werden **dürfen?**

____

c) man belegte Brote **nicht** im Unterricht essen **sollte?**

____

d) Schüler (in Zukunft) bestraft werden, wenn sie nicht tun, was die Lehrer sagen?

____ 18 P

III. Vocabulary

Fill in the English expressions of the German words within brackets.

It is difficult for John to ______________ (Freundschaft schließen) because he often feels ________ (verlegen). Sometimes he is even __________ (niedergeschmettert) when other pupils say that he is crazy or mad, that he is " ______________ " (verrückt) as they express themselves. Last Monday __________ (während) break some pupils tried to __________ (überreden) him to __________ (in Brand stecken) a waste-paper basket. To impress them, he ________ (grinsen) and agreed. He ______________ (zulaufen auf) the nearest waste-paper basket with a box of matches in his hand. But thanks to our ____________ (Fernsehüberwachungsanlage) he could be stopped in time. 10 P

IV. Imagine you are on holiday in London. 30 P

Write a letter to your American pen-friend in which you talk about your stay in the British capital. Choose two famous sights and give three pieces of information about each sight and talk about the Notting Hill Carnival (about four sentences)! Do not forget the formal aspects of a letter to a friend!

____

____

____

____

____

____

____

I. Reading comprehension (Green Line Unit 3/4)

1066: Early in the year 1066, the last Saxon King of England, Harold, was crowned in Westminster Abbey, the beautiful church which had then only just been built. In September of the same year William of Normandy, who believed he was the true King of England, had an army ready in the North of France. He only needed a wind from the South to take him across the Channel and invade England.

Harold knew that England was in danger. But the Normans were not the only ones he was frightened of. The King of Norway, who wished to conquer the country, landed with more than 300 ships on the English coast, and late in September Harold and his army met them near the town of York.

Only a week after the English had won this battle, news arrived from the South that the Normans had landed near Hastings with about 8000 men. Harold, 250 miles away, now went south to London, where he got together an army to fight the Normans, and in the middle of October the English were on a hill near the town of Hastings. Their position was so good that they drank a lot that night to celebrate it.

The battle next day was hard. The English had sharp farm equipment to fight with. When they felt the Normans were losing the battle, they ran down from their hill, but this was a bad mistake. Now the arrows showered down on both sides. Harold died from an arrow in the eye, and when the English saw that their king was no longer alive, their hope was lost. William had won and England had been invaded.

1. Right or wrong? Correct the wrong statements.

a) Westminster Abbey had been built long before 1066.

______________________________ 2 P

b) William of Normandy believed he was the true King of France.

______________________________ 2 P

c) The King of Norway was the only danger England had at that time.

______________________________ 2 P

d) At the beginning of the Battle of Hastings the English army's position was very good.

______________________________ 2 P

e) William died in the Battle of Hastings.

______________________________ 2 P

2. Answer in complete sentences.

a) In autumn 1066 William had an army in the North of France. Why did he want to invade England?

______________________________ 3 P

b) How did Harold die?

______________________________ 3 P

c) How did the English army feel after Harold's death? Why?

______________________________ 4 P

II. Grammar

1. A mother's thoughts. Fill in.

a) If Lisa were in the school play, I __________________ (watch) it. 1 P

b) My husband wouldn't be so tired if he __________________ (not/work) so much. 1 P

c) If Tim did more homework, he __________________ (can/have) better marks at school. 1 P

d) I __________________ (be) bored at home if I didn't work. 1 P

e) If I __________________ (have) more time, I could visit my friends more often. 1 P

2. Simple past, past perfect simple or past perfect progressive?

Last week Alan __________ (meet) Mary at a business meeting. Before Alan, Mary __________ (never/know) anyone so fascinating. Alan __________ (invite) her to lunch after the meeting __________ (end). Mary was so nervous that she __________ (cannot/eat) anything. After they __________ (go) out together a few times, Alan decided to marry her. Then Mary __________ (find) out something about Alan from a friend: Alan __________ (be) married for seven years. Angrily she __________ (go) to see Alan. When she __________ (arrive) he __________ (talk) on the phone to his wife for one hour. He __________ (want) to tell her about Mary. 12 P

3. The prop-word "one". Fill in.

a) "What sort of house do you live in?" – "In __________________ ". („einem alten") 1 P

b) "How many rooms are there upstairs?" – "Only two bedrooms – very __________________". („kleine") 1 P

c) "Most English people hate blocks of flats, especially the __________________ ". („großen") 1 P

III. Wie sagst du auf Englisch, dass... 20 P

a) es viele Aktivitäten gibt, an denen behinderte Menschen teilnehmen können?

____

b) Professor Hawkins infolge einer Krankheit seine Stimme verlor und einen neuen Weg fand, sich zu verständigen?

____

c) blinde Leute in vielen Kunstgalerien Skulpturen halten und fühlen dürfen?

____

d) neue Gebäude entworfen werden müssen, so dass Rollstühle ein- und ausgehen können?

____

Dictation, Listening comprehension und Reading comprehension haben eigene "Spielregeln", die im Detail von Schule zu Schule unterschiedlich sein können. Grundlegende Informationen zum Diktieren (wie oft, Sätze und Sinnabschnitte, Zeichensetzung usw.) haben wir auf unserer Homepage www.verlag-bauer.de zusammengestellt.

Falls Sie, liebe Eltern, in Englisch nicht so fit sind, bitten Sie eine andere Person, ihrem Kind zu diktieren. Alternativ finden alle Diktate sowie Listening Comprehensions auf unserer Homepage als Audiofiles zum Download. Weitere Hinweise finden Sie im Elternheft auf Seite 9.

I. Listening comprehension (Green Line Unit 5)

Text: Drake and Magellan explore The New World (Elternheft Seite 26: der Text wird vorgelesen)

Answer the questions in complete sentences.

1. What did Spanish ships do in South America in the 16th century?

____ 2 P

2. What did Drake's ships do on the South American coast?

____ 2 P

3. What did Queen Elizabeth think of Drake and why?

____ 2 P

4. What did the King of Spain want Magellan to do?

____ 2 P

5. Why did Magellan not return from his excursion which started in 1519?

____ 2 P

II. Grammar

1. Bob and Tim were new at Haywood last September.
   They had no idea how they should **do the exercises,** whether they should **ask again** and when they should **hand in** their homework.
   Use this information and make sentences with **question words + infinitive.**
   Use the English equivalents of the German „sich fragen ob"/„nicht sicher sein"/„nicht wissen".

   a) Bob and Tim ________________________________ 2 P

   b) They ________________________________ 2 P

   c) They ________________________________ 2 P

2. The teachers said to them that they:
* had to read the information
* had to stay in the classroom in bad weather
* weren't allowed to eat during lessons
* should bring a drink

Use this information to make sentences with **verb + object + infinitive.** Use the English equivalents of the German „erwarten"/„bitten"/„nicht erlauben"/„raten".

a) The teachers ______________ Bob and Tim ______________________________________ 2 P

b) The teachers ______________ them ______________________________________ 2 P

c) The teachers ______________ them ______________________________________ 2 P

d) The teachers ______________ them ______________________________________ 2 P

3. A dialogue some time later. Fill in – self, - selves or each other if necessary.

Tim: Will we meet ____________________ tonight at my house? We haven't seen ______________ for some time!

Bob: No, I can't come. I hurt ____________ this morning.

Tim: I wonder ________________ how it happened.

Bob: I cut ______________ badly with a knife. So I'd better stay at home. But I hope you and the others will enjoy ________________ .

Tim: Tina wants to come, too. She has short hair now. She has changed ______________ a lot. 7 P

III. Wie sagst du auf Englisch, dass...

a) man heute keine neuen Kontinente entdecken kann?

____

b) wasserdichte Kleidung auf Ausflügen notwendig ist?

____

c) Pilze gefährlich sein können?

____

d) gute Rucksäcke und Schlafsäcke wichtig sind?

____

e) man unnötige Dinge zuhause lassen muss?

____ 19 P

I. Reading comprehension (Green Line Unit 6)

A new bed: A long time ago there was a King and his wife, the Queen. They were a happy couple and they had everything in the world. However, when the Queen's birthday came near, the King had a problem. What could he give to someone who had everything? The King thought – until suddenly he had an idea. He would give the Queen a bed. The Queen did not have a bed because at the time there were no beds. So even someone who had everything did not have a bed.

The King called his Prime Minister and asked him to have a bed made. The Prime Minister called the carpenter (Schreiner) and asked him to have a bed made. The carpenter called his boy and told him to make the bed. "How big is a bed?" asked the boy, who did not know because at the time nobody had ever seen a bed. "How big is a bed?" the carpenter asked the Prime Minister. "A good question!" said the Prime Minister. And he asked the King: "How big is a bed?" The King thought - until suddenly he had an idea. The bed must be big enough to fit the Queen (including the crown which she sometimes liked to wear in her sleep).

The King called the Queen. He told her to put on her new pyjamas and told her to lie on the floor. The King took off his shoes and with his big feet walked carefully around the Queen. He found out that the bed must be three feet wide and six feet long to be big enough to fit the Queen (including the crown which the Queen sometimes liked to wear in her sleep). The King said "Thank you" to the Queen. And told the Prime Minister, who told the carpenter, who told the boy: "The bed must be three feet wide and six feet long," the boy said. When the King saw the bed, he thought it was beautiful. He could not wait for the Queen’s birthday. Instead he called the Queen at once and told her to put on her new pyjamas. Then he brought the bed and told the Queen to try it - but the bed was much too small for the Queen.

The King was so angry that he immediately called the Prime Minister, who called the carpenter. They punished the boy, who was very unhappy. The King thought - until suddenly he had an idea. A bed that was three King's feet wide and six King's feet long was naturally bigger than a bed three boy's feet wide and six boy's feet long.

He explained this to the carpenter, who explained it to the Prime Minister. He took off one shoe and called a famous sculptor (Bildhauer). The sculptor made an exact marble (Marmor) copy of the King's foot. This was sent to the boy. The boy took the marble copy and measured three feet wide and six feet long and made a bed for the Queen. The bed was ready just in time for the Queen's birthday. The King called the Queen and told her to put on her new pyjamas. Then he brought the bed and told the Queen to try it. The bed fitted perfectly (including the crown which she sometimes liked to wear in her sleep).

The King was very happy. He immediately made the boy a Royal Prince. And ever after anyone who wanted to measure anything used a copy of the King's foot.

1. True or false? Correct the false statements.

a) The King wanted to give his daughter a new bed because her old bed was broken.

____ 2 P

b) The Prime Minister made the new bed.

____ 2 P

c) The Queen always slept with her crown.

____ 2 P

d) The Queen got the first bed on the day of her birthday.

____ 2 P

2. Answer the questions.

a) Why did the Queen have to lie on the floor in her pyjamas?

____ 3 P

b) What did the King think when he first saw the first bed?

____ 3 P

c) What did the sculptor have to do?

____ 3 P

d) What happened to the boy in the end?

____ 3 P

3. Tell the story as if you were the boy. Use about 100 words and use the past tense.

____

____

____

____

____

____

____

____ 20 P

II. Grammar

1. Put the following information given in 2007 into reported speech.

"Traffic is now so bad during the morning and evening rush hours that the city has to do something to reduce it. The programme will begin next month. – A fire started a little after midnight and fire-fighters arrived within minutes. They got everybody out of the building quickly and nobody died in the fire." Start like this: The speaker said that ... Use three different introductory verbs ("say" and three others!) in your text.

____

____

____

____

____

____ 14 P

2. A journalist's questions to a sportswoman (Reported questions). Use the English equivalents of the German words "fragen", "wissen wollen" and "sich fragen".

a) Why did you walk across Australia?

________________________________ 2 P

b) What are your plans? ________________________ 2 P

c) Are you very tired? ________________________ 2 P

III. Wie sagst du auf Englisch, dass... 15 P

a) es sehr wichtig ist, sich nach einem Marathon zu erholen?

____

b) viele Schiedsrichter Leichtathletik mögen?

____

c) es wirklich unfair ist, jemanden absichtlich zu verletzen?

____

d) Golfplätze oft trotz starken Regens voller Leute sind?

____

Stegreifaufgabe 1 ✓ 20 / ⌛ 15 / 📖 101

I. Put the following sentences into the passive. Be sure to use the correct tense and use the by-agent only when needed.

1. In 1666 a great fire destroyed London.

London was destroyed in 1666 by a great fire 2 P

2. They couldn't finish the London Eye before the celebrations of the millennium.

The London Eye couldn't be finished before the celebrations of the millennium. 2 P

3. It takes tourists up to a height of over 120 metres.

Tourists are taken up to a height of over 120 metres. 2 P

4. You needn't book tickets in advance.

~~Book~~ tickets ~~aren't needed~~ needn't to be booked in advance 2 P

5. But you can buy tickets at the ticket office.

~~It~~ But ~~can~~ tickets can be bought at the ticket office. 2 P

6. They have made many changes in the Docklands in the last few years.

Many changed have been made in the Docklands in the last few years 2 P

7. I think they will make many more changes in London in the near future.

I think many more changes will be made in London in the near future. 2 P

✓ 20 / ⧗ 15 / 🕮 101 **Stegreifaufgabe 1**

II. In English, please.

The teacher is giving instructions to his pupils. Use a passive in each sentence.

1. Dieser Text muss von allen Schülern gelesen werden.

____ 3 P

2. Die Lateinhausaufgabe darf nicht in der Englischstunde gemacht werden.

____ 3 P

✓ 25 / ⧗ 15 / 🕮 101 **Stegreifaufgabe 2**

I. Make correct sentences.
"+" means that you must add the English equivalent (Entsprechung) of the German "seit".

1. The Morgans/to play football/+ two o'clock

____ 2 P

2. Ceri/already/to score/two goals

____ 2 P

3. Question: How long?/Ceri/to be interested in football
   Answer: + four years

____ 3 P

4. Owen/to play football/+ he was little

____ 2 P

5. When?/Gareth/to start playing football

____ 2 P

II. Translate the following sentences into English.

1. Seit drei Wochen kenne ich ein walisisches Mädchen, das seit Weihnachten in München wohnt.

____

____ 6 P

2. Ich traf sie am 4. November in einer Kneipe.

____ 3 P

3. Jetzt weiß ich, dass die Waliser seit der Zeit von König Artus walisisch sprechen.

____

____ 5 P

Stegreifaufgabe 3 ✓ 12 / ⌛ 15 / 📖 102

I. Form correct if-clauses (pattern II).

a) Tom is not very good at football. If I ____________ Tom, I ________________________ every day to become better. 2 P

b) Jane cleans her bike every week. If she ________________________ her bike every day, it 1 P

________________________ dirty. 1 P

c) Tim has got a computer. He ________________________ what to do in his free time, if 1 P

he ____________________ a computer. 1 P

II. Answer the following questions using a prop-word in each sentence.
Do not use the bold expressions in your answer.

a) Tim: "Did you get a **cheap flight** to New York, Tom?"

Tom: "No, I only got ________________________________." 2 P

b) Tim: "Did you watch an **interesting film** during the flight?"

Tom: "No, we could only watch ________________________." 2 P

c) Tim: "Did you buy **normal clothes** in New York?"

Tom: "No, I think I bought __________________________." 2 P

Stegreifaufgabe 4 ✓ 30 / ⌛ 15 / 📖 102

I. In English please.

A handout gives you tips about a camping trip to Yosemite National Park. Use a question word + an infinitive in each sentence.

It tells you

- ____ (wandern gehen/mit wem) 2 P
- ____ (Abfall entsorgen/wo) 2 P
- ____ (im Rucksack mitnehmen/was) 2 P
- ____ (ein Zelt aufstellen/wo) 2 P
- ____ (Bären fernhalten/wie) 2 P

II. Some more tips. Translate the following sentences into English.

a) Denk daran, eine Pfeife für Notfälle mitzunehmen, wenn du in der Wildnis wanderst.

____

____ 5 P

b) Ein erfahrener (experienced) Ranger rät dir, das Fleisch auf eine Aluminiumfolie (aluminium) zu legen, bevor du es grillst.

____

____ 5 P

c) Die Ranger wollen nicht, dass die Wanderer wild (wachsende) Früchte und Pilze essen.

____

____ 4 P

d) Sie bitten die Touristen, keine Äste abzubrechen oder Blumen zu pflücken.

____

____ 3 P

e) Und die Wanderer erwarten, dass die Zeltplätze sauber sind.

____ 3 P

✓ 40 / ⌛ 15 / 📖 103

Stegreifaufgabe 5

I. Reflexive pronouns: Different usages. Fill in.

Yesterday Jane and John ____________________ (sich treffen) in front of the cinema. They 1 P

__________________________ (sich anschauen) for a second and at once started to 2 P

__________________________ (sich fragen) what was wrong. 1 P

Jane: "Something seems to be wrong with me. What is it, John?"

John: "I can't tell you. It's a bit embarrassing."

Jane: "Why not? __________________________________ ? (Worüber beklagst du dich?) 2 P

I have always ________________________ (sich benehmen) correctly towards you." 1 P

John: "Well, I can't tell you. But go to the bathroom and ____________________ 1 P

______________ (sich im Spiegel anschauen). __________________ (sich beeilen)!" 1 P

A minute later:

Jane: "What a shame! Who has written 'I have ______________________________ (sich 1 P

verlieben) with John' on my face? Somebody must have done this while I was sleeping. By the

way, go to the bathroom ________________ !" John: "Oh Jane! I ________________ 2 P

_____________ (sich nicht erinnern können) reading a more beautiful sentence in my life.

And it's true. I'm really fond of you."

II. Translate the following sentences into English.

The teacher is talking to his pupils.

a) Ich weiß nicht, was ich mit euch machen soll. Ihr könnt euch nicht konzentrieren.

____

____ 4 P

b) Ich kann euch nicht hören. Ich will nicht, dass meine Schüler die ganze Zeit flüstern.

____

____ 4 P

Stegreifaufgabe 5 ✓ 40 / ⧗ 15 / 📖 103

c) Ich rate euch, nicht mit euren Nachbarn zu sprechen. Ihr werdet nichts verstehen.

____

____ 4 P

d) Es ist wichtig, dass man nicht vergisst, die Hausaufgaben zu machen.

____

____ 4 P

e) Ich erlaube euch nicht, dass ihr im Klassenzimmer esst.

____

____ 4 P

f) Ich bitte euch aufzustehen, wenn ich hereinkomme.

____

____ 4 P

g) Und meine Schüler können von mir erwarten, dass ich meine Unterrichtsstunden gut vorbereite.

____

____ 4 P

Stegreifaufgabe 6 ✓ 25 / ⧗ 15 / 📖 103

When Peter Dust was seven years old he was interviewed by a Latin teacher. Put this dialogue into reported speech. Use four different introductory verbs.

Teacher:	Have you ever done Latin, Peter?
Peter:	No, I haven't.
Teacher:	This is a Latin grammar! Learn this lesson! I will be back in 30 minutes.
After 30 minutes.	
Teacher:	Have you learnt the lesson?
Peter:	I think I can say it but I don't know what it means.
Teacher:	It means what it says.
Peter:	Why does "fenestra!" mean "Oh, window!" and what does "Oh, window!" mean?
Teacher:	You are a bad boy! If you continue to ask questions, you will be punished.

____

____

____

____

____

____

____

____

____ 25 P

Noten für Lehrerinnen und Lehrer?

Wen reizt es nicht, seinen Lehrern Noten zu geben – also den Spieß umzudrehen: nicht nur selbst benotet zu werden, sondern die Leistung des Lehrers zu bewerten?

Rechtmäßigkeit der Lehrerbeurteilung im Internet

Im Internet ist dies möglich: Auf www.spickmich.de könnt ihr euch zu ihren Lehrern äußern. Diese Möglichkeit besteht schon seit Februar 2007 und wird von vielen Schülerinnen und Schülern inzwischen regelmäßig genutzt.

Viele Lehrkräfte halten es nicht für richtig, dass sie einer Beurteilung durch Schüler unterzogen werden, die auf Kriterien wie „witzig", „cool" und „faire Noten" beruht. Diese Kriterien sind vielen Lehrkräften zu oberflächlich, zu nichtssagend und zu subjektiv. Manche befürchten auch, Schüler würden ihre Lehrer gar nicht sachlich beurteilen wollen, sondern nur Frust ablassen.

Als unlängst eine Lehrerin gegen das Internetportal spickmich.de geklagt hat, musste der Bundesgerichtshof in Karlsruhe darüber entscheiden, ob die Beurteilung von Lehrern im Internet weiterhin erlaubt sein soll. Am 23. Juni 2009 ist das Urteil gefallen; es lautet sinngemäß: Die Beurteilung von Lehrern im Internet ist rechtens, Schülerinnen und Schüler dürfen ihre Lehrer im Internet benoten.

Fairer Umgang miteinander

Es stellt sich jedoch die Frage: Was bringt eine Benotung im Internet? Wäre es nicht sinnvoller, mit den Lehrern direkt Kontakt aufzunehmen, wenn man Anregungen hat oder Kritik anbringen will? Auch dafür gibt es an vielen Schulen schon praktikable Modelle, z. B.:

- Rückmeldungen über die Abi-Zeitung (die aber meist zu spät herausgegeben wird),
- klassen- oder jahrgangsbezogene Lehrer-Schüler-Gespräche zu aktuellen Themen,
- Fragebogenaktionen (z. B. zum Termin des Zwischenzeugnisses).

Alles in allem ist es sicher sinnvoller, mit seinen Lehrern direkt zu sprechen, als sie im Internet zu benoten (auch wenn das vielleicht Spaß macht). Will man seinen Lehrern tatsächlich Informationen zukommen lassen (im Sinne einer Verbesserung des Unterrichts oder des Lehrer-Schüler-Verhältnisses), ist der persönliche Kontakt unumgänglich.

Doch auch die Lehrerbewertung in Internetportalen kann sinnvoll sein, wenn sie fair und nicht nur eine billige Retourkutsche für schlechte Noten oder den letzten Verweis ist.

Wo gehobelt wird, da fallen Späne:

Wenn Ihr, liebe Schüler/innen oder Sie, liebe Eltern und Lehrer Fehler in unserem Heft finden sollten: Bitte informieren Sie uns. Sollten wir etwas übersehen haben, werden wir dies auf unserer Homepage www.verlag-bauer.de veröffentlichen.

Dort finden Sie auch die jeweils gültigen Lehrpläne sowie die Aktualisierung von schulrechtlichen Bestimmungen, falls sich seit der Drucklegung des Heftes Änderungen ergeben haben. Auch für Anregungen sind wir dankbar.

WANTED!

Übersichtlich und praktisch: Schülerheft im DIN A4 Format, 128 Seiten
Lösungen und Bewertungsmaßstab für jedes Fach im integrierten Elternheft, 104 Seiten

Deutsch	**8 Schulaufgaben:** Beispielaufsätze aus den Bereichen Protokoll, Inhaltsangabe, Steigernde Erörterung; Aufsatz-Tipps **Schulinterner Test:** Texte lesen und verstehen; Sprachkompetenz; **Jahrgangsstufentest**
Englisch 1. Fremdsprache	**4 Schulaufgaben, 6 Stegreifaufgaben, 9 Übungen:** Dictation; Grammar; Mediation; Reading comprehension; Textproduction; Listening comprehension; Vocabulary; Translation; Word order; Letter writing; Mixed Exercises
Latein 1. Fremdsprache	**4 Schulaufgaben, 3 Stegreifaufgaben:** Übersetzung in die lateinische Sprache; Übersetzung aus dem Lateinischen; Grammatikbegriffe; Fremdwörter; Singular/Plural; Konjugation; Zeiten
Mathematik	**6 Schulaufgaben, 4 Stegreifaufgaben:** Proportionalität; lineare Funktionen und Gleichungssysteme, LAPLACE-Experimente; gebrochen rationale Terme; Ähnlichkeit; **Intensivierung**; **Jahrgangsstufentest**
Physik	**4 Schulaufgaben, 3 Stegreifaufgaben:** Energieerhaltungssatz; Aufbau von Materie; Wärme; elektrische Energie
Latein 2. Fremdsprache	**12 Schulaufgaben, 7 Stegreifaufgaben** (Lehrbücher Cursus, Prima, Auspicia)
Französisch 2. Fremdsprache	**4 Schulaufgaben, 10 Grammatikübungen:** Dictée à trous; Grammaire et vocabulaire; Test de compréhension oral; Dialogue; Production de texte; Traduction; Lire et écrire
Englisch 2. Fremdsprache	**4 Schulaufgaben, 6 Stegreifaufgaben:** British history; Grammar; Vocabulary; Reading comprehension; Translation; Listening Comprehension

Bestellungen beim BAUER-VERLAG, Gennachstraße 1, 87677 Thalhofen, Tel. 08345/1601
oder über den Buchhandel: ISBN 978-3-934509-99-3, 1. Auflage 2009, 14 EURO